2/22/11
$24.95
Amzn
AS
1-day

3/11

D1736727

Why America Is Not a New Rome

Also by Vaclav Smil

China's Energy

Energy in the Developing World (editor, with W. E. Knowland)

Energy Analysis in Agriculture (with P. Nachman and T. V. Long II)

Biomass Energies

The Bad Earth

Carbon Nitrogen Sulfur

Energy, Food, Environment

Energy in China's Modernization

General Energetics

China's Environmental Crisis

Global Ecology

Energy in World History

Cycles of Life

Energies

Feeding the World

Enriching the Earth

The Earth's Biosphere

Energy at the Crossroads

Creating the 20th Century

Transforming the 20th Century

Energy: A Beginner's Guide

Energy in Nature and Society

Oil: A Beginner's Guide

Global Catastrophes and Trends

Why America Is Not a New Rome

Vaclav Smil

The MIT Press
Cambridge, Massachusetts
London, England

For information about special quantity discounts, please email special_sales@mitpress.mit .edu.

This book was set in Sabon by SNP Best-set Typesetter Ltd., Hong Kong.
Printed and bound in the United States of America.

Library of Congress Cataloging-in-Publication Data

Smil, Vaclav.
Why America is not a new Rome / Vaclav Smil.
    p. cm.
Includes bibliographical references and index.
ISBN 978-0-262-19593-5 (hardcover : alk. paper)
1. United States—Civilization. 2. United States—Foreign relations. 3. United States—Economic conditions. 4. United States—Social conditions. 5. Power (Social sciences)—United States. 6. Rome—History—Empire, 30 B.C.–476 A.D. 7. Power (Social sciences)—Rome. 8. World politics—21st century. 9. Comparative civilization. I. Title.
E169.1.S5948   2010
973—dc22
                                                                                    2009019763

10 9 8 7 6 5 4 3 2 1

Hoc genus in rebus firmandumst multa prius quam
ipsius rei rationem reddere possis . . .

In matters of this sort full many a truth
Must needs be firmly established ere thou come
To spell the secret of the thing itself . . .

—Lucretius, *De rerum natura* VI
(Charles E. Bennett translation)

Contents

Preface

Comparisons of the Roman Empire, the most powerful state of classical antiquity, and the United States, the most powerful republic of the modern world, have been around for long time, but in a muted, off-center way. Soviet propagandists and European leftists used such comparisons (focused on expansion and far-flung empire building) for decades, but only a combination of events and trends that were too unexpected to be anticipated (and too strange to be invented) made the notion almost commonplace. The key event was the sudden (and amazingly nonviolent) demise of the Soviet empire before the end of 1991. The key trend, preceded by America's speedy and decisive victory in the Gulf War, was also unexpected: after the hardships of the 1980s America enjoyed vigorous economic growth during most of the 1990s, the shift powered primarily by the diffusion of microchip-based manufacturing, commerce, communication, and personal computing.

As a result, the world's richest large economy reached a seemingly unchallenge-able position of strategic superiority and unprecedented level of average affluence. But these admirable achievements had their obverse in rising trade deficits, growing private indebtedness, retreat of manufacturing, and excessive consumption; and these trends were accompanied by ubiquitous gambling, endless spectacles of tele-vised violent "sports" (including extremely popular displays of fake, but nonetheless brutal, wrestling), drug addiction affecting millions, and the inescapable presence of celebrity worship. No wonder that many commentators saw in these displays clear parallels with the excesses and vices of ancient Rome.

But then the years of America's vigorous economic growth and irrational expec-tations (published books expected that the Dow Jones index would reach not just 40,000 but even 100,000) was ended abruptly with the deflation of the aptly named dot-com bubble in 2000 and, much more tragically, the attacks of 9/11 and the U.S. invasion of Afghanistan in October 2001, followed less than a year and a half later by the drive to Baghdad. Again, many commentators saw these events, particularly the invasion of Iraq, as quintessential imperial actions worthy of comparison with the ancient empire. And as that seemingly endless and bloody Iraq stalemate continued year after year, reminding many of Rome's protracted and costly engagements with the barbarians, another trend reminiscent of that empire's chronic troubles unfolded as the unchecked flood of illegal barbarians across America's no longer defensible borders added to the depressing perception of America as a new Rome.

Consequently, that grand analogy was sustained as much by new perceptions of America's profound challenges and visions of its impending decline as by the former similarities of great-power superiority. The earlier image (corresponding to Rome ascendant) was that of America as a great power with many enemies but with no equal, a dynamic society with fabulous domestic riches and aggressive ingenuity. The new image (corresponding to Rome in retreat) saw all of that transformed into ineffectual, impotent irrelevance as a once great polity yielded to excesses of obesity, gambling, and debt even as it confronted the suicidal Islamist challenge: in short, an empire in obvious decline.

The list of prominent U.S. intellectuals who have not surfed this fashionable wave may be shorter than the list of those who have published such facile comparisons. Empire allusions, comparisons, columns, editorials, and reviews have been proffered by people as different in their views as Joseph Nye, dean of Harvard's Kennedy School of Government; Charles Krauthammer, columnist for the *Washington Post*; and Cullen Murphy, for two decades editor at the *Atlantic Monthly*, who in 2007 published a book of some 200 pages to answer the question *Are We Rome?* The comparison has attracted opinion makers across the political spectrum, such as Gore Vidal and Tom Wolfe, the *New York Review of Books* and the Heritage Foundation.

Not surprisingly, European intellectuals did not need any prompting to (re)join that chorus. When, in 2002, Jonathan Freedland canvassed Britain's leading historians of the ancient world for his documentary on Rome as the model empire, he found that they were "struck by the similarities between the empire of now and the imperium of then." In 2003, Peter Bender, a leading German historian and journalist, wrote nearly 300 pages on America as the new Rome. In 2005, Giovanni Viansino drew direct parallels between *ideologie e prassi* of *impero Romano* and *impero Americano*. And, inevitably in this age of electronic logorrhea, one could spend many hours trolling through Web sites and chat rooms with such titles as *American Empire* and *America Is the New Rome*.

Much of this could be dismissed as just a fashionable wave of insufficiently informed commenting, irrelevant private scribbling, or superficial comparisons that pick out as singularly revealing some commonalities shared by virtually all complex societies, juxtapose a few analogical habits and preferences, and conclude that they imply identical long-term outcomes. But it is undeniable that the comparison does resonate for a variety of reasons and hence its validity (or lack of it) deserves a closer critical look.

I wrote this book to provide a corrective, not by criticizing prevailing comparisons but by concentrating on several fundamental realities: the very meaning of empire; the actual extent and nature of Roman and American power; the role of knowledge and innovation in the two states; the roles that machines and energy sources played in their quotidian lives; and their demographic and economic realities, comprising population dynamics, illness and death, and wealth and misery.

Not surprisingly, the complex and contradictory nature and achievements of the two great societies suggest many intriguing parallels and some amusing as well as disconcerting similarities. But a systematic appraisal of fundamental realities exposes truly profound differences that make casual comparisons of the two empires at best misplaced but more often irrelevant. Understanding this is important—important in order to avoid misleading parallels, and important in order to look ahead without the burden of false and counterproductive analogies. Superficial (albeit often clever) comparisons may make for provocative remarks on talk shows and intriguing essays or interesting books, but a systematic deconstruction of these recently fashionable preoccupations shows them to be wide of the mark.

At the same time, I have no illusions about the effect this book, or any similarly corrective exercise, will have in changing the public discourse.

Marcus Fabius Quintilianus (Quintilian; 35–95 C.E.)—a famous oratory teacher during Vespasian's and Domitian's rule and the mentor of both Gaius Plinius Secundus (Pliny the Elder) and the future emperor Hadrian—captured this challenge perfectly in the fifth book of his *Institutio Oratoria* when he wrote about dealing with dubious arguments that have little or no individual force based on their merit but that acquire great weight because of their numbers:

Individually, these points are trivial and commonplace, but taken together they are damaging—not like a thunderbolt, but like a shower of hail (*Singula levia sunt et communia,
universa vero nocent etiamsi non ut fulmine, tamen ut grandine*).

How commonplace the mistaken notion of America as a new Rome has become is readily ascertainable by searching the Internet. A search for "American inventiveness" and "American productivity"—two attributes that have been essential for the country's ascendance—elicited in 2009, respectively, about 500,000 and about 5 million Google hits. In contrast, "America as a new Rome" produced nearly 22 million returns, and a query for "American Empire" came back with more than 23 million—a shower of hail indeed, and one so intense that even scores of rational correctives akin to this book are unlikely to attenuate its impact.

1

America as a New Rome?

Quid enim simile habet civitatium earum quas comparasti causa?

For what similarity is there in the cases of those states which you have brought into comparison?

—Titus Livius, *Ab urbe condita* XXXV:xvi (Cyrus Edmonds 1850 translation)

The undeniably impressive extent and longevity of the Roman Empire and, arguably, its prestige, might, and glory (some of it real enough, much of it greatly misunderstood and often uncritically exaggerated, not a little of it entirely undeserved) created an irresistible standard of comparison for all subsequent powerful and expansive states of Western civilization. Some of these states pursued policies that were deliberately fashioned to invite positive comparisons with the great classical model (a quest that ranged from high-minded actions to tragicomic gestures); others unintentionally evolved in ways that made analogies inescapable to many classically educated minds as well as to superficially informed opportunistic commentators on modern affairs. All of these comparisons have shared a key generic problem: the singularity of their complex subjects.

There has never been any other powerful state whose politics, ethos, militancy, durability, and legacy would closely resemble the unique conglomerate of attributes that defined the *imperium Romanum*, and the same is obviously true about such modern entities as the British Empire, the USSR, or the United States. Commonalities can be always found, but singularities are more important than any similarities. Contrasting modern states with Rome has at least two other specific drawbacks. First, Rome was one of the most enduring states in history, one that underwent profound transformations during more than a thousand years of ascent, perpetuation, and retreat. This invalidates many generalizations about Roman conduct or makes them highly suspect. Second, given the time span that must be bridged by comparisons of modern states to Rome (nearly two millennia have elapsed since

Rome's greatest reach), we do not know enough about many essential aspects of Roman society and hence cannot fully understand its *modus operandi*.

But making comparisons is a universal propensity of our species, and I will exercise it by focusing on a limited number of significant concerns, comparing well-defined factors, and calling attention to their links and functions in the two societies. Consequently, this is not a book of comparative history—not *histoire comparative* but *histoire comparée* using Marc Bloch's (1928) classic distinction—and not one preoccupied by any specific methodological concerns or written to meet the approbation of professional reductionist historians. As to the best approach, I agree with Raymond Grew (1980, 773) who in his thoughtful inquiry into comparing histories concluded that they are most enlightening when shaped in terms of general and significant problems and "when the elements compared are clearly distinguished, and attention is paid to the intricate relationships between the elements compared and the particular societies in which they are located."

Perhaps one more prefatory note: this is not a programmatic book, it was not conceived with any ideological message in mind, and its intent is not to offer any grand lessons. As a lifelong student of complex systems, I have approached the writing of this book much as I have done with all similar challenges: without any preconceived conclusions and without any agendas (the Romans had a phrase for this attitude: *sine ira et studio*). My only goals are to inquire, illuminate, and explain and thus, I hope, to understand.

I

Nihil Novi Sub Sole

...the attention will be excited by an history of the decline and fall of the Roman empire; the greatest perhaps, and most awful scene in the history of mankind.
—Edward Gibbon, *The History of the Decline and Fall of the Roman Empire* (1788)

America has been the latest great power whose intents, accomplishments, and failings have been compared to the actions of the Roman Empire and whose future has been foreseen as a variant of Rome's decline and fall, the description of the demise of a powerful state that Edward Gibbon's lifework inseparably attached to the most extensive and longest lasting of all Mediterranean empires.[1] Inevitable comparisons with its achievements began just a few centuries after the transformation of the Western Empire into a group of smaller Christian kingdoms with Charlemagne's (742–814) effort to consolidate some of these states into a new political entity that was considered to be a continuation of its august predecessor.

Four other states, or at least some of their rulers or political or ecclesiastical elites, have attempted to pattern explicitly some of their actions on Roman precedents, or have claimed to be in some important ways the inheritors or perpetuators of Rome's grand mission. After the demise of the Byzantine Empire some wanted to see Czarist Russia as the Third Rome; Napoleonic France chose explicitly Roman symbols and procedures in the aftermath of revolution and terror; the British Empire based its claim above all on the extent of territories under its rule of law; and Mussolini created a short-lived caricature of an imperial order that was, after a lapse of nearly 1,500 years, once again based in Rome.

Exempla Trahunt

Charlemagne's empire was deliberately fashioned to be seen as Rome's direct descendant. Pope Leo III crowned Charlemagne in St. Peter's Basilica on Christmas

Day of 800 as Imperator Augustus, bestowing on him the same name the Roman senate granted in the same city to Octavianus, the first *princeps*, in 27 B.C.E. But it is the year 962 (coronation of Otto I) that is usually taken as the formal beginning of *Sacrum Romanum Imperium*, the Holy Roman Empire (Bryce 1886; Heer 1968). Its language was Latin, its laws rested on Roman foundations, until after 1500 its emperors were crowned in Rome, they did not shun expansionary warfare, and the empire was long-lived: its official dissolution took place nearly 850 years after its establishment, in 1806, when the Habsburg Emperor Francis II renounced the title. But profound differences between the two empires have always made for only a superficially valid and ultimately unconvincing set of parallels.

The dates for the duration of the Holy Roman Empire bracket the history of something that was more an aspiration, a lofty concept, than a well-integrated political, strategic, or economic entity. The empire was far too splintered (it eventually consisted of more than 300, mostly small, principalities), and its always complicated internal politics and testy relations with Rome were far too unruly for that: "Neither holy, nor Roman, nor an empire," was Voltaire's famous verdict.[2] And even at the time of its greatest extent its territory embraced only a fraction of the original Western Roman Empire, cutting a wide swath across the central part of Europe from the Baltic to the Tyrrhenian Sea (figure I.1).

Its power came overwhelmingly from the multitude of its German jurisdictions, hence its common name *Heiliges Römisches Reich deutscher Nation* (Holy Roman Empire of the German Nation). But this was an inaccurate description because the empire also included entire territories of the ancient kingdom of Bohemia and Moravia (those were never part of the Roman Empire),[3] Austria, Switzerland, today's Belgium and the Netherlands, and parts of northern and central Italy. As a result, the empire had also governed Czechs, Slovenes, French, Dutch, Italians, and Jews. France (except for a strip along German, Swiss, and Italian borders), the Iberian Peninsula, and England were entirely beyond the empire's reach, as were any territories in Eastern Europe.

The notion of Russia as the Third Rome (*tretii Rim*) was considered to be a part of the Russian national idea, and some saw it as a major impetus for Russia's imperial expansion. The reality was different. Expansion from the medieval central Russian core (all the way to the Pacific Ocean by the mid-seventeenth century, followed by the penetration of Central Asia to the borders of Iran and Afghanistan during the nineteenth century) was not driven by such considerations. Russia as the Third Rome was primarily an ecclesiastical idea that was born after the conquest of Constantinople and the demise of the Eastern Roman Empire in 1453. It was

Figure I.1
Holy Roman Empire at the end of the Thirty Years' War in 1648.

based on the fact that Russia then became the largest Orthodox state (and a spiritual successor of the fallen Byzantine Empire), and it was given additional support by the marriage of Czar Ivan III to Sophia Palaiologos, a niece of the last (Eastern) Roman Emperor.

The idea of *tretii Rim* was formulated in some detail at the beginning of the sixteenth century by Filofei, a monk in Pskov. As Rowland (1996) noted, it has been irresistibly appealing to historians (some of them compiled extensive references to its use), but its original mission was not to justify expanding the empire but to strengthen the position of the Russian patriarchate with the Eastern Orthodox Church and to limit rather than increase the country's secular powers. As such, the concept did not have notable imperial influence, and it was later much criticized in Russia itself, but at the same time it has always retained some of its vague mythical appeal. That is how we should understand the references to the Third Rome that continue to appear in modern Russian publications (Panarin 1996; Luks 2002).

The French Revolution followed the sequence from Roman republic to new empire as its guiding political example, right down to the first consul's being elevated to emperor by the *senates-consulte*. Huet (1999) described all the deliberate parallels between the rise to power of Augustus and of Napoleon Bonaparte (consul for life in 1802, emperor in 1804) and the myth of Napoleon as a Roman emperor, a delusion that cost Europe several million lives (Ribbe 2005). Compared to Napoleon's brief rule of excess, the British Empire of the nineteenth century had a much better claim for a meaningful comparison with the Roman achievements.

In 1831 the first edition of *Encyclopedia Americana* noted that "imagination sinks under the idea of this prodigious power in the hands of a single nation [Rome] . . . But another paramount dominion was yet to be created of a totally different nature; less compact, yet not less permanent, less directly wearing the shape of authority, yet, perhaps, still more irresistible; and in extent, throwing the power of Rome out of all comparison—the British empire. Its scepter is influence." And that was decades before Britain acquired and consolidated its vast (Cape-to-Cairo) African possessions.

The comparison came naturally to many of those who ran the British Empire, a small group of classically educated officials and top military men who enlarged it and administered it for generations (Gilmour 2007).[4] Gilbert Murray (1866–1957) made the imperial comparison explicitly (if inaccurately): "At home England is Greek. In the Empire she is Roman."[5] Alfred Lyall (1835–1911), after long service in India (he ended his career in 1887 as the lieutenant-governor of North West Provinces and chief commissioner of Oudh) believed that future historians would see the British Empire "as a second remarkable illustration of the force with which a powerful and highly organized civilization can mould the character and shape the destinies of many millions of people" (1906, 348). Those who think this statement hubristic should consider the profound cultural impact the empire had on its most prized possession, India (Mustafa 1971; Wild 2001).

In an essay published in 1908, Evelyn Baring (Lord Cromer, 1841–1917, who was consul general in Egypt for nearly 25 years) approved of Lyall's search "in the history of Imperial Rome, for any facts or commentaries gleaned from ancient times which might be of service to the modern empire of which he was so justly proud," and he believed that "the intentions of the British, as compared with the Roman Government are, however, noteworthy from one point of view, inasmuch as from a correct appreciation of those intentions it is possible to evolve a principle perhaps in some degree calculated to avert the consequences which befell Rome, partly by reason of fiscal errors (1908, 21)."

In 1912, Charles Lucas (1853–1931) completed *Greater Rome and Greater Britain,* and two years later a jurist and historian, James W. Bryce, (1838–1922) published a long essay comparing the Roman Empire and the British Empire in India. Its first paragraph affirmed the exceptionalism of the two phenomena (1914, 1):

There is nothing in history more remarkable than the way in which two small nations created and learnt how to administer two vast dominions: the Romans their world-empire, into which all the streams of the political and social life of antiquity flowed and were blent; and the English their Indian Empire, to which are now committed the fortunes of more than three hundred millions of men. A comparison of these two great dominions in their points of resemblance and difference, points in which the phenomena of each serve to explain and illustrate the parallel phenomena of the other, is a subject which has engaged the attention of many philosophic minds, and is still far from being exhausted.

He could not know that in just two generations the British Empire would have shrunk to less than a score of small insular outposts. There is, of course, no universally accepted starting date of the British Empire. Its beginning may be seen in bold trans-Atlantic forays of Elizabethan explorers (Francis Drake, Martin Frobisher, Henry Hudson, Walter Raleigh) during the closing decades of the sixteenth century; in the founding of the East India Company (it obtained its Royal Charter in 1600); or in the nearly concurrent setting up of the first American colonies (Jamestown in 1607, Plymouth in 1620). Following Cain and Hopkins (2001) and taking the revolutionary year of 1688 as the origin of British imperialism, there are almost exactly two centuries to the empire's apogee in the year 1897, when Britain celebrated its monarch's Diamond Jubilee and when invocations of the analogies between the two empires became commonplace. At that time the two key simple quantitative comparisons clearly favored the new empire.

At the peak of its power Rome controlled a territory of no more than about 4.5–5 million km^2 (with modern Turkey, modern France, the Iberian peninsula, and Italy as its largest components).[6] In contrast, after the end of World War I (WW I) the British Empire covered about 30 million km^2 (figure I.2). Even when that total is reduced by subtracting uninhabited or very sparsely populated deserts of Britain's African possessions (Egypt, Sudan, and South Africa), the arid interior of Australia, and the sub-Arctic and Arctic near-emptiness of Canada, the remainder of at least 15 million km^2 was roughly three times as large as the lands under the Roman Empire.

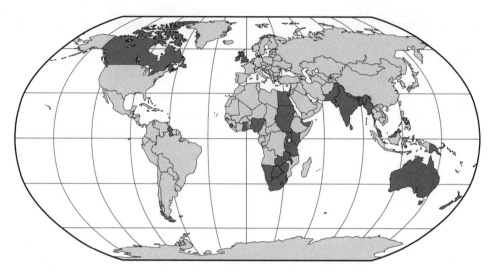

Figure I.2
British Empire after WW I. At this scale, many small island possessions cannot be shown.

In terms of population totals, the best estimates for the Roman Empire at the beginning of the fourth century C.E. (under Constantine, the first Christian emperor) are fewer than 60 million people, with roughly a 40/60 split between the western and eastern parts (Russell 1958). In contrast, at the beginning of the twentieth century the British Empire had a total population of almost 400 million people. The famous eleventh edition of *Encyclopaedia Britannica*, published in 1911, offered an improbably precise total of 388,712,785 people, of which three-quarters lived in the Indian subcontinent; the 1901 census counted 294,191,379 people, compared to the United Kingdom's total of less than 42 million (Lugard 1910).

But in the longevity comparison the British Empire came up short. If 1897 was its peak, the decline set in almost immediately afterward with the defeats during the Boer War in battles at Magersfontein (December 1899) and Spion Kop (January 1900). As the British troops were leaving the Southampton docks in October 1899 to fight that distant war, Thomas Hardy wrote of their embarkation with a distinctly martial Roman allusion (1901, 116):

Here, where Vespasian's legions struck the sands,
. . . .
Vaster battalions press for further strands,
To argue in the self-same bloody mode
Which this late age of thought, and pact, and code,
Still fails to mend.

The Boer rebellion was over by 1902, but soon came the mass slaughter and entrenched exhaustion of British troops during WW I (1914–1918), followed by India's relentless unrest as Britain became engaged in the existential struggle of World War II (WW II). Concurrently, the Arab-Jewish conflict in Palestine worsened after 1938 and became intolerable after 1945, leaving Britain eager to relinquish its mandate. The formal beginning of the empire's end came just 50 years after Victoria's Diamond Jubilee, with the withdrawal from India (on August 15, 1947) and the subcontinent's tragic partition (Khan 2007). If one takes 1688 as the empire's beginning and 1947 as its de facto end, the British Empire spanned about 260 years, a quite respectable run as far as the longevity of empires is concerned but far short of the persistence of power of ancient Rome.

After leaving India it took Britain about two decades to divest itself of all sizable African possessions: Bechuanaland (Botswana) was the last major colony to get independence, in 1966.[7] And almost exactly 50 years after leaving India, on July 1, 1997, came the British retreat from Hong Kong, the empire's most lucrative Asian outpost, held since the Opium War of 1842. That withdrawal has left Britain in the possession of only ten small inhabited island colonies whose total population in 2008 was about 180,000 people, the most populous being Bermuda (about 60,000), the least populous a tiny Pitcairn in the vastness of the South Pacific halfway between New Zealand and South America with some 50 people (mostly the descendants of *Bounty* mutineers who landed in 1790).

If Britain carried the imperial comparison as a consequence of its indisputable achievements and as a mark of its far-flung obligations, Benito Mussolini (1883–1945) was delusionary enough to insist on a re-creation of the Roman Empire itself. Indeed, his quest went even deeper as *Romanità* (Romanness), a multifaceted heritage from the classical Roman past, had a central place in legitimizing fascist rule (Nelis 2007). On April 21, 1922 (Birthday of Rome, a holiday created by Mussolini), *il duce* presented an abstract version of Rome as the foundation of his fascist state: "Rome is our point of departure and reference; it is our symbol or, if you wish, our myth. . . . Much of what was the immortal spirit of Rome, resurges in Fascism. . . . Roman is our pride and courage: Civis Romanus sum" (cited in Nelis 2007, 403).

In 1925, three years after he took power, Mussolini envisaged a Rome that must appear not just marvelous to all the peoples of the world but also vast, ordered, and powerful as it was at the time of Augustus (Minor 1999). Augustus was Mussolini's model (in 1937, to commemorate the two thousandth anniversary of the first emperor's death, *il duce* restored his mausoleum on the Campus Martius)[8] and fascism meant for him above all the "will to empire." Roman symbols—fasces, eagles, and short swords (*gladia*)—appeared on buildings and propagandistic posters, and architects began to design modern versions of such quintessential Roman structures as triumphal arches, heroic mosaics, and monumental marble statues.

A new forum (Foro Mussolini, now Foro Italico) included Stadio Mussolini built of traditional marble and brick and surrounded, like the ancient circuses, by white heroic male statues symbolizing virility and strength. The forum also had an obelisk inscribed *Mussolini Dux* (Mras 1961; Minor 1999). In April 1934, Mussolini unveiled four large marble maps on the wall of the Basilica of Maxentius along the newly created Via dell'Impero (now Via dei Fori Imperiali), which he ordered built between Piazza Venezia and the Colosseum so that his victorious armies could parade in view of great monuments, much like the Roman legions during their triumphal parades staged by the emperors after faraway conquests.

The maps are still there, marking the progression of the Roman Empire from a single white dot in the eighth century B.C.E. to the empire's greatest extent under the emperor Trajan by 117 C.E. (figure I.3). In October 1935 the Italian army invaded Ethiopia in order to add a major colonial possession to the territories of Somalia and Eritrea, which Italy had controlled since 1889, and Libya, which it had occupied as a result of the war with Turkey in 1911. Addis Ababa fell just seven months later, on May 5, 1936, and Mussolini's proclamation of the new empire on May 10, 1936, was obviously patterned on *adlocutio cohortium* (a speech given by an emperor to his legions).[9] He made the connection between the two empires explicit (cited in Minor 1999, 154): "raise high—legionaries—your standard, your weapons, and your hearts, and salute, after fifteen centuries, the reappearance of the Empire on the predestined hills of Rome."

In October 1936 a fifth map was put up on the Via dell'Impero showing the white-marbled Italy, Libya, Eritrea, Ethiopia, and Somalia, a new *impero del'Italia fascista*; Albania was added after Italy occupied it in 1939 (figure I.4). And, in a truly pathetic display of me-too craving, in 1937, Mussolini, copying the habitual Roman thefts of Egyptian antiquities, ordered the looting of a massive obelisk from Axum in northern Ethiopia and its removal to Rome, where it was installed in front of a newly built Ministry for Colonies.[10] But Mussolini's new *impero* lasted less than nine years, and the fifth map was broken up and removed from the wall.

Figure I.3
Marble maps of the Roman Empire placed on the wall of the Basilica of Maxentius by Mussolini in 1934. Photo by V. Smil.

Imperium Americanum

The United States, initially reluctant to enter yet another world war, emerged from the war against Germany and Japan as the world's greatest economic power and as the only possessor of nuclear weapons. But the USSR, despite the enormous destruction it suffered during the war, became an aggressive competitor. The Cold War was on, and it brought forth vituperative parallels between the behavior of the ancient Roman Empire and the might and mores of the United States. The Stalinist propaganda of my grade school years (when I lived in the westernmost outpost of the Soviet empire) and its much less odious Khrushchevian-Brezhnevian version of the late 1950s and the 1960s saw the U.S. military bases surrounding the USSR and the "expansionist" wars in Korea (never mind that Stalin's consent started that

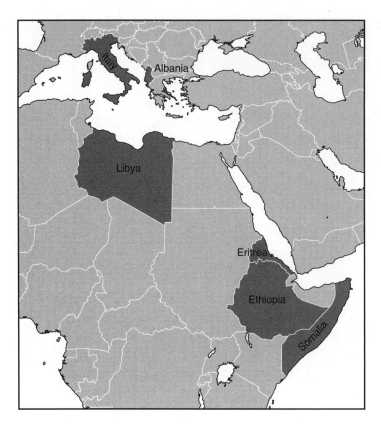

Figure I.4
Mussolini's *impero del'Italia fascista* included Libya, Eritrea, Ethiopia, Somalia, and Albania.

one),[11] Vietnam, and the Middle East (by proxy, via Israel) as signs of America's grand imperial design to dominate the world and to "enslave progressive forces" fighting for social justice and self-determination.

Communist propagandists saw a militaristic, expansionist, and enslaving Washington as an inheritor of evil Roman ways, and the European left (from French Stalinists to radical Scots Labourites) held similar views. In the United States itself this comparison and the search for analogies and similarities between the two societies, separated by two millennia of time, was hardly center stage until a mélange of events and trends made the notion almost commonplace; empire is currently part of a new political and cultural vocabulary used by liberals and conservatives alike. The shift began with a rapid unraveling of Soviet power during the late 1980s that culminated in the dissolution of the USSR in 1991, a remarkably peaceful process that was formally sealed on December 8, 1991.[12]

Less than ten months before this epochal event America's military dominance and unmatched strategic might were confirmed by a victory of the U.S.-led coalition over the Iraqi army in the first Gulf War, which lasted only six weeks (January 17–February 27, 1991). This was not just a swift and lopsided war but one that ended with the utter destruction of the enemy on the battlefield, an achievement symbolized by the mass of obliterated hardware as the U.S. Air Force demolished the retreating Iraqi Army along the infamous "Highway of Death" north of Kuwait City. The war's offensive operations were actually cut short in order to prevent the continuation of this "turkey shoot."[13]

This victory, a triumphant demonstration of America's superpower status, was potentiated by two remarkable economic retreats, those of the country's foremost strategic enemy (USSR) and of its most worrisome economic competitor (Japan). The collapse of the Soviet command economy and the rise of mafia-like business structures in the post-Soviet society were marked by a substantial decline of Russia's GDP: it fell by 5% in 1991, 14% in 1992, 9% in 1993, and 13% in 1994, and it did not bottom out until 1998, when its per capita rate was (in inflation-adjusted monies) just 60% of the 1991 level (figure I.5) and its average real income about half of the peak Soviet rate (Smil 2008b).

As for Japan, the Nikkei index (its leading stock market indicator) rose from a bit over 13,000 by the end of 1985 to nearly 39,000 in December 1989, and it was widely expected that the country would emerge as the world's leading economy in the early twenty-first century. But it was a classic bubble economy, and it burst in spectacular fashion: by the end of 1990 the Nikkei index fell to less than 24,000, and by the end of the 1990s it was below 14,000 (see figure I.5).[14] There is no historic precedent for such a rapid move from globally admired economic superpower to floundering society enmeshed in a prolonged socioeconomic crisis. But America's economic performance looked good not only in comparison with the much weakened post-Soviet states and with Japan's deflating economy.

During the 1990s the perception of America's unique imperial status was boosted by the country's vigorous economic sprint, led by innovative high-tech companies whose efforts helped to turn microprocessors, computers, and the newly commercialized World Wide Web into products and services that formed the admirable New Economy of the 1990s. This was a surprising development because it followed the troublesome 1980s, when Japan's economic power appeared to be unstoppably ascendant and America seemed destined to become a marginalized, has-been power

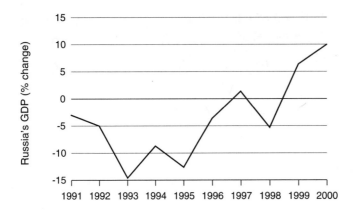

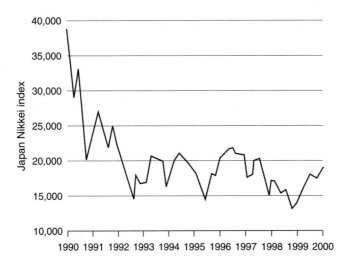

Figure I.5
Aftermath of an empire and the retreat of a great economic power: Russia's declining GDP and Japan's falling stock market of the 1990s. Plotted from data available at Russia's Federal Service of Government Statistics and Nikkei Net Interactive.

in the new century (Smil 2008b). This included a widespread belief that America would lose its leadership in electronic innovation.

But during the 1990s U.S. GDP grew by an average of 3% per year, a satisfyingly high rate for such a large economy. Moreover, the U.S. share of global economic product (expressed in market exchange terms) rose from nearly 26% in 1990 to about 31% by 2000. And added to America's newly enhanced military and economic might was the influence of its soft power, the worldwide appeal of its ideas, inventions, products, and way of life.[15] Some of these soft power influences have clearly been detrimental (for instance, the diffusion of fast food served in gargantuan portions), others naive (a computer for every child is no guarantor of true literacy). No matter—they were all addictive, diffused rapidly, and once abroad appeared irrepressible.[16]

While America thus advanced abroad, at home its wealth created excessive consumption that spread far beyond the traditional high spenders. Steadily falling savings rates and readily available credit made it possible to supersize the American dream (the common use of the verb *supersize* was itself notable). By 2005 the average size of all newly built houses reached 220 m^2 (an area 12% larger than a tennis court), and the mean for custom-built houses surpassed 450 m^2, equivalent to nearly five average Japanese dwellings.[17] Houses in excess of 600 m^2 became fairly common, and some megastructures of *nouveaux riches* covered 3000 m^2 or more.

All these homes became crammed with consumer products ranging from miniature electronic gadgets to in-home movie theaters, from sybaritic marble bathrooms to granite-top counters in kitchens some of whose center islands were larger than entire kitchens in small European apartments. These new palatial villas came to be situated further from city downtowns and were reached by driving ever larger SUVs, vehicles connected neither to sport nor to any rational utility. There is surely no need for more than 1 tonne of steel, aluminum, plastic, rubber, and glass to convey one woman to a shopping center, but vehicles in common use weighed 2–3 t and in the case of the Hummer, a restyled military assault machine, nearly 4.7 t. Ownership of these improbably sized vehicles became the ostentatious symbol of the decade, whose other marks of excess were ubiquitous gambling and mass addiction to (not uncommonly drug-fueled) performances of televised baseball or fake wrestling.

Although the decade saw a temporary reversal of governmental budget deficits (from a shortfall of more than $220 billion in 1990 to a surplus of nearly $240 billion in 2000), this relief was accompanied by steady increases of trade deficit that quadrupled from $111 billion in 1990 to $455 billion in the year 2000.[18] But at the beginning of the new century the U.S. economy appeared to be relatively invulnerable: after all, it had created the world's "only remaining superpower." That all changed in a matter of hours on the morning of September 11, 2001, but it is too early to tell if that attack on the iconic buildings of America's economic and military might accelerated the American retreat or actually postponed it.

The swift toppling of the Taliban regime in Afghanistan and the launching of a (grandiosely named) global war on terror were essentially defensive/retaliatory reactions, yet they almost instantly strengthened the notion of America's premeditated imperial behavior. Martin Walker, a journalist who worked for the *Guardian* and UPI, wrote (seemingly unaware of precedents) that "the new-Rome analogy that began as a journalist's flippant conceit more than a decade ago has flourished into a cliché, and I'm now feeling a degree of remorse" (2002, 37). He explained that his writings on the parallels between ancient Rome and America had their origin in a talk he had with Adam Michnik, a Solidarity activist, at a conference in Moscow in 1989, a month before the Berlin Wall came down.

A list of (superficial and questionable) similarities between Rome and America that they discerned included culture that is robust and populist yet deferential (to, respectively, the Greeks and the Europeans); roads and highways; and a "common obsession with central heating and plumbing." A few years later Walker returned to the topic in a book (1994), and he revisited it again in 2002:

The case for the analogy is easily stated. The U.S. military dominates the globe through 200 overseas bases, a dozen aircraft carrier task forces, and a unique mastery of the new high technology of intelligent warfare. This universal presence is buttressed by the world's richest and most technologically advanced economy, which itself dominates global communications and the world's financial markets, their main institutions based—and their rules drafted—in Washington and New York. (2002, 36)

This is a standard recital, but Walker (2002, 37) also made an acutely correct observation: "The comparison is as glib as it is plausible, and there has always been something fundamentally unsatisfactory about it."

Such doubts have not crossed the minds of literati from across the entire intellectual spectrum who began to fill their books and essays (Bacevich 2002; 2003; Bacevich and Mallaby 2002; Ikenberry 2002; Wade 2003; Cohen 2004; Falk 2004; Johnson 2004) with imperial (and that often meant Roman) allusions and parallels. Of course, not everyone brought in the ancient parallels. For example, Ikenberry (2002) made no Roman comparisons. Similarly, Bacevich and Mallaby (2002, 50), while welcoming a newly found readiness to consider American empire on its own merits and acknowledging that "the notion that the United States today presides over a global imperium has achieved something like respectability," found little to connect it to any predecessors; they saw America as a uniquely "informal empire" and "an empire without an emperor."

But there has been no shortage of commentators who drew imperial parallels. Litwak (2002, 76) began his essay by noting that "America's global dominance prompts popular references to a latter-day Roman Empire." Joseph Nye, dean of Harvard's Kennedy School of Government, summarized the key points of this book *The paradox of American Power* (2002b) in *an Economist* article titled "The New Rome Meets the New Barbarians." Unequivocal about the degree of U.S. dominance, Nye was apprehensive about the eventual outcome: "It is true that no nation since Rome has loomed so large above others, but even Rome eventually collapsed."

Appraising the analogies of the two most often repeated factors in the Roman demise, internal decay and "a death of thousand cuts from various barbarian groups," Nye did not see anything pointing strongly in the direction of internal decay but thought it was harder to exclude the barbarians, "particularly given the rise of transnational domains and the possibility of massive destructive power in the hands of small groups." His conclusion: "The paradox of American power in the twenty-first century is that the largest power since Rome cannot achieve its objectives unilaterally in a global information age."

Writing in *New Perspectives Quarterly* (2002), Paul Kennedy, a professor of history at Yale and the author of a widely read book, *The Rise and Fall of the Great Powers* (1988), shared Nye's opinion of America's status as "the greatest superpower ever" but evoked Rome only by citing Rousseau's question, "If Sparta and Rome perished, what state can hope to endure power?" His concern about the future was primarily economic because "America's present standing very much rests upon a decade of impressive economic growth." He concluded that if this growth dwindled and budgetary and fiscal problems multiplied over the next 25 years, "the threat of overstretch would return."

In June 2002, Lind noted in the *Globalist* that comparisons between the United States and the Roman Empire were coming from both the right (Max Boot of the *Wall Street Journal* calling for a "benign" American imperialism) and from the center left, from commentators he called "humanitarian hawks" who were anxious to launch preemptive attacks to destroy hostile regimes. Indeed, empire allusions were made by writers as different in their viewpoints as Charles Krauthammer, a conservative columnist for the *Washington Post*, and Gore Vidal, a doyen of America's liberal thinkers.[19]

Institutional opinion makers partial to imperial analogies spanned a similarly broad range. The left-of-center *New York Review of Books* published in its February 28, 2002 issue David Levine's caricature of President Bush in legionnaire's garb carrying the scales of justice in his right hand and the presidential shield (behind which protruded an assortment of tiny rockets) in the other. This is art truly in the spirit of that great Soviet satirical weekly, *Krokodil*, whose cartoonists depicted U.S. presidents with rockets and bombs sticking from their pockets.[20] Yet another Levine caricature, in the issue of October 23, 2003, *New York Review of Books* portrayed the president in a modern flight suit but clad in a Roman mantle and plumed Roman helmet (*cassia*), a pistol tucked in his belt, right hand ready to draw, left one holding a miniature missile.

The unswervingly conservative Heritage Foundation invited J. Rufus Fears, a professor of classics, to give a lecture on the lessons of the Roman Empire for America. He claimed that "Rome of the Caesars and the United States today are the only two absolute superpowers that have existed in history" and concluded with a flatteringly inspirational comparison:

So we must ask ourselves the question: Are we willing to follow that path of empire? Do we have the reserves of moral courage that the Romans did to undertake that burden of empire? And what will be our legacy? For I am quite convinced that of all the people who have passed through the Middle East, of all the people who have passed through history, there has been none so generous in spirit, so determined to leave the world a better place, and so imbued with the technology and the wealth and the opportunity to leave a legacy far more enduring and far better than that of the Romans. (2005, 8).

But great-power analogies were not the only ones that captured American attention; soon came the talk of another imperial fall. The economic gains of the 1990s were rapidly transformed into economic worries as the runaway stock market retreated in 2000 and the threat of terrorist attacks introduced new uncertainties. The U.S. budget balance turned from surpluses of $237 billion in fiscal year 2000 and $127 billion in 2001 to deficits (figure I.6); in fiscal year 2008 the deficit approached half a trillion dollars ($455 billion), and the stimulus spending designed to reverse a major economic downturn pushed the deficit well above $1 trillion for fiscal year 2009.

Concurrently, the country's trade deficit widened from $455 billion in 2000 to $787 billion by 2008 (see figure I.6).[21] At the same time, income inequalities, after narrowing for a time, began to widen during the last three decades of the twentieth century. Between 1966 and 2001 the median U.S. income rose by 11%, but the increase was 58% for people in the 90th percentile and 121% for those in the 99th

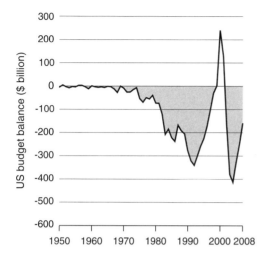

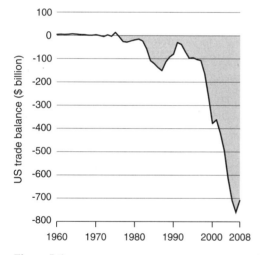

Figure I.6
America's double deficit: budget (1950–2008) and trade (1960–2008) balances. Plotted from data available at Office of Management and Budget, the White House.

percentile (Dew-Becker and Gordon 2005). The fraying of the middle class has certainly been the most worrisome consequence of this trend (Lardner and Smith 2005).

Corporate scandals that involved fraudulent business deals and frank embezzlement (exemplified by Enron's Kenneth Lay and Tyco's Dennis Kozlowski and, ultimately, by Bernard Madoff) reached into billions, even tens of billions of dollars. This all began to evoke images of Roman excess. Here is a typical encapsulation (2009) of these analogies from the Web site *Roman Empire—America Now!*

Why is America now like the Roman Empire? Because it's conquering the world? No. Because Americans are like Romans? Some are; some are like the Roman Senators of the fifth century, one of the most rapacious and ruthless ruling classes that ever held power. Think Mafia. For the amount of wealth: think billionaires today. . . . The Roman Empire fell because it was bankrupted by its leaders; well, look at the red ink now! Budget deficits, trade deficits, a huge national debt. . . . Does anyone remember when we were actually paying down the debt? Both Romans and now Americans have had the misfortune of being ruled by a Selfish Class. Rome fell because of it. Will America replay the Fall of Rome?

Given the often reflexive anti-Americanism of European intellectuals, it is hardly surprising that after 9/11 they eagerly added to comparisons of Roman and American transgressions. When Freedland (2002a; 2002b) was making a documentary film on the topic, he found "without exception" that Britain's leading historians of the ancient world were "struck by the similarities between the empire of now and the imperium of then." And when promoting the broadcast in the *Guardian*, that great standard-bearer of the British left, he came up with a clever title "Rome, AD . . . Rome, DC?" and wrote that "the word of the hour is empire," that "sole superpower" is an "oddly modest" term to label America's new imperial role, and that "the idea of the United States as a twenty-first-century Rome is gaining foothold in the country's consciousness."

Freedland ran through a predictable list of the similarities between the two empires, starting with overwhelming military strength and conquering and colonizing habits (albeit in America's case "we don't see it that way"). His list included superb road systems (he claimed that today's information superhighways are the counterpart of Roman *viae*); a mixture of hard and soft power used in advancing the imperial design (togas, baths, and central heating as the tools of "enslavement" deployed by the Romans, and Starbucks, Coca-Cola, McDonald's, and Disney as America's "similarly coherent cultural package" used to dominate the world); and reliance on puppet governments (U.S. support for the Shah as a signal example). He also found both states adept at mythologizing the past and invoking supreme powers (deifications of emperors, "God bless America" at the end of political speeches, "In God We Trust" on the currency) and sharing the belief in "a mission sanctioned from on high."

Less predictably, Freedland concluded that the gladiatorial games in the Colosseum and Hollywood shoot-'em-ups serve the same function ("Both tell the world: this empire is too tough to beat"), and searching for a historical analogy to a recent atrocity, he suggested that Romans had their 9/11 when a Pontic king, Mithridates, implored his subjects to kill the Romans across Anatolia in 80 B.C.E. and they massacred some 80,000 people. Such a list should make even readers only slightly familiar with Roman and American realities highly suspicious of the appropriateness of the comparisons. Leaving aside the left-leaning opinions of most of Hollywood's producers and celebrities, what insight is gained by confusing Hollywood movies with U.S. policy? And how meaningful is a comparison between an indiscriminate slaughter of a population seen as an occupier in a time of war and an ideologically motivated terrorist attack on carefully chosen symbols of a superpower?

Peter Bender, one of the doyens of German journalism and international studies, identified two great resemblances between ancient Rome and the United States as similar paths to dominance and historically unprecedented positions as world powers of their time. He detailed his thesis in *Weltmacht Amerika das neue Rom* (2003a). English readers can get all of its principal arguments in a paper that Andrew I. Port of Yale translated for *Orbis* (Bender 2003b). Bender's approach differs quite a bit from Freedlander's, and he is careless in claiming that "the Roman Empire included almost the entire then-known world; the United States dominates almost the entire globe since the collapse of the Soviet Union" (Bender 2003b, 145). I deconstruct both these assertions in chapter II.

Bender put a great deal of emphasis on geopolitics.[22] Most notably, he saw a formative commonality shared by Italy and the United States: both should be seen as insular nations. Obviously, they are not islands, but Bender claimed that because of their long coastlines their history has been molded more by the fact that they are surrounded by seas rather than by interactions with their neighbors. As a result, both Romans and Americans "were for long time insular in their thoughts and feelings" (Bender 2003b, 146). On the question of why both abandoned this insularity, Bender conjectured that they did so once "the oceans ceased to offer protection, or so it seemed" (2003b, 148). For the Romans that moment came during the First Punic War, for the United States it was the Pearl Harbor attack. A third similarity is that neither empire was created by a great conqueror (a charismatic leader, in the modern parlance); their power increased gradually but steadily until they became dominant.

A new chapter of imperial comparisons was opened by the U.S. invasion of Iraq in March 2003. A swift conquest was followed by a seemingly endless sequence of killings by suicidal al-Qaeda bombers and sectarian militias as well as by criminal and extortionary gangs. By the end of 2007 this quotidian violence was responsible for deaths of nearly 4,000 U.S. soldiers, tens of thousands of Iraqi police and military, and of a much disputed but undoubtedly high number of civilians.[23] These years of violence produced nothing better than a bloody stalemate, exposed the limits of U.S. military power, and abruptly shifted the perception of America as an ascending empire to America trapped in a painful, costly, and eventually futile effort to prevent its loss of great-power status. As the Iraq stalemate continued, the new imperial analogy was supported as much by the similarities of once seemingly invincible great-power superiority as by the expectations of impending retreat from that unique status.

The image of America as a great power—a state with many enemies but, much as the Roman Empire, with no equal, a dynamic society with fabulous domestic riches, organizational ingenuity, and aggressive drive—was replaced by impressions of a society slowly coming apart under the stresses of Islamist attacks and Iraqi "quagmire" (a favorite term that defeatists borrowed from the Vietnam War era). By 2006 talking heads and op-ed writers were eager to prophesy the end of American empire in the sands of Mesopotamia. Adding to the perceptions of America in its twilight phase was the insidious "takeover" of the country (as some saw it) by tens of millions of new "barbarians" flooding across the country's borders as well as such home-grown signs of decay as gross obesity, rising debt, and runaway trade deficits.

The opinion-making chorus began to intone in a near unison: an empire that is unmistakably in decline. And once the idea of decline gains broad acceptance, the notion of fall cannot be far behind. This reasoning may turn out to be yet another fine illustration of a logical fallacy that the Romans knew as *post hoc, ergo propter hoc* (after this, therefore because of this). On the other hand, it might be an accurate anticipation of events because decline does usually precede fall. Not surprisingly, some European commentators firmly believe that the latter is the correct interpretation, and they have been eager bearers of the message.

Both the elite and public perceptions of U.S. actions and verdicts on America's future became highly negative, even hostile, in the two greatest continental powers, Germany and France, as well as in most of the smaller nations. Of course, anti-Americanism is nothing new in France—for example, Julien (1968) wrote about

American empire 40 years ago—and after 2003 the sentiment found unusually widespread acceptance everywhere in Atlantic Europe. In Italy, Viansino (2005) published an explicit comparison of *impero romano* and *impero Americano*, and Italians familiar with the history of the Roman Empire have been eager to contribute their condemnations in an online discussion of *U.S.A. e Impero Romano* on the Web site *Forum di Riflessioni*.

Russian accusations of America's imperial intents, honed to perfection during the Stalinist years and toned down by the late 1980s, made a strong comeback under Putin. Even Mikhail Gorbachev, who presided over the demise of the Soviet empire, sees it that way. In a BBC interview in June 2007 he said,

We lost 15 years after the end of the Cold War, but the West I think and particularly the United States, our American friends, were dizzy with their success, with the success of their game that they were playing, a new empire. I don't understand why you, the British, did not tell them, "Don't think about empire, we know about empires, we know that all empires break up in the end, so why start again to create a new mess."

Many American commentators concurred. Weigel (2007, 1), asking if America is a new Roman Empire, answered, "Yes, obviously it is," and noted that "our confidence leads us to make the same kinds of military blunders as the Romans, and the only argument is whether Iraq is our Teutoburg Forest or our Adrianople—if we've learned our lesson and will stop pushing outside our boundaries, or if we've used up all our get-out-of-jail cards and are primed for a fall."

An editorial in *Financial Times*, August 18, 2007, was nearly as gloomy:

Comparisons with Rome's later periods of imperial excess and hubristic over-expansion are more popular. Some point to Rome's institutional decay. . . . Others dwell on its military misadventures, in particular the perennial failure to subdue Mesopotamia. . . . The question "Are we Rome?"—long a national fascination—has become shorthand for "Are we doomed?"

But the editorial offered a way out:

Rather than lamenting a slide into decadence, the U.S. could remind itself of strengths it shares [with the Roman Empire]—social mobility, an ability to assimilate newcomers of different races, and a talent for making life pleasant for its citizens, whether with aqueducts or circuses.

A similar recipe for preventing decline was offered by Cullen Murphy in *Are We Rome?* (2007). The book's overall tilt and tone are clear from its subtitle: *The Fall of an Empire and the Fate of America*, and from the précis on the cover flap, which claimed revelations of "a wide array of similarities between the two empires: the blinkered, insular culture of our capitals; the debilitating effect of venality in public life; the paradoxical issue of borders; and the weakening of the body politic through various forms of privatization."

Murphy found six principal parallels between the two states: as centers of the world; as military superpowers; as states poorly served by privatization of public services, beset by corruption in government and degradation of civil society; as polities ignorant and dismissive of the outside world; as states with major border problems; and as societies that find it impossible to manage their overwhelming complexity. Nevertheless, he summoned a vigorous dose of American optimism that made him see a fundamental difference between Rome, which "dissolved into history just once" (albeit successfully, given its heritage), and America, which "has done so again and again":

The genius of America may be that it has built "the fall of Rome" into its very makeup: it is very consciously a constant work in progress, designed to accommodate and build on revolutionary change. . . . Are we Rome? In important ways we just might be. In important ways we're clearly making some of the same mistakes. But the antidote is everywhere. The antidote is being American. (206)

I find this faith breathtaking: Americans making all those mistakes that can be avoided by being American.

The Comptroller General of the United States David Walker joined the argument by using the parallel of decline:

The Roman Republic fell for many reasons, but three reasons are worth remembering: declining moral values and political civility at home, an overconfident and overextended military in foreign lands, and fiscal irresponsibility by the central government. Sound familiar? In my view, it's time to learn from history and take steps to ensure the American Republic is the first to stand the test of time. (USGAO 2007, 11)

This survey of recently published imperial analogies and parallels could continue, and such writings will keep on appearing. Moreover, on the Internet, one can find every kind of imperial comparisons, questions, warnings, and dire prophecies— laudatory, condemnatory, condescending, inspirational, pretentious, ignorant, officious, incoherent, facetious (Latin adjectives all)—on Web sites and chat rooms like *American Empire, The American Empire Project Forum, America Is the New Rome,* and *Roman Empire—America Now!* By mid-2009 a Google query for "American Empire" elicited more than 29 million hits, and "End of American Empire" came back with more than 22 million.[24]

But there is one group of Americans who do not think their country is the new Rome. America's conservative premillennial Protestants—the label Herman (2000) used for those who believe in the Bible's literal truth and the coming end of time—

take strong exception to the idea; instead, they see a unified Europe as a new Roman Empire. They believe that the Revelation of John mandates the revival of the Roman Empire: "Five kings have already fallen, the sixth now reigns, and the seventh is yet to come, but his reign will be brief" (Rev. 17:10; Arterburn and Merrill 2004 translation). Egypt, Assyria, Babylon, Medea-Persia, and Greece are interpreted as the five fallen kingdoms; Rome was the ruling power when John's vision took place; and a revived Roman Empire is yet to come, which will be ruled by a trinity of Satan, Antichrist, and Beast.

Many fundamentalists believe that the reunification of Europe—starting with a highly symbolic Treaty of Rome in 1957, which set up the European Economic Community, and progressing to the European Union, which stretches from the Atlantic to Russia's borders—constitutes a clear step toward the fulfillment of that prophecy. Curiously enough, a 2004 exhibit in Brussels that was coordinated by the European Commission and sponsored by the European Council, openly affirmed the goal of a new Rome (*sans* the Satan part, naturally). Its organizers articulated the European Union's ambition in a remarkably uninhibited way: the euro will break the monopoly of the dollar by 2010, and the Roman Empire will return as the EU expands deep into Eurasia, North Africa, and the Middle East and becomes the world's premier superpower and the dominant force in global affairs because of its vast legal and moral reach (Evans-Pritchard 2004).

From a historic point of view, these sentiments, combining quasi-Napoleonic hubris[25] and reflexive anti-American animus, are much easier to understand than the reasoning of American fundamentalists. Those exegetes equate opaque biblical phrases ("And he was given authority to rule over every tribe and people and language and nation" (Rev. 13:7)) and mythical creatures (the Beast with "two horns like a lamb and spoke like a dragon" (Rev. 13:11–14)) with the process of European unification and with the diabolical powers of Brussels bureaucrats (figure I.7). How they arrive at such interpretations is a mystery to which only they possess a key. In any case, many (most?) of the 31% of Americans who believe that the Bible is the actual word of God to be taken literally may have no problem in accepting these conclusions.[26]

A leading American prophecy writer, Hal Lindsey, had no doubt that the Antichrist would emerge "out of the culture of the ancient Roman Empire" (1970, 113) to lead Europe into its final battle, in which it would be defeated by the returned Jesus and "and there will be no more death or sorrow or crying or pain. For the old world and its evils are gone forever" (Rev. 21:3–4). Ever since, many writers espousing biblical inerrancy have foretold the emergence of the Antichrist from the

Figure I.7
Detail of the seven-headed beast in Dürer's rendering from his 1498 woodcut series illustrating the Revelation of St. John (Apocalypse). All of Dürer's woodcuts can be found in Kurth (1927).

EU: Meredith (2004), Rast (2003), and Gillette (2007) exemplify these convictions. Their reasoning echoes the Church of God Daily Bible Study explanation that describes "the New Rome, the real Rome, which will be based in *Rome* (that's what *Roman* Empire means)" as "the very formidable opponent of the USA in the end of time—which is not theory or conjecture . . . war with the EU will be an *unavoidable* clash of titans"; the new "Roman Empire will get much of its military and religious power from Satan . . . that is *reality*, based upon the whole history" (Blank 2004, 1).

Intentio Libri

This book is for those with whom I share an inadequate power of imagination to equate the EU with a beast risen up out of the sea (with "seven heads and ten horns, with ten crowns on its horns" (Rev. 13:1)) and hence to state with confidence that the pursuit of Roman-U.S. analogies is an entirely misplaced endeavor because a new Rome has already risen on another continent. As noted in the preface, the recent ubiquity of imperial analogies between Rome and America could be dismissed as merely a fashionable bandwagon, but the comparison of the two states is not entirely inapt, and its validity (or invalidity) deserves a closer critical look. The best way to explain why America is not a new Rome is not a direct approach, not, as the Romans would have said, jumping *in medias res* by offering a list of major putative differences with apposite comments.

A better way to pursue this task is by following the Lucretian advice that I chose as the epigraph of this book: by establishing first many a truth and approaching the heart of the matter by a winding path. Several reasons make this approach necessary. Perhaps most notably, the ground must be prepared because America's understanding of a society whose apogee came nearly two millennia ago is a simplistic caricature fed by Hollywood extravaganzas and repeated phrases about military overextension, imperial excesses, and decline and fall.

Europeans should have a somewhat richer understanding of Roman realities, but when they, and the Asians, make the imperial comparisons involving the United States, their judgments are all too often no less questionable. America's commonly simplistic image of the outside world and of the distant past finds a worthy counterpart in the outsider's endless biases concerning America. This glibly professed European and Asian understanding of the United States is particularly exasperating, even infuriating, because it does not stem from simple ignorance or a lack of information but is so often rooted in a mixture of condescension, disdain, and even hatred mixed with envy.[27]

In the quest for a better understanding of Roman matters, all but a tiny share of Americans (as well as other speakers of non-Romance languages) share a disadvantage that can be fixed only by years of dedicated learning and a lifetime of devotion: the intricate, disciplined, parsimonious yet extravagant *lingua Latina* does not speak to them. This is, of course, only part of a much larger missing parcel: linguistic innocence is an American norm that extends even to the astonishingly inadequate Arabic and Farsi capabilities of the U.S. government's intelligence agencies. As a result, even the simplest of all Latin words, *et*, is constantly and inexplicably mispronounced by legions of opinionated TV experts as "ek."[28]

No less important, for all but a small fraction of Americans the names on the map of the Roman world evoke no recognition and carry no meaning; they are nothing but alien terms unconnected to any recognizable features (be they of a mundane or magnificent aspect). They do not produce images of natural grandeur (such as erupting volcanoes or gales checking the flow of a mighty river, both so memorably described by Lucretius),[29] or recall admirable achievements of bold engineering designs (tall arches of the *Aqua Claudia* marching unswervingly across the Roman *Campagna* would be an excellent example). Only the names of a few cities resonate, but how many would those be besides Rome itself, Pompeii, and

Figure I.8
Details of Trajan's column (completed 113 C.E.), a 30-m tall structure on an 8-m pedestal base, built of 20 Carrara marble drums and decorated with a 190-m winding frieze commemorating the emperor's Dacian wars (101–102 and 105–106 C.E.). Photo by V. Smil.

perhaps Carthage and Alexandria? How many Americans know of the importance of Augusta Treverorum or Dura Europos?[30]

I suspect that among the scores of experts who virtually live on the screens of ponderous political TV shows and who casually mention Roman-American parallels hardly anyone could locate the forests of Tarraconensis, the fields of Paphlagonia, and the shores of Syrtica on a blank map of lands surrounding *mare nostrum* (as Romans proprietarily called the Mediterranean).[31] And how many of them command any Braudelian *longue-durée* perspectives or have a secure understanding of key historical realities? How many editorial writers (now joined by masses of utterly unqualified bloggers) who pontificate on America's decline and Rome-like fall could confidently say which emperor came first—Trajan, whose victories in Dacia are commemorated on a splendid marble column that the Roman senate ordered to be built on his forum (figure I.8), or Marcus Aurelius, who set down (in idiomatic Greek) his Stoic thoughts while defending the empire's northern border among the Quadi at Granua?

Three generations ago a fairly solid knowledge of these matters was still *de rigueur* among European intellectuals, but it is no longer so in the EU of the early twenty-first century, and I have no illusion that the unprecedented numbers of European tourists visiting Rome take home any better appreciation of Roman history. Noting these weaknesses in basic understanding (*lacunae* is a fitting Latin word here) is not a matter of pedantic and irrelevant insistence on trivia or marginalities whose grasp (or lack of it) has no bearing on one's ability to understand and comment on Roman matters, to interpret their meaning and import, and to use them in historic analogies. *The opposite is true: an appreciation of the language, a feel for the lay of the Roman lands, a solid grasp of the glories and blunders of the empire's long history are among a few quintessential markers of necessary Latin/ Roman/imperial homework well done.*

In their absence it is not surprising that so many commentators can get away with trotting out obvious, generic realities as if they were brilliant, insightful observations; unfortunately, most of their readers, viewers, or listeners apparently take this verbal fluff for learned Roman-American analogies. And even more exasperating is the casualness with which the instant experts put together a few vague analogies about habits, preferences, or trends in two societies separated by two millennia in time and conclude that these will bring about similar long-term outcomes.

In this brief book I confirm the limited validity of some of these parallels, but its main aim is to diligently deconstruct most of that misleading comparative edifice that pictures America as a new Rome. I try to convey the complex and contradictory nature and achievements of the two great societies. I point out some valid parallels and similarities as well as fundamental differences.

In the second chapter I first explain the meaning of *empire* and assess how the U.S. realities do not fit the definition. This is followed by contrasting the territorial extents of the two states and by the examining America's peculiar global hegemony. In the third chapter I compare the inventiveness of the two societies and the power of their prime movers and energy sources. The fourth chapter focuses on the vastly different population dynamics of the two societies, on their experiences of illness and health, and on their distinctive patterns of wealth and misery. Finally, in a brief closing chapter I reassess the most commonly cited similarities between the two societies and recapitulate those fundamental differences that make Roman-American historical analogies dubious.

The Romans had an apt phrase, proverb, or poetry line for everything. *Homines libenter quod volunt credunt* (men believe what they want to), wrote Terentius; and

Seneca said that *fallaces sunt rerum species* (the appearances of things are deceptive). While it may not be possible to change the first reality, I try my best to go beyond surficial and deceptive appearances in order to clear away some misconceptions and fallacies and to demonstrate that America is not a new Rome. That is actually an easier task than to be able to say, with some certitude, what modern America is. Marcus Tullius Cicero knew that state of mind well: *Utinam tam facile vera invenire possem quam falsa convincere* (I only wish I could discover the truth as easily as I can uncover falsehood).

2

Why America Is Not a New Rome

Nam dempto hoc uno fulgore nominis Romani, quid est cur illi vobis comparandi sint?

For, setting aside only the splendour of the Roman name, what remains in which they can be compared to you?
—Titus Livius, *Ab urbe condita* XXI:xliii (Cyrus Edmonds, 1850 translation)

Chapters II–IV, the centerpiece of the book, answer the epigraph's question by restating, defining, redefining, questioning, criticizing, deconstructing, and rejecting some of the most important analogies and parallels that are made between Rome and America, and they detail a number of fundamental differences that make any meaningful comparisons questionable. I divide these matters among three broad categories and, for a closer topical examination, subdivide each into three subcategories. This division has nothing to do with any triadic preferences (not uncommon among Romans and even more favored in the Chinese numerology)[1] and everything to do with imposing necessary brevity. Matters tend to get out of hand when scholars deal with the history of the Roman Empire; they have suggested scores of reasons for its fall, ranging from indisputable to frivolous (Rollins 1983; D. Kagan 1992; Heather 2005).[2]

The recent flood of commentary devoted to the rise of American empire and its impending demise presents a similarly daunting array of reasons and causes behind these trends. Consequently, if the task were to be approached in an exhaustive manner, it would necessitate dealing with an encyclopedic range of subjects. Instead, I restrict my treatment to a relatively small number of fundamental realities and processes that best capture the internal dynamics and external affairs of the two states. With this choice I follow the ancient Roman admonition *non multa sed multum* and try to keep the task within reasonable limits. Even so, my topics range from the borders of the Roman Empire to the misfortunes of America's foreign policy, from childhood mortality to ingenious machines.

But before I introduce brief descriptions of the three central chapters, I must stress my commitment to definitional clarity. Using terms with clearly determined meaning is the mainstay of modern scientific inquiry, and it has been my practice in more than 40 years of research and writing. But this imperative is commonly ignored by many of those who deal with historical analogies. Even if we agree with Kamiya's (2007, 1) description that comparisons between two historical epochs are just "an excellent intellectual parlor game," we would still need some basic rules to play by. For any serious, systematic inquiry, an unambiguous understanding of essential terms is a necessary precondition of all meaningful comparisons; yet the relevant definitions are almost never supplied by those who casually measure the actions and the travails of today's America using the yardstick of Rome's ancient ways and accomplishments.

The first broad category of my inquiry concerns the extent and the power of the two great states. In the second chapter I begin these appraisals and contrasts by answering a key question: What is an empire? The term has been used casually in referring to the current actions and policies of the United States, as if its meaning were generally so well understood that it could go undefined. I examine it by explaining the dual meaning of the original Latin word *imperium*, by offering multifactorial definitions of the term, and by demonstrating that *empire* is not suitable for labeling the intents and actions of the modern American republic.

Only then do I contrast the often exaggerated power of the two states. I describe the borders and size of the Roman Empire in order to show that Rome, contrary to repeated assertions, did not control most of the world known in antiquity, and that the empire had contemporary peers. Paradoxically, it is on both of these accounts, and contrary to the commonly held notion of U.S. global supremacy, that the Roman-U.S. analogy works with near perfection. The United States also has never had any truly global political, strategic, or economic control (again, I am using the word *global* in its correct scientific sense). And ever since it emerged victorious from WW II the country has faced enormous military, economic, and ideological challenges not only from other major powers but also from determined adversaries in control of smaller states and more recently also from more nebulous, but no less deadly, terrorist organizations; unfortunately, a sober conclusion is that all these challenges may only intensify in the future.

In the third chapter I leave the mainstream of historical studies and concentrate on the biophysical fundamentals of the two states, on forces that circumscribe the achievements of all societies, be they military conquests, economic advances, or prevailing levels of individual well-being. The first section of chapter III contrasts the truly incomparable roles played by invention and innovation in the history of the two states, the second details their vastly different reliance on machines, and the last compares the energetic foundations of the two societies that circumscribe the scope and mode of strategic and economic action.

The fourth chapter looks at the most fundamental differences in quotidian lives of ordinary Romans and Americans. Its first section contrasts the population dynamics of the two societies, their vital statistics, life expectancies, and age structures in order to illustrate disparities whose magnitudes create profoundly different demographic and hence human and socioeconomic realities. The second looks at illness and death in the Roman Empire in general and in the capital megacity in particular in order to portray the reality of ubiquitous suffering and truncated lives. The last section is once again a foray into unorthodox history by using the best available evidence to contrast the magnitudes and distribution of wealth and misery in the two societies.

These two chapters—chapter III on inventions, machines, and energy sources and chapter IV on population dynamics, standard of living, and basic economic realities—could be criticized for engaging in anachronistic exercises or for being simply superfluous. How can we put the accomplishments and capacities of an ancient state on the same scale as those of a modern society that is two millennia younger? Is not the fact of dramatically different lives in the Roman world and in the modern United States a truism not worth belaboring? And can not one grant all these fundamental technical, demographic, and economic differences and still argue, as so many have done, that Rome and the United States enjoyed, in their respective (yet very different) worlds, similar positions of imperial power (however defined)?

There is perhaps no better quote to disarm the anachronism argument than to repeat what Scheidel (2003, 160) pointed out when explaining why a comparison of Roman and modern hygiene is not misplaced, even though the Romans were obviously not aware of bacterial infections or communicability of diseases: "It is exactly *because* the Romans were unaware of modern notions of hygiene that we must apply our own deliberately anachronistic standards in ascertaining the probable consequences of their absence." Similarly, a relative deficit of Roman inventiveness, marginal reliance on machines, low levels and inefficient modes of energy use, and a near-subsistence standard of living for most of the empire's citizens had immense consequences for the empire, and hence all of them must be examined (and wherever possible quantified) from modern perspectives.

Ignoring these contrasts between the ancient Romans and modern Americans because they seem obvious produces a comparison devoid of any attention to a critical set of fundamental factors that shape history and delimit the power of states.

Criticizing their inclusion because they are simply a part of well-appreciated differences between life in antiquity and modernity is to argue in favor of unrealistic, selective, and biased comparisons. It is one thing to grant this acknowledgment tacitly and without any examination or to do so in broad qualitative terms, and quite another matter to explore these differences (in inventiveness, reliance on machines, energy use, population dynamics, and economic performance) in as much quantitative detail as the combination of first principles and available historical sources allows.

Only such quantitative appraisals can make it clear if we are dealing with two societies whose differences in energetic, demographic, and economic matters are largely irrelevant for a comparative examination of their respective imperial postures, or if these biophysical fundamentals are (once they are properly taken into account) so unlike that focusing the comparison only on the political-military sphere does not make much sense. An excellent modern example of the failure to appreciate critical demographic and economic differences (or just acknowledging their existence in broad terms without in-depth specific inquiries) is the misleading nature of the standard comparison of the United States with the USSR.

Expert analysis agreed that the Soviet per capita GDP (even using the Central Intelligence Agency's highly exaggerated aggregates) was lower than the U.S. rate, that the Soviet economy was generally less flexible, and that Soviet citizens had a shorter life expectancy than Americans, but all these acknowledgments were perfunctory compared with the obsession about the numbers and capacities of the Soviet nuclear warheads, bombers, fighter planes, tanks, and troops. As a result, the USSR was seen even a few years before its dissolution as a very formidable superpower whose seemingly unstoppable ascent warranted higher military spending; during President Reagan's two terms the Pentagon's budget increased by about 40%, and the United States launched "Star Wars," a technically questionable missile defense program.

And yet a proper comparison would have shown that by the mid-1980s the USSR was an economically and demographically failed state, a state where the average life expectancy was actually declining and whose economy could not satisfy even the basic daily needs of its citizens. The result was inevitable—a collapse of that state brought about by its fundamental internal weaknesses, not by foreign determination. How different the U.S. posture vis-à-vis the USSR could have been if it had been genuinely appreciated that its citizens had an average standard of living commensurable with a second-rate regional power and that its demographic indicators pointed to a combination of quantitative and qualitative decline unparalleled in any other industrialized nation.

II

Empires, Powers, Limits

His ego nec metas rerum nec tempora pono;
imperium sine fine dedi . . .
Romanos rerum dominos gentemque togatam: sic placitum.

To these no period nor appointed date,
Nor bounds to their dominion I assign;
An endless empire shall the race await . . .
The Romans, rulers of the land and sea,
Lords of the flowing gown. So standeth my decree.

—Virgilius, *Aeneidos* I:278 (E. Fairfax Taylor translation, 1907)

There is nothing new about the uncritical elevation of Roman achievements or the hyperbolic admiration with which so many Western historians, novelists, and producers of films and TV series have echoed the judgment of classical writers (be they Roman or Greek) regarding the Roman Empire's extent, durability, and power.[1] Too many commentators have recently succumbed to a similarly uncritical appraisal of America's reach and might, a habit symbolized by unending references to the "only remaining superpower" and casual use of the term "American empire." Perhaps the most notable difference is that the latter label has been used as much in awe as with unease, and frequently with disapproval if not frank abhorrence by many foreigners and some fierce domestic critics.

But what is an empire? What if a closer examination shows that America does not have, and indeed never had, one? Would adding an adjective (*informal*) qualify the empire more accurately? Would hegemony be a more fitting label? Such questions are not a matter of irrelevant semantics or idle academic quibbling. Even a cursory consideration of these fundamental definitional differences makes it clear that *empire* and *hegemony* are not synonyms and that to explain the distinction requires more than citing a dictionary entry. Given their importance for the subject of this book's inquiry, I attempt to answer these questions in some detail.

In the real world empires or (if such descriptions better fit a complex reality) hegemonies do not last, and only a few of them ruled or dominated significant portions of the world for relatively long periods of time. But even such a seemingly straightforward task as coming up with a definite time span to be used in historical comparisons presents a challenge. This is particularly true in the Roman case: the state's long history poses problems of periodization, and selection of marker years has to consider disparities, uncertainties, and inconsistencies. Most of the published pontifications on America as a new Rome ignore these matters; they simply do not bother to explain what is being compared. Are we comparing the entire lifespans of the two political entities, or are we contrasting only clearly defined periods? The latter option would appear to be more logical, coherent, and manageable, but it still does not eliminate many challenging questions of historical periodization.

As for the United States, is it generally understood that references to America are limited to the country's recent history? If so, then when was the first time that America showed its imperialistic intents, or when did most of the commentators, foreign and domestic, conclude that its actions deserved such a label? Surely it was not only in 1991, after the first Gulf War and with the demise of the other superpower, when the talk of empire became so common. Was it, then, in 1945, when the United States emerged from WW II as the world's leading economic and military power and the only possessor of nuclear weapons? And would it not be logical to see the roots of America's imperial policy in the late 1890s, when the country took its first colonial step during the Spanish-American war as it engaged the declining Spanish empire both in the Caribbean and in the Pacific?[2]

But was not the country's first colonial step the support the U.S. government gave in 1893 to a revolt led by Samuel Dole (his eponymous company is still a great power in the global fruit trade), which deposed Queen Liliuokalani and resulted in the seizure of Hawaii by American planters? Or should the war with Mexico (1846–1848), which ended with a massive enlargement of the United States with the westward addition of lands between Texas and California and as far north as southern Wyoming, be seen as the first demonstration of America's imperial ambitions (figure II.1)?[3]

Analogical questions and even greater uncertainties apply to Roman history. Even if it is agreed (as is usually implied) that only imperial Rome is the subject of comparison, then it is still necessary to be familiar with the essential features of the long republican period that preceded it because it was during those centuries when a determined, coherent polity centered on Rome prevailed first over its immediate neighbors, developed its governance, strengthened its economic and military

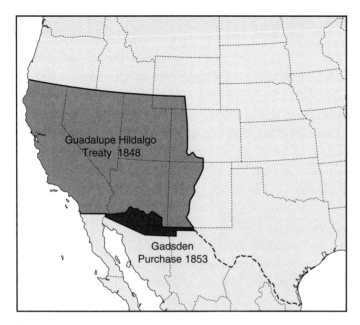

Figure II.1
America's territorial gains from the war with Mexico, 1846–1848.

capability, and began its protracted territorial expansion. Do we thus delimit the span under consideration by starting with the traditional date for the foundation of the Roman Republic (509 B.C.E.), or do we begin only during the middle of the third century B.C.E. at the time of the First Punic War (264–241 B.C.E.), when Rome began the campaigns to acquire possessions beyond the Italian peninsula?[4]

The next step would be easy only if the formal means of governance could be equated with imperial intents and goals. Historians often argue about the periodization of major epochs (the Renaissance and the Industrial Revolution are the two spans that are perhaps the most difficult to delimit to everyone's satisfaction), but dating the beginning of imperial Rome (*sensu stricto*, as the beginning of monarchy) is not a highly contentious matter, at least not in the sense that the two obvious dates fall within the same generation. Years of deepening political and personal divisions, increased violence, military intimidation, rebellions, and rioting led first to a large-scale civil war (49–45 B.C.E.) between Gaius Julius Caesar and Gnaeus Pompeius Magnus (Pompey) and his son Sextus, then to Caesar's brief rule, followed by the second triumvirate (Octavianus, Caesar's adoptive son; Marcus Antonius [Mark Antony]; and Marcus Lepidus), a new bout of civil war that ended in the defeat of Antony (31 B.C.E.) and the elevation of Octavianus to *princeps* by the senate in 27 B.C.E.[5]

Consequently, the earliest date for the formal beginning of the empire is 45 B.C.E., when Caesar became a virtual dictator (de facto end of the republic), and the latest one is 27 B.C.E., when Octavianus received supreme power from the senate as Augustus; the latter is the generally acknowledged beginning of the principate that survived afterward in various forms (sometimes gloriously but often as nothing but a seemingly unending series of plots, counterplots, and assassinations) for almost exactly 500 years. But to equate the onset of monarchy with the onset of imperial behavior (*sensu lato*) would be a patent error: the beginnings of that behavior must be traced to the emergence of imperial core-periphery relations between Romans and allies/subjects that define the Roman Empire.

And the empire's ending date is perhaps even more problematic. The least part of it is choosing 476 C.E., when Odoacer deposed Flavius Romulus Augustus, or 480 C.E., when the never enthroned Julius Nepos was assassinated. Those two exits were to the end of the Western Empire what the departure of a last few lingering attendees is to emptying a large sold-out theater after a lengthy and, as the end approaches, unremittingly bloody play. Should we not reduce the empire's effective span by a century, to the year 378 C.E. when the emperor Flavius Julius Valens was killed by the invading Goths at Hadrianopolis? After that time the empire never regained its previous (albeit often dented) integrity as it entered a period of near-continuous dismemberment with large swaths of its territory repeatedly overrun or continuously ruled by the irresistibly advancing Vandals, Goths, and Huns.[6]

On the other hand, there is the problem of what to do about the Eastern Empire, which became permanently separated after Theodosius's death in 395 C.E. but whose distancing from the center began officially more than a century earlier, when Diocletian divided the *imperium* in 286 C.E., and was strengthened by Constantine's establishment of a new eastern capital in 330 C.E. That empire—Βασιλεῖα τήυ Ρωμαίων (Basileia tōn Rōmaiōn) in its eventual old-new official language—was a richer part of the former whole; it carried on with most of the long-established norms, and it survived for nearly another thousand years (albeit in increasingly truncated forms) after the demise of the Western Empire (figure II.2).

Because of this combination of continuity and longevity the cutoff at 476 C.E., logical and obvious as it seems from some perspectives, cannot be a satisfactorily conclusive solution but merely an expedient choice. The most famous (but given its length not necessarily the most often read) account of the Roman Empire's decline and fall, Gibbon's narrative, rejects it and opts for the imperial continuity; Gibbon

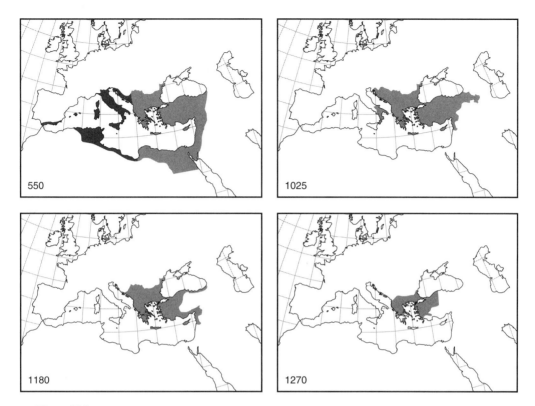

Figure II.2
The changing extent of the Eastern Roman Empire. Compiled from various maps. Temporary reconquest of parts of the Western Empire by Belisarius is shown in a different shading.

ends the story in 1453 as the forces of Mohammed II finally breached Constantinople's massive walls and killed the last of the Roman emperors.[7]

And given the longevity of the Roman Empire, it is possible to select either a period of relative stability and prosperity or one of deepening loss of control as the Roman comparative yardstick. In the first instance, Gibbon's influence has been decisive; perhaps none of the sentences in his massive opus is quoted more often than this elegant conclusion:

> If a man were called to fix the period in the history of the world during which the condition of the human race was most happy and prosperous, he would, without hesitation, name that which elapsed from the death of Domitian to the accession of Commodus. (I, 70).

This period, between 96 and 180 C.E., spanned the rule of just five emperors,[8] the last one, Marcus Aurelius, being perhaps the empire's most sympathetic ruler

Figure II.3
Marcus Aurelius, emperor of Rome (161–180 C.E.). His grand equestrian statue is on the Capitoline Hill, the original in the Palazzo Nuovo and a replica in Michelangelo's Piazza del Campidoglio. Photo by V. Smil.

(figure II.3), and it was undoubtedly imperial Rome's golden age of extended peace and orderly transfer of power.

But choosing it as a yardstick for historical comparisons would be no less problematic than selecting the fourth century C.E., filled with imperial assassinations and territorial disarray, or, to give a modern example, claiming that the 1990s (with the Evil Empire unraveled, Japan's economy in retreat, oil prices low and stable, U.S. military power supreme in the wake of the Gulf War, and the country's economy prospering) provide a definitive comparative yardstick for the achievements of modern America.[9] On reflection, rigid period truncations are undesirable.

My references to Rome are overwhelmingly to the centuries of the principate, the period of peak but also contested Roman power; moreover, today's public knowledge of that period (as caricatured as it may be) is comparatively greater than for either earlier or later eras. Similarly, in order to make sense to readers, my references to America are generally to the post–WW II era, when the United States became an undoubted but also variously challenged superpower. At the same time, it should be kept in mind that during its middle to late republican period Rome was every bit as "imperial" (above all, territorially expansive) as during the later monarchical era, and that U.S. "imperialist" activities, such as they were (see the next section), peaked around 1900.

Answering the question about the extent of an empire (the lands directly controlled by a central administration) and its relations with the lands outside its borders (some not beyond its influence, others far away and yet a source of feared incursions and attacks) may seem a much easier task. And it would be so if it were limited just to descriptions of expanding or contracting territories, and if we were comparing two very similar political entities. Unfortunately, neither is true in this case. To begin with, the task is greatly complicated by the interpretation of such operative (but inevitably loaded) words as *control*, *boundaries*, and *domination*. Control may range from a firm physical possession of a territory and unimpeded exercise of central power to a questionable rule by proxy using a weak local regime whose own control may not extend much beyond a capital.

Although the Romans divided their known world starkly between *imperium* and *barbaricum*, the second realm was subject to many gradations of attitude, ranging from the cultivation of friendship, cooperation, and tolerance with associates and friends (*socii et amici*) to fear of and enmity toward strangers, no matter if they resided just across a border or rode in from afar to breach the empire's borders and conquer its lands. In contrast, the U.S. hegemony has never relied on extensive occupation of foreign lands, and this reality does not make any simple comparisons of the territories dominated by the two societies very meaningful. At the same time, Americans have also experienced a full range of attitudes toward their *barbaricum*, ranging from a generously rapid embrace of former enemies to long-lasting enmity and from muted concerns to panicky fears.

But the military origins of the two states are very different. The powerful Roman Republic was created by a lengthy series of wars, first on the Italian peninsula and later throughout the neighboring Mediterranean lands, and these conquests were extended into deep hinterlands of *mare nostrum* (and even beyond them) during the last decades of the republic and the subsequent centuries of imperial rule. The American republic is also a product of wars, first the War of Independence (1775–1782), then the great internal conflict of 1861–1865, which opened the way for the country's rapid modernization. But its global reach is the outcome of participation and victories in the two world wars of the twentieth century, which it entered only reluctantly and after being provoked or attacked.

My appraisal of modern (post–WW II) American power (military, economic, or cultural) will be counterintuitive. I do not join the chorus of those who repeat the refrains about "the greatest superpower ever," about the United States "dominating the globe" (or "nearly the entire globe"), about "no nation looming so large" since Roman times, about an "unprecedented power" and "the wonder of the world." Instead, I survey a multitude of America's weaknesses and vulnerabilities in order to show that such commonly overawed assessments are but flawed perceptions of a much less powerful nation whose past choices displayed little if any true imperial behavior and whose options have become more restricted even as it has grown stronger in absolute terms.

What Is an Empire?

When comparing the two powerful societies that are the subject of our inquiry, the terms *Rome* and *America* are readily (and correctly) understood to be shorthand for the ancient Roman state and for the United States of America. Unfortunately, there is no comparably intuitive understanding or ready agreement regarding the definition of *empire*. This is no problem for commentators who, as I noted in the previous chapter, see *empire* as a fitting label for the actions and intents of the modern United States, and hence they feel that it provides a perfect categorical analogy for comparisons with the ancient Roman state. Many of these commentators take the imperial status and ethos of the modern United States entirely for granted and concentrate on exploring and explaining its political, military, economic, and social implications.

A few representative citations illustrate this school of thought. Perhaps most notably, more than 2,400 American historians believe that America has an empire whose further expansion must be stopped: by the end of 2007 that many had signed an online petition against the war in Iraq that was first circulated in September 2003.[10] According to Buchanan (1999), much of U.S. foreign policy during the twentieth century was undesirably imperial. Johnson (2000) focused on the imperial "blowback," on the costs and unintended consequences of American actions abroad. Bacevich (2002) edited a volume of 20 essays that examined various aspects of the prospects and problems of American empire. Ryn (2003) wrote about the ideology of American empire, and Mann (2003) had no doubt about its existence based on "ruthless arrogance" and about its incoherence.

Ferguson (2004) favored the imperial label for anything from making sea lanes secure for international trade to the exports of U.S. consumer goods and entertainments; by such a definition the United States must be an empire many times over. Gowan (2004, 491) concurred, stating that the United States "possess strong elements of what we have called a capitalist world empire." Morgan (2006, 215) echoed a widely held perception when he concluded that "American empire has put strain on the military, which, like the Roman legions of past millennia, is the ultimate means of enforcing the imperial will."

Sale (2005) looked ahead with an unequivocal catastrophism in a book review entitled "Imperial Entropy: Collapse of the American Empire". His last sentence left no room for alternatives: "Hence no chance to escape the collapse of empire." Not surprisingly, after the U.S. invasion of Iraq, Britain's leading leftist historian wrote about the empire expanding "wider and wider" and ascribed to it a goal unprecedented in history: aiming at global domination and going about it by "an extraordinary, ruthless, antagonistic flaunting" of power (Hobsbawm 2003, 3).

I would need several paragraphs just to list other titles of recently published comments that predict an imminent collapse of American empire due to the imperial overstretch of the superpower that is "already clearly past its zenith" (Hiro 2007, 5) and that has no chance to be an exception to the age-old pattern of imperial demise. But one more judgment should not be missed, that of Gore Vidal, whose writings have promoted the idea of ruthless, predatory, conspiring American empire for decades. According to Vidal, the American empire "was carefully thought out by four men"—Alfred Thayer Mahan, Brooks Adams, Theodore Roosevelt (figure II.4), and Henry Cabot Lodge—during the 1890s, worked out largely in secret, and accomplished by means of the Spanish-American War.[11] Vidal's conclusion in an essay published in 1986: "Despite the criticism of the few, the Four Horsemen pulled it off. Then United States was a world empire" (2005, 49).

Its expansion followed, but Vidal, always an incisive thinker, had actually parted with the notion of an aggrandizing empire in 1985, long before most of the commentators embraced it:

On September 16, 1985, when the Commerce Department announced that the United States had become a debtor nation, the American Empire was as dead, theoretically, as its predecessor, the British. . . . Like most modern empires, ours rested not so much on military prowess as on economic primacy. (2005, 41)

A pretty definitive description of *imperii finis*. The future that Vidal foresaw was Asiatic, a combination of Japan's technical prowess and China's "resourceful

Figure II.4
Theodore Roosevelt, a leading promoter of war with Spain in 1898 and the twenty-sixth U.S. president (1901–1909). Courtesy of Library of Congress, LC-DIG-pga-02409.

landmass" with Europe and the United States "simply irrelevant to the world that matters" (2005, 43).[12]

Remarkably, all these commentators proceeded with their analyses without ever defining the meaning of empire. Do they believe that a uniform notion of this obviously complex concept is shared by all their readers? If so, why did Vidal terminate the empire in 1985 while others are still using the term, including nearly 2,500 professional historians, who protested its post-2001 "expansion"? And what if there has been no American empire, what if (as argued by some historians and students of international politics and strategy) that term should be dismissed as a clearly inappropriate choice for America's actions compared to Roman realities?

This would turn Roman-U.S. imperial analogies into misplaced exercises based on forcing fundamentally different realities into preconceived ideological molds. Unless one unquestioningly accepts the ideological biases of those for whom the very existence of an (undefined) American empire is a foregone conclusion, it is imperative to take a closer look at the etymology of that noun, come up with its sensible modern definition, and then apply it to the recent actions and intents of the United States. Obvious starts are not helpful. Standard definitions are either tautologous (and hence entirely unsatisfactory: "a monarchy with an emperor as head of state" or "a domain ruled by an emperor or empress"), or they require additional definitions of other key terms.

If an empire is "a group of countries under a single authority" then, given the very large number of legally binding directions that incessantly reach the member states from Brussels, the EU would surely qualify. And Taagepera's (1978, 113) definition of empire as "any large sovereign political entity whose components are not sovereign, irrespective of this entity's internal structure or official designation" rests on a contentious interpretation of *sovereignty*. Is Canada an empire because Quebec's status as a nation, recognized on November 27, 2006, even by the federal House of Commons (albeit as a nation within Canada), is not accompanied by exclusive control of its destiny (a long-sought aim of the separatist *Parti Québecois*) and because its northern territories (Northwest, Yukon, and Nunavut) have no inherent jurisdiction?[13]

I find Schroeder's (2003, 1) definition best: "Empire means political control exercised by one organized political unit over another unit separate from it and alien to it." Schroeder rightly stresses that while many factors enter into empire (ranging from economic and technical matters to ideology and religion), "its essential core is political: the possession of final authority by one entity over the vital political decisions of another." But his definition does not fit perfectly all historical realities because some empires—including the chaotically managed Roman Empire after the third century C.E., the Byzantine Empire, or China at any time after the unified Qin period (third century B.C.E.)—did not have a clearly defined core that lorded it over other political systems.

But Schroeder's definition clearly excludes Canada as an empire, and it perfectly describes the Roman Empire at the height of its centralized power as well as the Soviet empire in whose westernmost outpost I grew up. When the three states on its western European flank attempted to chart a more independent course, the ultimate arbiter intervened, with a bloody suppression of the Hungarian uprising in 1956, a massive occupation of Czechoslovakia in 1968, and the suppression of the Polish Solidarity movement under martial law in 1981. And, to illustrate another important reality of imperial control, the rule does not have to be direct because local collaborators can administer imperial outposts with exemplary zeal, even with fanaticism matching or surpassing that of their distant overlords; again, the post-1948 history of the country where I grew up offers a perfect illustration.[14]

Figure II.5
Gaius Julius Caesar Augustus, Rome's first emperor. This marble statue, in the Vatican
Museums, is a replica of a lost original found in 1863 in Prima Porta near Rome.

Linguistically, the term *empire* presents a fundamental definitional duality (which
is readily explained) and a challenge of actual application (a matter that is not so
easily settled). The first problem arises from the contrast between the original and
the later, derived, meaning of the term. This complication is due to "a shift, or
more precisely an extension of meaning" (Richardson 1991, 1). In its original sense
the noun simply described the right to command (*imperare*) within the Roman
state. Understood in its widest sense, *imperium populi Romani* "was the power
Romans exercised over other peoples" (Lintott 1981, 53). Early Roman kings held
the *imperium*; under the principate it was vested in the magistrates (consuls and
praetors) during their brief time in power (one year) or in promagistrates (pro-
consuls and propraetors) during the time they fought abroad or administered
conquered territories. And so Augustus, the first emperor (figure II.5) and the only
one whose autobiographical recital of accomplishments was preserved (in *Res
Gestae Divi Augusti*), could say that in his nineteenth year, after raising an army
at his own expense and freeing the state, "the senate enrolled me in its order ...
assigning me the place of consul ... and gave me the imperium" (*imperium
mihi dedit*).

This right of *imperium* clearly extended to the ultimate matters of life and death,
and it always contained an element of the mysterious.[15] While this exalted sense of

imperium was never lost in the Roman understanding of state affairs, by the second half of the first century C.E. the noun acquired its concrete meaning as the political and spatial designation of a powerful state in control of extensive territories, and *imperium Romanum* came to be used much as we now use the term. Because all but a tiny share of its modern users are not even aware of the broad, fundamental, and mysterious meaning of *imperium*—for them the term simply evokes a far-flung and usually aggrandizing, if not outright aggressive, state—it is easy to argue that the historical comparisons have only the concrete image of a territory-bound empire in mind.

The term has been used in this sense quite commonly to label numerous entities that preceded the *imperium Romanum* (Sumerian, Egyptian, Akkadian, Harappan, Shang, Zhou, Hittite, Assyrian empires), that were its contemporaries (Parthian, Sasanid, Qin, Han), and that followed it (Byzantine, Sasanid, Muslim, Tang, Holy Roman, Mongol, Yuan, Ottoman, Ming, Spanish, Qing, Russian, British, Soviet). And it is obvious that the term has been used rather indiscriminately; it has been applied, particularly in the case of ancient states, without any attention to the longevity or the territorial extent of those states.

Barfield's (2001) classification of empires imposes a much needed order on this incoherence. In his classification primary empires are states established by conquest that exercise sovereignty over large (subcontinental or continental) territories inhabited by substantial and diverse populations (at least 10^6, more often 10^7, people) by relying on centralized administration. The Roman Empire and China's successive dynasties are perfect examples of this category. In contrast, secondary, or shadow, empires take a variety of outward forms, ranging from mirror empires (which pressure neighboring primary empires for tribute payments, a model deployed by many nomad states on China's northern and western borders) to maritime trade empires (which use relatively small armed forces and limited territorial control in order to leverage rich economic profits).[16]

Barfield (2001) also noted that empires tend to increase diversity, and that their need for effective transportation and communication arrangements (in order to promote economic activity and project their cultural identity) leaves legacies beyond their eventual duration. Again, both the Roman Empire and the Chinese dynasties illustrate these realities. The obvious question, then, is the suitability of the imperial label for describing the past and present actions and intents of the United States. The first choice is obvious: the United States is not, *pace* Barfield, a primary empire. Even Hobsbawm (2003), writing from an uncompromisingly leftist perspective, had to admit that the United States has actually never practiced colonialism. The territories it seized during its nineteenth-century expansion were either incorporated into the federal state (albeit not immediately) or set free. California, ceded by the Guadalupe Hidalgo Treaty in 1848, became the thirty-first state in 1850; Nevada became a state in 1864, Utah in 1896, and Arizona and New Mexico in 1912.

Congressional consent for the war against Spain forbade any annexation of Cuba (Teller amendment), and cuba regained its independence by the Treaty of Paris in December 1898. The postwar history of the Philippines is often considered America's first real colonial/imperial experience. The Philippine War of Independence (1899–1902) followed the Spanish defeat, and America's military response actually shared some similarities with the conquest of Iraq and its aftermath.[17] But no permanent colonial regime followed the war's end; by 1902 the U.S. Supreme Court made the U.S. Constitution applicable to the islands, and the Philippines became independent in July 1946.

As for the other two gains from the Spanish War, Guam and Puerto Rico eventually became "organized but unincorporated" territories of the United States, and Puerto Ricans have repeatedly rejected (by votes in 1967, 1993, and 1998) either statehood or independence. Hawaii became the fiftieth state in 1959. Consequently, even during the aftermath of the Spanish-American war, when the United States was in temporary control of distant territories, its actions conformed only very feebly to what some definitions (Doyle 1986; Schroeder 2003) consider a key imperial attribute, a dichotomy between a ruling core and a ruled periphery.

After its victory in WW II the United States did not behave like an imperial power: it did not annex any foreign territories or impose any direct permanent military rule in the defeated countries. Even in the two countries whose defeat cost the United States more "blood and treasure" than any other conflict in the nation's history, the U.S. occupation powers ended fairly soon: in Japan in 1952 and in West Germany in 1954. And while significant numbers of U.S. military forces remain in Germany and Japan, the United States has no control of the political process and no legal authority over the citizens of the two countries (just the opposite is true; U.S. servicemen are now judged by local courts for their crimes).

There was never any intent to subject South Korea after 1953 to U.S. military or civilian rule, and nobody has suggested creating the American equivalents of *France outre-mer* (Guyana, Guadaloupe, Martinique, etc.) by administratively taking over the two small countries that were temporarily invaded by U.S. troops (Grenada in 1983, Panama in 1989). In the case of the two latest military engagements, the United States insisted on the earliest possible elections and transfer of power to national governments: a new Afghani government led by Hamid Karzai was sworn in December 2001, and a new Iraqi government under Ayad Allawi took over 15 months after the fall of Baghdad, in March 2003. President Bush affirmed in his graduation address at West Point in June 2002 that "America has no empire to extend or utopia to establish. We wish for others only what we wish for ourselves—safety from violence, the rewards of liberty, and the hope for a better life."

And there is simply no factual basis for the often repeated claim of America as a global (using that word in its strict spatial sense) hegemon or the world's dominant power. This claim is usually supported by pointing out the large number of the U.S. troops deployed abroad and the many U.S. military bases around the world: Walker (2002) had the U.S. military dominating the globe through 200 overseas bases, and Viansino (2005), through 800 bases in 130 countries. These claims are wrong; it is easy to check the reality. Even with the wars in Iraq and Afghanistan there has been no indication of expanding military reach; in 2005 neither the total number of troops deployed abroad nor their share of the overall count were at unprecedented levels, and there were only 14 countries with large U.S. troop deployment (more than 1,000), half the total of the late 1950s (figure II.6).

The Department of Defense annual *Base Structure Report* contains detailed information that dispels the notion of U.S. military tentacles embracing the planet. As of the end of 2005 the United States had 3,731 military bases, 2,888 in the United States, 77 in the U.S. territories, and 766 abroad in 31 countries and territories, not counting the bases in Iraq and Afghanistan, the two countries where its troops were in combat (USDOD 2006). But 91% of all foreign bases were small installations, and in 12 countries or territories such bases consisted of fewer than 50 people, including one man on the Bahamian island of Andros, where the U.S. Navy stills owns a single building. Only Bahrain, Serbia (where the troops were peacekeepers), and four NATO countries (Belgium with NATO headquarters, Iceland, Spain, and Turkey) hosted between 1,000 and 2,000 members of the U.S. military, and more than 10,000 U.S. army, navy, or marine personnel were only in the United Kingdom, Italy, South Korea, Japan, and Germany.

The last three countries contained about 70% of all U.S. overseas bases, with 80% of all military personnel abroad (this comparison excludes the changing totals of combat troops in Iraq and Afghanistan). There are, of course, U.S. marines guarding many embassies and military personnel engaged in training or technical assistance (as is true of numerous Brits, Frenchmen, or Russians), and that is how the claims of countries with a U.S. military presence are boosted to well over 100. But a detailed perusal of the base report makes it difficult to see how seven people on

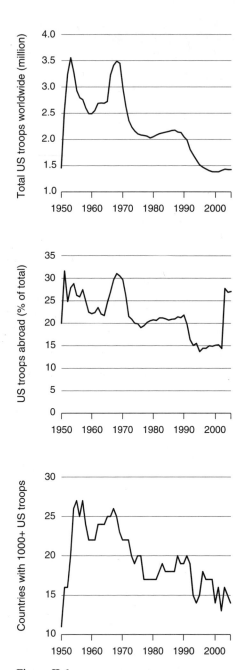

Figure II.6
U.S. troops deployed abroad (absolute numbers and shares of totals) and number of countries with more than 1,000 U.S. troops, 1950–2005. Plotted from data in Kane (2006).

St. Helena or 12 people in Norway, one man in Bahamas, and two in Oman, and a few hundred people in Portugal and Cuba (Guantánamo Bay) make the United States a global hegemon.

The three countries with the largest numbers of U.S. military bases and noncombat troops obviously do not take orders either from local commanders or from the Pentagon, unless one believes that the United States prefers to have a key European ally governed for decades by a Socialist party, now also with generous additions of *die Grüne*, and widespread anti-American sentiment (as has been the case in Germany); or a leadership that has often gone against U.S. desires in its soft treatment of its irrational neighbor (as in South Korea); or a country that has been allowed unlimited access to U.S. markets but has practiced unfair and multifaceted protectionism at home (as even a reforming Japan still does).

Even in Latin America, in the hemisphere claimed by the venerable Monroe doctrine as the sphere of America's special influence, the United States is hardly in control. It has chosen to live with a number of signal defeats and disappointments since 1945, most notably Fidel Castro's decades of Communist rule in Cuba (figure II.7) and most recently with open insults from the president of Venezuela. And even the most leftist anti-American intellectuals would not make the argument that the United States somehow controls or dominates China, India, and Russia, countries that now account for two-fifths of humanity and whose combined economic product (expressed in purchasing power parity) is larger than that of the United States. Nor could they, particularly not after 9/11, assert that the United States has any hegemonic powers in the Muslim world.

But should not the United States be seen as a special variant of a maritime trade empire, leveraging its military power (without protracted direct rule and controlling occupation of large territories) and technical prowess to harness large economic benefits in the global marketplace? Yes, there can be no doubt about the truly global roles played by U.S. innovations in the transportation, communication, and information sectors; the era of unprecedented globalization seems unimaginable without such U.S. multinational companies as Boeing, IBM, Intel, GE, or Microsoft.[18] These corporations have been obvious beneficiaries of globalization, but has the country (which has lost millions of well-paying jobs and is sinking ever deeper into debt) really benefited? The argument about America as a new species of maritime trade empire would work if the United States had a large trade surplus and if its currency were an indisputable standard of global trade.

There is yet another special imperial category claimed for the United States. Some of those who advocate the notion of American empire maintain that the United

Figure II.7
Fidel Castro, who ruled Cuba for 48 years (January 1960 to February 2008, when he ceded power to his brother Raul), was a deeply irritating reminder of the limits of U.S. power. Photo from Prensa Latina.

States does not need to occupy and control large territories because it is a de facto empire that functions without direct (administrative and political) involvement in foreign countries and imposes its designs and goals by a combination of military, economic, and cultural means that creates compliant client states. This use of *empire* as a metaphorical label for American aims and intentions has become commonplace, but there are two fundamental problems with this reasoning, one generic, the other specific.

All powerful nations have always furthered their goals by a combination of means at their disposal. Is then France—with its troops stationed permanently in Senegal, Gabon, and Djibouti; with a new permanent military base in the United Arab Emirates; with its paratroopers repeatedly dispatched to trouble spots in its former African colonies; with its efforts to bind the French-speaking world with cultural and technical cooperation through the creation of what eventually became *Organisation internationale de la Francophonie*—an empire? Does India qualify because it helped to create a new, less hostile, state on its eastern border when Indian troops invaded East Pakistan and their intervention led to independent Bangladesh by the end of 1971 and thus weakened India's principal enemy, Pakistan? Or because of its active diplomacy aimed at influencing its neighbors and nearby states as well as gaining the approval of the United States for its nuclear status?

A close examination of modern U.S. history makes it clear that the United States has been anything but omnipotent in imposing its designs (a point I make in detail in the third section of this chapter). Consequently, it is impossible to disagree with Robinson (2005, 42–43), who argued that hegemony (Greek *hēgemonía*, ἡγεμονία) is a much more fitting description of the U.S. role than empire: "If we are to pay any attention to the root meaning of our words, hegemony makes a much better descriptor than empire." Schroeder (2003, 1) argued along the same lines: "A hegemon is first among equals; and imperial power rules over subordinates . . . imposes its decision when it wishes." And Scheidel (2006a, 12) made it clear, after examining the recent arguments about America as an "imperial republic," that *empire*'s "suggested conceptual synonymity with, and semantic superiority over, *hegemony* remains wholly unsupported."

Clearly, the United States does not rule and it does not command. It leads; it has allies, not subjects; and a leader, unlike an absolute sovereign, cannot demand submission. Schroeder (2003, 1–2) sees a hegemonic power as "the one without whom no final decision can be reached within a given system; its responsibility is essentially managerial, to see that a decision is reached." Based on this definition, the post–WW II United States has not even been a strong hegemon because it has had frequent problems exerting its authority and has repeatedly failed to obtain general (or even dominant) consent even among its closest allies.

The second, specific, reason that the United States is not a de facto empire is logically even more compelling than the absence of territorial control or repeated failures of consent and cooperation. Its essence was captured perfectly by Schroeder (2003, 2): "Those who speak of an American empire bringing freedom and democracy to the world are talking of dry rain and snowy blackness. In principle and by definition, empire is the negation of political freedom, liberation, and self-determination." And historic evidence also provides plenty of examples of empires as aggressive, and sometimes brutal, tools of exploitation: Spain's post-1519 actions in America, Belgian rule in Congo, and Japan's Greater Co-prosperity Sphere in WW II Asia are just three infamous cases of this behavior.

Roman rule, even during the two most assertive centuries of the principate, may have been less systematically exploitative, but there is no doubt that the Roman Italians did not pay (much) for their empire but their provincial subjects did. In contrast, during the twentieth century the supposedly imperial United States paid a considerable price not only for the liberation of their European and Asian allies (and enemies) but also for their postwar defense. Those countries—most prominently Germany, France, Britain, Italy, Japan, and South Korea—continue to reap enormous economic benefits by not having to pay adequately for their own protection or to transfer resources to the "imperial" protector. In that sense, as Scheidel stresses, the United States is the *exact opposite* of the Roman Empire.

America, eager to expand the benefits of personal liberty and functioning democracy, can be accused of many things—of naivete or arrogance, of misreading the history and culture of distant lands, or of engaging in inappropriate state building—but it cannot be accused of being imperial. If words are to retain their consistent meanings, if definitions are to be based on realities and not on fanciful interpretations, then the verdict is clear: the United States has never been an empire, and the fact that some commentators claim it has been, ascribe to it the most sinister intents, and eagerly anticipate its demise does not make it so. On the other hand, it is sensible to use the hegemony label for America's intents and actions as long as the term is qualified by noting that the United States frequently cannot assert its leadership and obtain desired consent even among its closest allies and that even such a relatively limited role is fiercely questioned and opposed by many Americans.

America's political strength, cultural allure, strategic might, and economic weight put the country into an extraordinary category for which *empire* may be an appealing, evocative label but one that is far from accurate. No matter how powerful America is, and no matter how much that power is welcomed or resented, it is America's influence, not dominance, its seriously strained and much contested hegemony, not its unchallenged dictates, that best describe the reality. There should be arguments about the real nature, actual reach and efficacy, and eventual durability of U.S. hegemony, but *imperium* (even with qualifiers like *indirect*, *de facto*, or *virtual*) is a patently false category for conducting such debates.

Roman Reach: Hyperboles and Realities

By Jupiter's decree the reach of the Roman Empire (in both space and time) was decided at the mythical beginning of the state when Romulus established the city of Romans. In Virgil's words (*Aeneidos* I:278), quoted in this chapter's epigraph, this was to be an *imperium sine fine* (empire without end).[19] Such a phrase may be a fine display of poetic license, but it is factual nonsense and obviously no basis for historical comparisons. Yet the hyperbolic but influential idea of Rome as an empire without end—a master of οἰκουμένη (*oikoumene*, the world's inhabited regions, Roman *orbis terrarum*)—had appeared long before the empire reached its greatest extent.

Polybius, writing sometime between 167 and 146 B.C.E. (that is, even before the conquests of two key large provinces of the future empire, Macedonia and Aegyptus, which were incorporated, respectively, in 146 and 30 B.C.E.), asked at the beginning of his *Histories* (I:1), "For who is so worthless or indolent as not to wish to know by what means and under what system of polity the Romans in less than fifty-three years have succeeded in subjecting nearly the whole inhabited world to their sole government—a thing unique in history?"

Two issues of *denarii* during the seventh decade B.C.E. have a figure of Roma wearing a diadem, fasces in her left hand and setting her right foot on a globe (Crawford 1974, 413). *Res Gestae Divi Augusti* (The Deeds of Divine Augustus, the autobiographical funerary inscription engraved on two bronze pillars in Rome in 14 C.E.) were those "*quibus orbem terrarum imperio populi Romanum subiecit*" ("by which he subjected the whole wide earth to the rule of the Roman people").[20] Incredibly, these hyperbolic claims of imperial hubris have survived the following two millennia quite unchanged; they continue to describe the ancient Roman reach.

For example, S. J. Harrison (1997, 75) ended his examination of the survival and supremacy of Rome by noting that far-flung dangers depicted on the Shield of Aeneas can be "seen as providing future perils and victories for Rome under Augustus' leadership, enabling it to extend its military supremacy to the global level." And similar hyperboles are now used to portray the magnitude of American power; the extraordinary extent of the two states is usually seen as their major shared attribute. To quote a typical example (emphasis supplied): "The Roman Empire included almost *the entire then-known world*; the United States dominates almost the *entire globe* since the collapse of the Soviet Union" (Bender 2003b, 145).

I chose this citation because it exemplifies the errors that are commonly committed in order to assert the validity of Roman-American comparisons. Such descriptions cannot be tolerated as just being creatively hyperbolic; they are demonstrably, and inexcusably, incorrect. Nor can they be dismissed or ignored by pointing out that the relative power of ancient states is better compared in terms of population under their control and that in this respect the Roman Empire's reach was quite impressive; it controlled perhaps as much as one-quarter of humanity, and an even larger share of people lived close enough to be under its partial or indirect influence.

Population may have mattered more than territory because of limited (or nonexistent) ability of ancient societies to extract valuable natural resources in regions remote from their core areas and because of slow, expensive, and unreliable means of long-distance transportation and communication, but this does not invalidate the importance of controlling (however tenuously) contiguous areas in far-flung states with widely separated centers of high population density. In any case, those who extoll the comparative greatness of Rome or who describe the magnitude of U.S. power do so overwhelmingly on the basis of territorial control, and hence the argument must be joined in those terms.

In the Roman case, the claim about "the entire then-known world" is easy to dismiss; the unfortunate phrasing is burdened with ethnocentricity (known by whom?); no Old World civilization knew anything about the Americas and Australia. But the claim is obviously false even if the known world is taken to be just that part of the *oikoumene* that was either well known (albeit with declining accuracy when moving further away from the Mediterranean) or correctly surmised by ancient geographers and historians. Indeed, it is wrong even when the extent of the then-known world is limited just to the states or organized populations that were the Roman Empire's enemies or with whom the Romans traded (directly or indirectly).

Despite the fact that ancient maps have not survived, we still have a fairly comprehensive record of the Roman knowledge of the Old World thanks above all to the geographies of two Roman Greeks, Strabo (64 B.C.E.–24 C.E.) and Claudius Ptolemaeus (Ptolemy; 90–168 C.E.).[21] Ptolemy compiled a lengthy listing of settlements and geographical features (with latitudes expressed in the modern manner as degrees from the equator, and longitudes measured from the Canary Islands, the westernmost territory known to the Romans) that enables us to reconstruct what was known during the second century C.E. about Europe, Africa, and Asia (Berggren and Jones 2000; figure II.8). Other detailed descriptions of the empire's lands, of its neighbors, and of distant reaches of the *oikoumene* are available in Polybius (203–120 B.C.E.), Pliny the Elder (23–79 C.E.), Titus Livius (Livy; 59 B.C.E.–17 C.E.) and, for the lands adjacent to the Red Sea and northern Indian Ocean, in *Periplus Mare Erythraei*.[22]

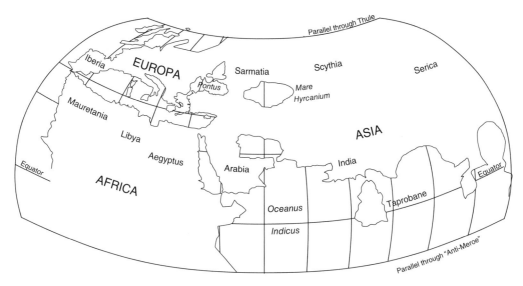

Figure II.8
A simplified version of a map by Claudius Ptolemaeus (Ptolemy) depicting the *oikoumene*, the world's inhabited regions known to the Romans during the second century C.E.

The empire's northernmost outpost was a line of Flavian watchtowers, forts, and fortlets built along the Gask Ridge between the Forth and Tay, just north of the *vallum Antonini* that cut Scotland along the Forth-Clyde isthmus (Fields 2005).[23] Roman legions most likely never landed in Ireland (Ivernia), they never reached Scandinavia, and the empire controlled only a relatively small part of Germania. A long-lasting longitudinal border was established along the Rhine and the Main (Rhenus and Moenus) and then, turning eastward, along Ister (Danube). Roman artifacts have been found in abundance not only in the immediately adjacent regions of Bohemia, Moravia, and Slovakia just north of the Danube but also in Denmark and throughout Poland, and some Roman traders made it all the way to the Baltic (Brogan 1936; M. Wheeler 1954).[24] But most of Germania (the Romans put its eastern borders as far east as the Vistula, today's Wisła running through southeastern and north-central Poland) remained beyond Rome's control.

The empire's northeastern border ran along the Danube (today's Slovakia was left out), but in central Pannonia (today's Hungary) it turned eastward to embrace Dacia (today's western and central Rumania), conquered by Trajan by 106 C.E. Roman borders reached the Black Sea (Pontus Euxinus) just north of the Danube delta at the mouth of Dniester (Tyras) at Olbia (near Odessa). The empire never held any territory on the plains and steppes of today's Poland, Ukraine, and Russia (known as Sarmatia by the Romans) or further east into Asia in the territories north and east of the Caspian Sea (Scythia, Sogdiana, and Bactriana).

The Romans made repeated attempts to set up a province in northern Mesopotamia and succeeded temporarily on at least four occasions, but their legions never penetrated further east than the northernmost shores of the Persian Gulf (Sinus Persicus), when, as Cassius Dio tells us, in 116 C.E., Trajan stood at its shore (of what is today Iraq's narrow access to the ocean), watched a ship leaving for India, and wished that he were as young as Alexander, whose armies penetrated nearly 3000 km further east to northwestern India.[25] But a Roman client state in southern Mesopotamia was given up the very next year, with Hadrian's accession in 117 C.E., and Trajan's foray remained unrepeated.

East of Sinus Persicus were the lands of the Persian Empire, Rome's perennial enemy. Parts of that empire became well known to those unfortunate Romans who ended up there as prisoners of war or as slaves. That empire, under the Parthian dynasty (247 B.C.E.–224 C.E.) and then under Sasanid rule (226–651 C.E.), extended from today's Armenia, northwestern Iraq, and the heart of Mesopotamia in the west through today's Iran and Turkmenistan to the river Oxus (the Amu Darya) and to what is now the western part of Afghanistan (see figure V.4). And east of the Parthian/Sasanid lands were the territories through which marched the warriors of Alexander the Great all the way to the Indus (Cummings 2004).

Beyond them was the mass of India whose coastline, reaching the mouth of the Ganges on the Bay of Bengal (Sinus Gangeticus), was well known to ancient sailors and geographers. Arikamedu, a major Roman trading station, was on India's eastern coast close to where in 1674 the French established another major trading port, Pondicherry (M. Wheeler 1954; Begley and de Puma 1991). Less was known about India's interior, the source of imported diamonds and spices, above all of highly valued pepper.[26] And beyond the Sinus Gangeticus and the Aurea Chersonesus (Golden Peninsula, the lands of Southeast Asia) was China (Sinae or Serica), about whose existence the Romans first knew thanks to indirect trade. Silk was the most desirable import from that distant land, although the first time the Romans saw it displayed was on an inauspicious occasion: Parthian riders unfurled silk banners before the battle at Carrhae (53 B.C.E.), where Roman forces led by Marcus Licinius Crassus suffered a major defeat.

More than 100 years later Pliny the Elder, in his *Historia Naturalis* (77 C.E.), got silk's origins wrong but correctly noted the Chinese lack of enthusiasm for foreign trade, a constant of China's policy that prevailed into the early modern era.[27] The silk trade between China and the Roman Empire, transiting the Kushan and Parthian empires, reached its height at about 90–130 C.E. (Thorley 1971; Christian 2000). Individual Romans, be it traders or captives, must have been reaching China for centuries, and the country was finally visited by a group of traders (it is unlikely that it was a formal Roman embassy) in 166 C.E. Chinese sources identify them as coming from the land ruled by Antun (we cannot be sure if it was Antoninus Pius or his successor Marcus Aurelius, whose full name was Marcus Aurelius Antoninus Caesar Augustus) during the reign of the emperor Huan (146–168 C.E.) of the Eastern Han dynasty (Young 2001). A Han envoy sent to Daqin (Chinese name for the Roman Empire) was dissuaded by the Parthians from going further west, but the Chinese had some basically correct information, as well as many mistaken notions, about Rome.

The Romans occupied for longer periods only a sliver of the Arabian Peninsula, a narrow coastal strip along the Sinus Arabicus (Red Sea) across from Sinai (Arabia Petraea). Finally, in Africa, Roman control never extended deep into the interior (M. Wheeler 1954; Kirwan 1957; Raven 1993). A Roman expedition penetrated as far south as Meroë, the capital of the Kushite kingdom (800 B.C.E.–350 C.E.), about 200 km northeast of today's Khartūm. Small groups may have traveled as far west as Darfur or even Tibesti in today's northern Chad, but the actual control extended furthest only along the Nile: there the southernmost boundary of Aegyptus reached Hiera Sycaminos at about 23° N, roughly halfway between Aswān and Wadi Halfa, that is, between the Nile's first and second cataract (now under the waters created by the Aswān Dam).

The Romans also controlled roads between the Nile and the Red Sea (Mare Erythraeum) the ports of Myos Hormos (close to today's al-Qusair in southern Egypt) and Bereniké, a further 300 km southeast along the coast near the Tropic of Cancer, where the Roman presence (port buildings, nearby forts, and watering stations) remained until the Arab conquest in 638 C.E. South of Aegyptus was vast Aethiopia, which encompassed today's Sudan, Eritrea, and Ethiopia. Because of long-standing trade the Romans knew of a passage through the Red Sea to India, and eventually (once they learned how to use the southwesterly monsoon to sail fairly directly from the mouth of the Red Sea to India) some of their ships joined other vessels on that route to bring in relatively large volumes of Indian imports. *Periplus Mare Erythraei* also provides the indisputable information that by the end of the first century C.E. the Romans knew the coast of East Africa as far south as Rhapta (today's Dar as-Salam in Tanzania) and later even further south to the shores of today's Mozambique.

West of Aethiopia were the vast deserts of Sahara sparsely inhabited by Gara-
mantes and Gaetuli in Libya interior, south of the coastal Roman possessions of
Libya, Syrtica, Tripolitana (today's Libya), Numidia (westernmost coastal Algeria),
and Mauretania (today's Mediterranean part of Algeria north of the Saharan Atlas
and central part of today's Morocco north of the Atlas Mountains). Roman control
never reached far inland; before the introduction of camels for transport in the
desert, the Sahara was a formidable barrier to any southward penetration.[28] The
Roman presence in Mauretania illustrates the limits and uncertainties of actual
control exercised by the imperial administration in the remotest provinces.

Alliances with local rulers and tribes rather than widespread military occupation
and direct rule were common along the border, and de facto control rarely extended
far outside principal cities or fortified outposts. Modern maps of Roman provinces
show the Romans controlling the territory up to about 200 km inland from the
African coast, but in reality (with a few exceptions of forward fortified positions)
the control extended only to the coastal plain and nearby valleys. In the Atlantic
the Romans knew of (but never occupied) the Canary Islands (Fortunatae Insulae)
but, curiously, they never sailed along the continent's western shores to get what
was the easiest access to sub-Saharan Africa (Harden 1962; Snowden 1970; Moscati
1999).[29]

But this brief summary of the Roman reach should not be seen as a description
of imperial frontiers. Imperial frontier was not a concept equivalent to a modern
frontier; the Romans tried to assert control over peoples and towns rather than
along precisely delimited lines (Isaac 1992). That is why the territorial limits of the
empire are commonly indicated only by vague descriptions of a few notable markers.
Firm control over an entire territory did not guide their military planning or administration; effective control could be achieved by very limited forces stationed in a
few garrison towns or by relying largely on allied support, but in other areas the
Roman army penetrated far beyond a border zone of a frontier province and maintained its presence there for long periods of time. A notable example of such
a prolonged foray was found in northern Hijaz: the Roman Legion Legio III
Cyrenaica left behind inscriptions in Medain Saleh (Hegra), about 900 km from its
main base in Bostra, in today's northeastern Jordan (Bowersock 1983; Millar 1993;
Young 2001).

Territories under the Roman control increased from slightly more than 2
million km^2 after Caesar's conquest of Gallia (completed 51 B.C.E.) to about 3.5
million km^2 by the time Augustus died in 14 C.E. and reached a peak of about
4.5 million km^2 at the beginning of the second century (figure II.9).[30] Even when it

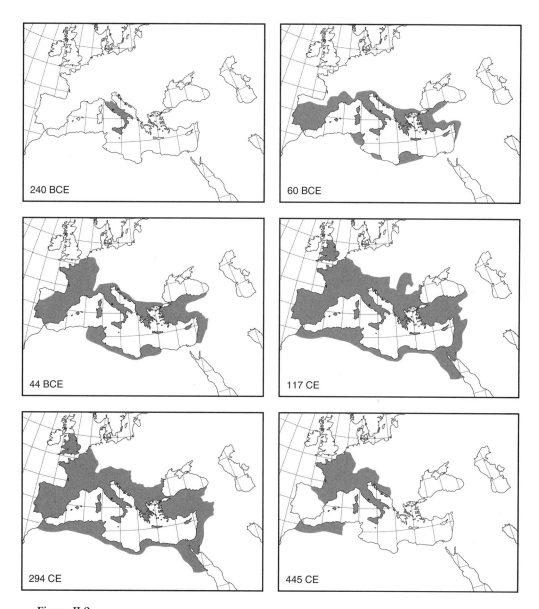

Figure II.9
Territorial expansion of the Roman Republic (240, 60, and 44 B.C.E.) and the changes during the mature (117 C.E.) and late (294 and 445 C.E.) Roman Empire. Compiled from various maps.

is assumed (conservatively and not entirely accurately) that on the three Old World continents the Romans knew virtually nothing of sub-Saharan Africa (except for Sudan, Ethiopia, and the East African littoral to about 10° S) as well as nothing of Siberia, northeast China, and Japan, their known world encompassed at least 32 million km^2. This means that even during their most expansive period (assuming about 4.5 million km^2 under Roman control) the empire covered less than 15% of the *oikoumene* known by the Mediterranean civilizations in antiquity, a far cry from any position of global dominance.

And just to complete the case, here are the global comparisons. Ice-free continents (that is, the potential planetary *oikoumene*) cover about 145 million km^2, and hence Rome, during the time of its greatest territorial reach, controlled no more than about 3% of it. Republican Rome's most powerful enemy, the Parthian empire of the Arsacid dynasty, controlled a larger territory until the middle of the last century B.C.E. and that *natio molestissima* remained a never-resolved worry for the Romans; vis-à-vis the Parthians, the Romans certainly did not feel like dominating superiors (for more on this centuries-long enmity, see chapter V).[31] And before the end of the fourth century both a weakening Rome and a new dynasty in China (Qin) were surpassed in size by a growing Sasanid empire, which controlled about 3.5 million km^2.

In contrast to the 3% of ice-free land under the Roman control, by the end of the nineteenth century the British Empire covered about 23%, and the Czarist empire and China's Qing dynasty claimed about 10% of all ice-free land. Rome's was the world's most extensive empire for only about 150 years, between 220 and 370 C.E. (figure II.10). Its great contemporary, China's Han dynasty, surpassed it in size (its territory grew to as much as 6.5 million km^2 by 100 C.E., and a century later it was still about 4.5 million km^2), and the two states were roughly matched in population, each having perhaps as many as 60 million people (Hardy and Kinney 2005). As I show in some detail in chapter III, Han China easily wins the imperial contest in terms of technical innovation and economic might.

Finally, I must note that in a systematic survey of empire sizes throughout history Rome does not make it even into the top 20, a set topped by the British (maximum of 34 million km^2), Mongolian (a short-lived maximum of 33 million km^2, longer control of 24 million km^2), and Russian (23 million km^2) empires (Taagepera 1978). Nor was the Roman Empire exceptionally long-lived. Its great Asian contemporary, China's Han dynasty, lasted 427 years (and, of course, the succession of other Chinese dynasties continued until 1279, when Mongols gained temporary control of that empire); the Sasanid dynasty ruled for 425 years, Byzantium (dating its

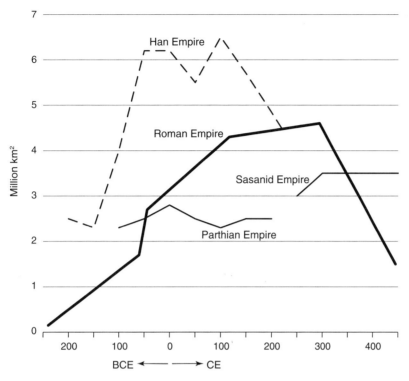

Figure II.10
Changing sizes of the ancient world's three largest empires, 250 B.C.E.–450 C.E.: Rome, Parthia/Sasanid Persia, and Han. Roman territories calculated from areas depicted in figure II.9; other territories plotted from data in Taagepera (1978).

beginning from 395 C.E.) survived for 1,058 years; and the Russian empire (after it reemerged from Tatar rule in 1480) persisted for 437 years and kept on expanding almost until the end of its existence.

The Roman Empire was neither the most extensive nor extraordinarily long-lived even when the comparison is limited to its contemporaries, and it definitely was not the most inventive and economically most productive state of antiquity (see chapter III). Dealing with the second hyperbolic claim—what seems to me to be a self-evident lie, namely, all those variants of the claim that the United States "dominates almost the entire globe"—cannot be done simply in terms of actual territorial control. Even the most biased critics of U.S. policy should admit that the United States does not behave as a primary empire eager to occupy, annex, and directly rule foreign territories. That is why a survey of U.S. territorial reach analogical to the exercise just performed for the Roman Empire, while easy to do, is not particularly revealing.

America's Peculiar Hegemony

America's sovereign territories of 9.37 million km^2 make it the world's fourth largest country, far behind Russia (17.1 million km^2) but close behind Canada (9.98 million km^2) and China (9.56 million km^2) and well ahead of Brazil (8.51 million km^2) and Australia (7.7 million km^2). Clearly, America's widely acknowledged hegemony (be it extolled, criticized, or resented) has no simple, direct relation to the country's size. Instead, its nature and limits have to be examined in terms of its relations with the outside world, by taking a critical look at the country's underlying economic and military powers.

I have already noted (while taking a closer look at definitions of empire) that American influence is not as dominant as is commonly assumed, even when that function is viewed in terms of hegemony, because America's leadership (in any case exercised only within a limited political realm composed predominantly of Western democracies) is repeatedly met with a great deal of doubt, dissent, and rejection. A closer critical look at U.S. power reveals the country to be a weak, ineffective hegemony that has little in common with all those tiresome labels about "only remaining superpower" and "global domination." In reality, U.S. power (properly understood as a combination of economic and military capabilities) has been evolving in two distinct ways: while many of its indicators have increased in absolute terms, it has been in gradual relative retreat for more than two generations.

We can actually pinpoint the precise date of its apogee: September 2, 1945, the day when Japanese representatives, led by the Foreign Minister Shigemitsu Mamoru, signed their country's surrender on board the USS *Missouri*, anchored in the Tokyo Bay (figure II.11). At that time the United States, after victory against Germany and Japan and after using nuclear bombs in Hiroshima and Nagasaki, was not only the world's sole nuclear power[32] but also by far the largest economy and an unrivaled symbol of hope, progress, and prosperity. In relative terms this position began to erode almost immediately—both by America's own actions and by the growing military capabilities of the USSR—even as the absolute indicators continued to rise, some quite impressively.

The country's GDP (expressed in constant monies) was 5.5 times greater in 2005 than in 1945, and even in per capita terms, as the population total grew from 132

Figure II.11
Japanese representatives signing their country's WW II surrender on the deck of the USS *Missouri* in Tokyo Bay, September 2, 1945. Photo from Naval Historical Center.

to 300 million people, this was a nearly 2.5-fold increase. America's armed reach became truly global with the introduction of strategic jet-powered bombers carrying nuclear bombs (the B-47 was the first such plane, in 1947), nuclear submarines (*Nautilus* was the first, in 1954), and intercontinental ballistic missiles (first deployed in 1959). The U.S. capacity for destruction reached obscene heights, with a maximum of 32,000 nuclear warheads of all sizes in 1966 and nearly 14,000 strategic warheads by the late 1980s (Norris and Kristensen 2006). In addition, America's technical leadership was immensely strengthened by its pioneering role in the electronic and information revolution: it gave the world the first transistors, integrated circuits, and microprocessors (Smil 2006).

But this absolute ascent was accompanied by a steady relative descent. I will chart first the economic component of this weakening. In 1945, America was responsible for about 35% of the world's economic product (Chase-Dunn et al. 2002). Prior to that only one country, Qing dynasty China at the peak of its powers between 1780 and 1820, came close to claiming such a high share, although it did not realize it and was quite content to exist in relative isolation.[33] As the United States began to use some of its riches to help the postwar recovery of Europe (Germany in particular) and Japan,[34] and as the economies of both its former adversaries and its allies began to regain some of their prewar strength, the U.S. share of world product began to fall even as America's economy continued to expand at a relatively fast pace. In constant monies (adjusted for inflation) it declined to 30% by 1960 and fell to just below 25% by 1970, reducing its weight in the global economy by nearly one-third in a single generation.

Since then the share has remained remarkably stable; the latest reevalution of national GDPs in terms of purchasing power parities puts the U.S. weight at 22.5% in 2005, with China a distant second (9.7%) and Japan (7%) third, followed by India, Germany, and Russia (World Bank 2008). Still, there is a huge difference between being first when responsible for more than one-third of the world's economic product and being first with only about one-fifth of it. Moreover, that simple comparison of national totals hides the fact that in per capita terms the distance between the United States and the rest of the Western world, which amounted to roughly 1 order of magnitude difference in 1945, shrank substantially. By 2005 the average per capita GDP of the three largest EU economies (Germany, Britain, and France) and Japan was only about 15% below the U.S. mean (World Bank 2008). More important, that falling share tells us nothing about the deterioration of America's economic fundamentals, a process that has now been unfolding for two generations and whose decisive reversal appears to be highly unlikely.

Even before the drastic economic downturn of 2008–2009 nothing in America's financial books provided any confidence as the country had enormous government budget deficits, soaring trade deficits, worsening current account balances, a deteriorating international investment position, excessive private indebtedness, and weakening currency. All these undesirable trends were punctuated by periods of recovery or rebound, but long-term directions have been disheartening. Despite a brief spike of budget surpluses between 1998 and 2001 the cumulative gross federal (public, national) debt doubled between 1992 and 2005 to about $8 trillion, or 65% of the country's GDP in that year (USDT 2008). By the end of 2007 the debt rose to $9.2 trillion, and its increase during that year ($843 billion) was larger (in exchange-rated terms) than Russia's annual GDP.

And then came the worst economic crisis of the post-1945 era and the repeated bailouts of financial institutions and stimulus spending began to add further deficit trillions in a matter of mere months. Yet the country's staggering public debt is actually less than the sum is actually less than the sum of America's privately held debt. Consumer credit (personal loans and car loans) reached $2.5 trillion by the end of 2007 (a nearly 30% increase in just five years), and outstanding mortgage debt surpassed $13 trillion, nearly doubling since 1999 and roughly equaling the total of the country's annual GDP (FRB 2008). To this should be added debt incurred by state and local governments (about $2 trillion) and the government's unfunded Social Security and Medicare/Medicaid liabilities, the latter total adding up to more than any other deficit item. The grand total of all these debts is already at least $25 trillion and possibly close to $50 trillion (at least four times the size of U.S. annual GDP) and still growing.[35]

Rising domestic debt has been accompanied by deepening imbalances in foreign trade. The last prolonged period of U.S. trade deficits, caused by rapid industrialization and enormous infrastructural needs, was after the Civil War. But in 1896 the United States began to run a surplus on its foreign trade and was able to maintain it (even through economic downturns and world wars) for the following 75 years. The country's trade balance began to turn negative during the early 1970s: in 1976 the deficit was only about $8 billion, but by 1990 it was ten times as large at $80.9 billion. And soon this slide turned into a free fall: the 1997 deficit more than doubled in just two years, the record 1999 deficit nearly doubled by 2003, and in 2006 it was almost ten times the 1990 level at $758.5 billion (USCB 2008; see figure I.6).

This means that the U.S. annual trade deficit has become larger than the annual GDP of Indonesia or Australia, indeed larger than the annual GDP of all but 14 of the world's nearly 200 nations. And while budget deficits can be cut relatively rapidly by a determined administration, in the near to medium term America has no choice but to continue its extraordinarily high dependence on energy imports, for which it cannot pay either by its disappearing manufactured products or by its food. In 2006 almost exactly one-third (32.3%) of the trade deficit was due to petroleum imports. This reality also has strategic implications; a nation that imports two-thirds of its crude oil is obviously highly vulnerable not only to sudden price spikes but to actual physical shortages of the fuel.[36] This concern is particularly acute given the fact that America's main oil suppliers are (with the exception of

Canada, the largest oil exporter to the United States) countries that are either politically unstable or profoundly corrupt or both.[37]

And while other affluent nations (Japan, South Korea, Taiwan, or Singapore) buy an even larger share of their energy demand abroad, they can pay for these imports by their exports of high value-added manufactures. America has lost this option. By 2006 the country had a deficit in 15 out of 32 major categories of capital goods and in all but 3 of 25 categories of consumer goods, where the only small surpluses came from toiletries and cosmetics, books, and musical recordings (USCB 2008). While manufacturing has declined in all affluent countries, the U.S. losses have been exceptionally large, from about 30% of all labor force during WW II to less than 12% by 2005, compared to 18% in Japan and 22% in Germany (USDL 2006). And it comes as a surprise to most people when they learn that the United States has been losing its previously huge agricultural trade surplus and that it is becoming a net importer of food, feed, and beverages; in 2006 its deficit in this category amounted to nearly $10 billion.

It is an even greater surprise that the United States has a considerable deficit in the trade of advanced technology products, about $44 billion in 2005, $38 billion in 2006 (USCB 2008). These trade deficits are the main reason for a steadily worsening current account balance that has been continuously negative since 1982. In that year it stood at less than –$6 billion, by 1990 it was –$417 billion, and by 2006 it reached –$811 billion, or nearly 6.5% of the country's GDP (BEA 2008). This shortfall absorbed some two-thirds of the aggregate worldwide current account surplus, a situation unprecedented in history. The outside world has thus been propping up the U.S. economy. By the end of 2008 foreign countries held nearly $2.9 trillion of U.S. Treasury securities; China led with nearly $600 billion, followed closely by Japan and the United Kingdom (about $350 billion), followed by the oil-exporting countries of the Persian Gulf, Brazil, Luxembourg, and the Caribbean banking centers (FRB 2008).

Ever since America's net international investment position turned positive by the end of WWI, the country was a paragon of global business domination. This impression may still linger, although the turning point came more than a generation ago, in 1986, when the country's international investment position turned negative (USCB 1976; C. L. Mann 2002; BEA 2008). The following two decades saw a stunning reversal of fortune. By 1990 the negative balance was about $250 billion, by the year 2000 it reached nearly $1.4 trillion, and by the end of 2007 it stood at $2.4 trillion, equal to nearly 20% of the country's GDP (BEA 2008).

Inevitably, these profound shifts had to weaken the formerly regnant U.S. currency. The beginning of its decline was brought about by a combination of excessive spending in the late 1960s and rising imports in the early 1970s. In 1971, before the Nixon administration severed the last tie with the gold standard and ended more than a quarter century of global financial stability set by Bretton Woods agreements in 1944, exchange rates were DM 3.48/$ and ¥358/$. In 1986, 15 years later, the U.S. dollar was worth just DM 2.17 and ¥160, and in 2000, before the introduction of the euro, the rates were just DM 2.07 and ¥120. These large devaluations against the Deutschmark and the yen, the currencies of the other two leading Western economies, and then against the euro brought the position of the U.S. dollar as the world's reserve currency into question (Kenen 2002; Papaioannou, Portes, and Siourounis 2006).[38]

The bottom line, and no pun intended, is that the U.S. economy has been living on borrowed time. Naturally, many commentators who surveyed this depressing economic landscape wondered how much longer it could remain so relatively undisturbed, and others concluded that a crisis ending is inevitable and will be severe. To be aware of these realities and still to argue that these economic foundations are good enough to maintain the country as "the only remaining superpower" or hyperpower or empire requires a great deal of wishful thinking. But could it be possible to argue that these dismal realities are somehow secondary, that it has been America's unprecedented military might that has made the difference and that still has a decisive role in international relations and in defining the country's stature? A critical look at America's use of military force reveals that it, too, has been on a troubled trajectory, that victory has been the rarest of the outcomes in all of its post-1945 engagements, and that the cost has been crippling by any rational measure.

My goal is not to label or classify America's military interventions by dividing them into wars justified by defense or overwhelming moral imperatives, defensive actions with an aggressive component, clear instances of aggression, or premeditated aggressions justified by claims that were known to be false. The historical literature is full of such classifications, often based on the ideological slants of the commentators, and with the invasion of Iraq these exercises in apologia or blame became ubiquitous though neither particularly useful nor analytically interesting.

What I find much more important is to adopt a historical perspective and to focus on the long-term consequences of these actions in order to see their actual results. Such an exercise is enlightening because it shows, again and again, the following

Figure II.12
Korean War (1950–1953) destroyed virtually the entire Korean peninsula and ended in a strategic stalemate that has not been resolved more than half a century later. Photo, from U.S. Army Center of Military History, shows a 105-mm howitzer crew in action.

traits: America's aversion to creating or maintaining an empire; its readiness to come to terms with peoples and regimes that only recently were enemies and to give them generous help; and the often meager rewards and substantial economic, political, and social costs of the country's armed interventions.

First, a brief review of America's post–WW II military experiences. The Korean War (figure II.12), the first major post–WW II conflict that involved U.S. forces, did not end in defeat, but after three years of heavy fighting, about 137,000 U.S. casualties (nearly 34,000 dead), and a cost of approximately $360 billion (in 2005 dollars), it was a mutual exhaustion that led to the armistice in July 1953 (Stewart 2005). The result of this inconclusive draw was to return the country to the status quo ante, but only after most of Korea's infrastructure had been leveled. Three years and three months after the Korean armistice the Voice of America was encouraging the Hungarians in their quixotic anti-Soviet fight, but President Eisenhower had no intention of using America's military might as the Red Army tanks crushed the Hungarian uprising (October 23–November 10, 1956). Nor was such a move considered in August 1961, as the East German Stasi regime built a wall dividing Berlin, or in August 1968, when the Warsaw Pact troops led by the Soviet Army occupied Czechoslovakia and ended Prague's brief spring and summer of hope.[39]

Figure II.13
Vietnam War (1964–1973) ended—after deep divisions at home made its continuation impossible—with ceding victory to the Vietcong and North Vietnam, withdrawing from the battlefield, and leaving Saigon (April 1975). Photo, from U.S. Army Center of Military History, shows an infantry division building a bunker on one of many defended hills in 1967.

Marine landings in Lebanon in July 1958 (aimed at stabilizing the pro-Western government of Camille Chamoun) are now remembered only by older Lebanese and by some American historians. When the marines withdrew in October, the immediate crisis was averted, but the action certainly did not provide any lasting stability to that hopelessly divided nation. A long civil war began in 1975 and lasted until 1990, and after a period of relative calm Lebanon continues to experience the same kind of instability in 2008 as it did in 1958. There is little need to expand on America's tragic involvement in Vietnam (figure II.13), a war that lasted more than a decade, that saw as many as 543,000, troops deployed at one time, whose death toll approached 50,000, and whose cost (in 2005 dollars) was more than half a trillion dollars.[40] The final drama of this tragedy came in April 30, 1975, as Vietnamese tanks crushed the gates of Saigon's U.S. embassy and frantic crowds of refugees tried to board the last helicopters departing from the embassy's roof (Butler 1985; Fenton 1985).

Four years later the United States only looked and protested (and canceled its participation in the 1980 Moscow Olympic Games) as the Soviet tanks drove to Kabul in December 1979. America's eventual response to that invasion turned out to be a blunder of monumental, epoch-making proportions. The training and arming of fundamentalist Muslim volunteers (Afghans as well as Arabs from many Middle Eastern countries) to fight the Soviets became—after the Soviet pullout from Afghanistan (completed by February 1989) and after Usama bin-Lādin began to resent the presence of the U.S. troops in Saudi Arabia—the very foundation of Al Qaeda's capability and the Taliban's eventual rise to power in Afghanistan.

Shortly before the Soviet invasion of Afghanistan, on November 4, 1979, young Muslim radicals took hostage 53 U.S. diplomats at the American embassy in Tehran, and Iran's new theocratic regime held them with complete impunity for more than 14 months (Bowden 2006). A poorly prepared rescue mission by the U.S. military (ambitiously named Operation Eagle Claw) ended on April 24, 1980, in a conflagration at the first desert staging area in southern Iran, destruction of seven Sea Stallion helicopters, and the death of eight Delta Rangers (Ryan 1985; Bowden 2006). American hostages got out only on January 20, 1981, as Ronald Reagan was sworn in as the fortieth president.[41]

Reagan's presidency is now often portrayed in heroic terms (he supposedly forced the USSR to its knees), but during his first term, with the country's military at its highest readiness and receiving an unprecedented share of peacetime budgets for arms buildup, the United States suffered a humiliating defeat that was not strategically decisive but that demonstrated the all-too-obvious limits of its might because it went, yet again, entirely unanswered. The event was the Hizbullah's suicide bombing of the U.S. marine barracks in Beirut on October 2, 1983, which killed 241 people.[42] Pro forma assurances that the United States would not be frightened into withdrawing lasted only for a few days; the marines were first moved offshore and then with drawn from Lebanon by the beginning of February 1984. There was never any retaliatory strike against Hizbullah, and nobody was court-martialed for the grossly inadequate security measures at the marine barracks.[43]

Other demonstrations symbolizing the limitations on U.S. power were the shooting down of a Blackhawk helicopter in Mogadishu and a 15-hour gunfight in the streets of the city on October 3 and 4, 1992, which ended in the death of 18 Rangers and the subsequent gruesome public dragging of dead bodies of U.S. soldiers by a mob of young Somalis (Bowden 1999; Stewart 2002). This in-your-face gesture (most likely organized by bin-Lādin) was followed by a prompt and complete U.S. withdrawal ordered by President Clinton on October 7. There was no retaliation, and there were no consequences for those who planned that botched Somali mission. More important, the first attack on New York's World Trade Center on February 26, 1993, was treated as a matter for minor police action even after Al Qaeda's plans spelling out the nature and ambition of future attacks became known by seizing the organization's training manuals, and even after a plot to bring down airplanes flying across the Pacific was accidentally uncovered in Manila, and after its mastermind, Ramzi Yusuf, was captured in Pakistan in 1995.[44]

The terrorist attacks of 9/11 exposed a fatal vulnerability because neither America's superpower status or its military capacity could prevent them. Not only did those attacks kill more people than did the Japanese bombing of Pearl Harbor, but they also carried an enormous economic price: as much as $95 billion for New York City alone (Thompson 2002) and about $500 billion for the entire nation (Looney 2002). That cost was contrasted by Usama bin-Lādin (2004, 3) in his message to the American people with the cost of $500,000 that al-Qaeda spent to launch the attack. He could thus brag that "every dollar . . . defeated a million dollars," that these attacks are "bleeding America to the point of bankruptcy," and that because of the U.S. president's response, a costly war on terror, both of them were playing as one team "towards the economic ruination of the country . . . even if the intentions differ." In economic terms, this might have been the most successful instance of asymmetric warfare in modern history.

Response to these killings and to America's global humiliation was prompt as the aerial attacks on Afghanistan began just 26 days after 9/11, but the Taliban's swift defeat was not achieved primarily by the deployment of the U.S. military but by basically enabling the country's warlords to reclaim most of the regional powers they had lost to the religious zealots. Eight years later the situation in Afghanistan remains precarious as large sections of the country remain in the Taliban's control, as warlord powers and religious intolerance continue to rule, and as al-Qaeda's top leaders, including bin-Lādin and his Egyptian deputy Ayman al-Zawahiri, still elude capture.

And then Colin Powell—the man who during the 1990s (when he was the chairman of the Joint Chiefs of Staff) nearly had (in his own words) an aneurysm when Madeleine Albright (at that time Secretary of State) asked, "What's the point of having this superb military that you're always talking about if we can't use it?" (Powell and Persico 1996, 576)—helped to lead the United States into Iraq, into a conflict where Americans have paid a much lower price in casualties than in the Vietnam War but whose financial costs will be second only to those of WW II.[45] By June 30, 2008 all congressional appropriations for the post-9/11 conflicts (wars in Afghanistan and Iraq and all other Global War on Terror operations) added up to about $775 billion in constant 2000 dollars (Belasco 2008).

This means that the Iraq war has already been more expensive than the Korean conflict, and in October 2007 the Congressional Budget Office put the war costs for the next ten years at an additional $570 billion even if troop levels were to be reduced to 30,000 by the year 2010, sending the overall cost above $1 trillion, or roughly twice as expensive as the Vietnam War.[46] And all of these expenses are incurred by a country whose combined annual budget and trade deficit now exceed two trillion dollars a year. Whenever I review and update these figures I marvel at the depth of ignorance of people who write about U.S. global dominance without knowing these facts, or at the extent of denial displayed by people who know them but still call the United States a hyperpower that dominates "nearly the entire world."

As with the country's economic foundations, those who believe America's post-1945 military engagements to be irrefutable demonstrations of a superpower capacity to change the course of would affairs as it sees fit must have an infinite capacity for delusion. A dispassionate appraisal sees all of them as severe, costly, and repetitive demonstrations of the limits of America's military might. But why not see the Korean War as a kind of victory because its eventual outcome was the creation of the world's thirteenth largest economy, a success by any measure? Similarly, why not argue that in the long run the Vietnamese victory was not a strategic defeat for the United States because Southeast Asia did not become a Communist stronghold (disproving the domino theory that played such a prominent role in America's entering the conflict) and Vietnam is now integrating its trade-oriented economy into the global market? A charge could also be made that I have deliberately ignored the Gulf War of 1991, America's swift and signal military victory at the head of an impressive multinational coalition, a clear case of a powerful hegemony in effective action.

But none of these arguments can do away with the following facts. The seemingly endless Korean stalemate has tied up a substantial chunk of the U.S. military for more than half a century and has been the direct cause of endless concerns about irrational North Korea, whose deliberately provocative actions (testing missiles and even a nuclear bomb, breaching nonproliferation treaty obligations), continuous lies about its nuclear program, and admissions of cheating have amounted to serial (and seemingly never-ending) demonstrations of America's impotence. The war in Vietnam divided America so deeply and so bitterly that more than two generations after its beginning, even the latest presidential campaign could not escape its reach, demonstrating a domestic trauma of historic proportions, a defeat by any measure.

And the Gulf War could be seen as just one last delayed, aberrant victory, a blip briefly interrupting the decline of America's effective military capability, but in retrospect it is more accurately classed as the beginning of America's intervention and long, extremely costly involvement in Iraqi affairs—so far the greatest strategic challenge America has faced in the new century. If America has had a difficult time imposing its designs on its enemies, the limits to its supposed global hegemony are no less revealingly illustrated by its inability to convince even its friends to follow its wishes or stand by it in times of need: its two largest NATO allies, Germany and Turkey, simply refused to join the "coalition of the willing" against Iraq in 2002–2003.

Germany was defeated by the United States in a protracted war (at a cost of more than 180,000 American lives), subsequently received America's generous aid to resurrect its formidable economic capacity, and is still a host to more than 60,000 American troops. Yet when its foreign minister[47] was asked to join the Iraq War coalition, he simply told the U.S. Secretary of Defense "Sorry, you haven't convinced me," and there the matter ended (Hockenos 2007).

No less tellingly, the Turkish government (with NATO's second largest standing army and after decades of a close relationship with the United States) forbade U.S. forces to use its territory for the invasion of Iraq, a move that complicated the drive to Baghdad and undoubtedly prolonged the campaign.[48] America in times of war and need thus could not count even on its two closest allies, but there was (adding "of course" seems to be irresistible here) no retaliation, no hint of indirect punishment such as economic sanctions or suspensions of certain relations. One could cite many other cases of allied refusal to join ranks or allied insistence on charting a separate course, both illustrating America's ineffective hegemony and nonimperial behavior.

Public opinion polls have shown a high degree of anti-American feelings as soon as America acted without the consent of most of its allies who refused to join in the overthrow of Saddam Hussain. By 2007 the only Western nations with a majority (barely) of the population having a favorable opinion of the United States were

Canada (55%), Italy (53%), and Britain (51%); analogical shares were 30% in Germany and 23% in Spain (Pew Research Center 2007). Widespread anti-American sentiments of populations (and openly scornful, patronizing, and insulting comments by the media) in the countries that have been America's most important military allies may be one thing, but deliberately contrarian actions by their governments (often expressed in terms of barely contained disdain) are another matter.

In 1991 the Philippine Senate rejected a new treaty extending the use of Subic Bay for another ten years, and the United States got an ultimatum to vacate the base within a year; it did so ahead of time (by November 1992), leaving behind usable assets worth some $8 billion, and the complex became a freeport zone with considerable foreign investment in new manufacturing. Clark Air Base, after volcanic ash from the eruption of Mt. Pinatubo had been cleared, became Diosdado Macapagal International Airport, Manila's modern alternative air transport hub. Similarly, the United States did not insist on maintaining control of the Panama Canal and returned it to Panama on December 31, 1999. Perhaps the symbolically most insulting older example of allied uncooperativeness is Charles de Gaulle's peremptory order to withdraw U.S. forces out of France and his decision to quit the military structure of NATO in 1966.[49] (France was the beneficiary of two critical interventions of U.S. forces during the two world wars.) The Americans simply assented and left.

Finally, a telling recent example. Would an imperial power allow a prime minister of a country that it had recently conquered (and whose reconstruction and defense cost it thousands of lives and hundreds of billions of dollars) to repeatedly visit a neighboring nation (which had been the great power's avowed enemy for more than a generation and which actually helped to kill some of its soldiers stationed in the neighboring land by providing lethal explosives) and to have a cordial *tête-à-tête* with its president, who openly calls for the destruction of the great power whose very existence he deems satanic?

The answer to this rhetorical question is an unequivocal no. But that is precisely what Americans could see on their TVs: the smiling Iraqi prime minister Nuri al-Maliki embracing Mohammed Ahmedinejad, president of a harshly anti-American fundamentalist Islamic theocracy in Tehran, on a visit to Baghdad. This is hardly an image illustrating U.S. imperial policy and confirming the claims of anti-American propagandists who see the Iraqi government as just a tool of U.S. occupiers. In nearly all these cases it is very hard to imagine that a real imperial power, even a true hegemon, would behave in such ways.

Analogical Roman situations—giving generous economic aid to aggressors whose defeat cost more lives and treasure than any other previous conflict in the country's history; leaving mass murders and gruesome desecrations of troops entirely unanswered; consenting to simply withdraw its legions and abandon its fortifications when asked to do so by former allies; taking no for an answer from its closest *socii et amici* when asking for help in the time of war; or letting allied governments cultivate friendly relations with Rome's enemies or be formed on anti-Roman platforms—are even harder to visualize. Perhaps the best conclusion is to agree with Scott (1990), who observed that true hegemony never really exists because smirks of resistance always hide behind the public mask of deference. Except that America's hegemonial powers are even more feeble than that, unable to elicit even publicly deferential behavior from its closest allies. Hers is perhaps the most peculiar—tenuous, soft, uncertain—hegemony ever seen.

III

Knowledge, Machines, Energy

At qui utrumque perdidicerunt, uti omnibus armis ornati citius cum auctoritate, quod fuit propositum, sunt adsecuti.

He who is theoretic as well as practical, is therefore doubly armed; able not only to prove the propriety of his design, but equally so to carry it into execution.
—Marcus Vitruvius Pollio, *De Architectura* I.1.2
(Joseph Gwilt translation, 1826)

Traditional historians have sought to explain the fortunes of nations by delving into social, cultural, religious, and military aspects of their evolution, and economic historians, in common with mainstream economists, have concentrated on capital and labor as the key organizing principles of productive activities. But to students of energy systems who trace energy flows through ecosystems, another relation is as trivially obvious as it is irreplaceably fundamental: all systems, be they grasslands or coral reefs, cities or civilizations, are nothing but highly organized (simple or complex) converters of energy (Smil 2008a). Levels of energy use (more precisely, the availability of useful energy) circumscribe the economic, military, and (to a lesser extent) social capacities of any society and are the key determinants of the prevailing quality of life (Smil 1994; 2008a). Higher, more varied, and more efficient energy throughputs result in more desirable, that is, richer and more differentiated, outcomes.

Consequently, this chapter highlights the profound disparities in the composition of energy sources used by ancient Rome and modern America as well as the enormous gaps that separate typical per capita levels of energy use and their prevailing conversion efficiencies. Most of these differences are explained by the extent and intensity of reliance on extrasomatic energies, that is, energy flows other than the muscle power of humans and animals.[1] In turn, increasing use of extrasomatic energies depends on the introduction and diffusion of mechanical prime movers, machines that are able to convert the chemical energy of fuels or the kinetic energy of moving media (water, steam, air, gases) into rotary or reciprocating motion that, in turn, can be harnessed for a multitude of tasks. That is why I briefly explain the reliance on machines in the Roman world and then contrast the truly incomparable roles that mechanical prime movers played in the two societies.

But I should start at the beginning. The introduction and diffusion of new machines is a direct function of the level of inquisitiveness that permeates a society, of its eagerness to innovate, of its support for such endeavors, and of its institutional arrangements that make it easier to convert brilliant ideas into practical and widely adopted processes. Modern Western societies in general, and the United States in particular, were created by a complex interplay of these factors, that is, by the interactions of science, industry, and commerce (Mokyr 2002; Smil 2005; 2006). The most commonly used distinction between invention and innovation is that the former is a new product or process with commercial promise (in the modern world it is almost always science-based), whereas the latter refers to the successful entry of a new product or service into a particular market (Branscomb and Auerswald 2002).

Innovation is necessarily gradual, although its pace varies from tardy to rapid. Similarly, not all inventions are a matter of sudden inspiration (*eureka!*); there are often substantial gestation periods and notable precedents. Nations that manage to be better at innovation than invention will harness greater economic and social benefit than countries where brilliant inventions are not in short supply but have a low chance of being commercialized. An excellent example of this contrast are the post–WW II technical histories of Japan (a great innovating society) and the USSR.

Science is an ancient human endeavor that became gradually elevated from isolated individual pursuits to the most dynamic productive force in history. Even the earliest urban societies left behind records of intellectual inquiries into the nature of physical reality, the properties of life, and changing environmental and social circumstances. In later, more complex, civilizations these efforts became more systematic and probing and were eventually classified into specific categories of basic sciences dealing with universal realities (mathematics, physics, astronomy, chemistry, biology) and applied endeavors ranging from agronomy (indispensable to sustaining good harvests) and medicine to various branches of engineering.

During the nineteenth century theoretical and experimental discoveries were increasingly produced by deliberate and systematic pursuit of knowledge, and once revealed they became subject to rapid commercialization and widespread diffusion as new tools, machines, and processes transformed the millennia-old pattern of predominantly agricultural societies into a modern urban-based, high-energy, machine-driven civilization. America has been the unsurpassed contributor to this epochal spark of innovation, benefiting (in Mokyr's felicitous phrase), from the richest gifts of Athena.[2]

How did the Romans acquit themselves in this respect? Were they uncommonly inventive or no more than competent in comparison to other ancient societies? Or did they have a deep curiosity deficit and a rather unremarkable innovation record? This question can best be answered by contrasting Roman achievements with the advances of one Rome's most illustrious predecessors, the Hellenistic civilization of the eastern Mediterranean of the third and second century B.C.E., and with the achievements of Rome's great Asian contemporary, China's Han dynasty.

Inventing New Worlds

The history of technical advances—of fundamental inventions and their subsequent diffusion and widespread commercial adoption—displays two very different patterns of progress. The first is akin to the classical (Darwinian) view of evolution: slow improvements (usually based on better empirical understanding and patient experimentation) result in noticeable gains in efficiency, utility, reliability, and durability. The declining use of charcoal per unit of smelted metal, the greater maneuverability of sails, and the higher efficiency and increasing power of water-wheels are three examples of this slow, cumulative progress unfolding on the scale of many centuries.[3] The second pattern is progress at uncommon speed, so fast that it warrants borrowing another evolutionary term: saltation, a relatively brief spell characterized by remarkable advances. These periods of uncommonly rapid and broad advances punctuate the much longer eras of cumulative progress, and they tend to raise societies to new plateaus of technical capability (much like the abrupt shifts of scientific paradigms so famously described by Kuhn (1962)).

Artistic creativity displays the same duality. The period between 1475 and 1550— a saltation encompassing the creations of Sandro Botticelli and Michelangelo Buon-arroti—contributed more to the evolution of Western art than an equally long early medieval span (say, 800–875) or a late Roman span (say, 300–375) (figure III.1).[4] These saltations (artistic, technical, or scientific) are not spatially widespread phenomena; they are limited not only in time but also in space, and in their initial phases they may be driven solely by a single society (even a single city), which thus temporarily gains an enormous comparative advantage over its peers.[5]

Figure III.1
Details of Botticelli's *The Birth of Venus* (c. 1485), *top*, and Michelangelo's *The Creation of Adam* (c. 1511) from the ceiling of the Sistine Chapel exemplify the astonishing burst of creativity that took place during the Renaissance.

With this reality in mind, I can proceed to formulate one of the fundamental differences between imperial Rome and modern America. The United States led both of the two latest grand technical saltations whose impact created the modern global civilization, first the unprecedented spell of innovations during the two generations that preceded WW I, then the era of impressive post–WW II advances. During the latter period the United States also occupied an unchallenged place of scientific excellence.

The Romans were undoubtedly accomplished engineers and capable builders, and the centuries of imperial rule were not as a devoid of innovation as has been claimed by those who see that era as one of prolonged technical blockage. But this does not change the fact that the Romans were neither impressive inventors nor the leading technical innovators of their time and that their legacy of systematic, incisive intellectual inquiry compares poorly with that of their Greek predecessors and their Chinese contemporaries.

American creativity has been a bright comet across the firmament of technical and scientific progress; the Roman innovations, only attenuated starlight. Perhaps no single sentence has captured that amazing vigor of the first great wave of American inventiveness better than Mark Twain's, spoken by a Yankee (at King Arthur's court) who learned to make anything, from guns to boilers: "Why, I could make anything a body wanted—anything in the world, it didn't make any difference what; and if there wasn't any quick new-fangled way to make a thing, I could invent one—and do it as easy as rolling off a log" (Twain 1889, 20).

There is no need for a lengthy itemization of the many scientific and engineering advances that took place during history's most impressive innovation era between the end of the U.S. Civil War and the beginning of WW I (H. M. Jones 1971; Smil 2005). What must be stressed is that America's contributions included not only fundamental inventions (such as those by Alexander Bell, Thomas Edison, Charles Hall, George Eastman, and Orville and Wilbur Wright) but also remarkable and truly epoch-making innovations in the organization of industrial and agricultural production, transportation, communication, marketing new products, and turning novelties into items of everyday use.

Two iconic examples should suffice. The first one combines brilliant invention with admirable organizational capacity. Edison's famous incandescent lightbulb was perhaps the least important of his numerous inventions; after all, he had many domestic and foreign competitors, and a new form of light was just one of many possible uses of electricity. But only Edison was able to put in place (between 1879 and 1882) an entire new industry, the world's first commercially viable system of

Figure III.2
Thomas Edison (1847–1931), *left,* and Henry Ford (1863–1947), two exemplars of Americans' inventive and innovative drive. Courtesy of Library of Congress, LC-USZ62-98067, LC-USZ62-78374.

electricity generation, transmission, and conversion.[6] The second example, Henry Ford's introduction of the automotive assembly line, is a prime case of fundamental innovation and manufacturing revolution. Edison's and Ford's success also symbolizes the uncommon propensity of American entrepreneurs for fusing an innovative spirit with profit-driven business calculations, a combination that has often helped them to best their European competitors (figure III.2).[7]

All that is required to appreciate America's effective combination of inventive spirit and commercial prowess, its leadership in the invention, diffusion, and adoption of new industrial processes, machines, and devices, is to consult one of the histories of twentieth-century technical advances (Constable and Somerville 2003; Billington and Billington 2006; Smil 2006). They show America's primacy in fields ranging from the new world of electronics and new means of long-distance transport to new ways of extracting and processing hydrocarbons and synthesizing nitrogenous fertilizers.

And there is hardly any need to belabor the dominant role the United States has occupied in the world of scientific discovery. One kind of evidence may be seen as biased or questionable, but when every relevant statistic makes the same case, the conclusion is undeniable. Here are three different kinds of persuasive evidence. In the 2007 annual ranking of the world's leading universities, U.S. institutions took 8 of the top 10 places and 18 of the top 25 (ARWU 2007). Scientists and engineers residing in the United States were granted 59% of patents awarded worldwide between 1963 and 2006 (USPTO 2008).

By 2004, 30% of the world's scientific publications were still authored by U.S. researchers, the share nearly seven times higher than the country's share of global population and a per capita publication output 20 times higher than in China (Zhou and Leydesdorff 2006). Between 1951 and 2005, U.S. scientists received 195 of 350 (or 56%) of all Nobel prizes granted in physics, chemistry, and medicine and physiology, and for the years 2006, 2007, and 2008 of the 16 science laureates 11 were Americans (Nobel Foundation 2008). These are all highly disproportional achievements when compared on a per capita basis.[8]

But America's unrivaled position in today's global technoscientific universe had no analogue in Roman achievements. Despite its long duration and no shortage of acute minds, the Roman Empire had an unremarkable (it would not be an exaggeration to say a truly minimal) record in advancing scientific understanding, and its overall contributions to technical and engineering innovations were (a few construction achievements aside) fairly limited. Indeed, this conclusion extends to cover the entire European antiquity, perhaps most famously and influentially in the writings of M. I. Finley, a leading classical historian of his generation.

Finlay's 1965 paper on technical innovations and economic progress in the ancient world opened with a devastating judgment:

It is a commonplace that the Greeks and Romans together added little to the world's store of technical knowledge and equipment. The Neolithic and Bronze Ages between them invented or discovered, and then developed, the essential processes of agriculture, metallurgy, pottery, and textile-making. With these the Greeks and Romans built a high civilization, full of power and intellect and beauty, but they transmitted to their successors few inventions. (29)

This interpretation has been widely accepted, and it has been supported by pointing to a relatively meager interest in the matters of scientific reasoning and technical innovation expressed in the surviving Roman literary sources and by noting a lack of archeological evidence demonstrating a common Roman reliance on machines other than those powered by animals and people.

Rome's surprising lack of systematic intellectual curiosity and the era's paucity of technical advances (especially given the obviously large needs for manufactures and food to supply large urban populations as well as to sustain large armies) have been most often explained by lack of economic incentives because of the presence of the dominant social arrangement: widespread reliance on slave labor militated against the invention of mechanical alternatives to human toil by suppressing investment in innovation and hindering the diffusion of new machines (Wilson 2002). Disparagement of practical applications of theoretical understanding, which was supposed to be common among Greek and Roman intellectuals, was another favorite explanation.[9]

In any case, Finley's (1965; 1973) conclusion about the technical blockage and lack of economic progress in the ancient world was particularly influential, and it only reaffirmed the existing predilection to see studies of Roman innovation and technical advances as of marginal interest when compared with work on Roman armies, borders, or satires. Finley's judgments were not as dogmatic as his critics made them out to be. At the very outset of his 1965 paper he wrote, "Paradoxically, there was both more and less technical progress in the ancient world than the standard picture reveals. There was more, provided we avoid the mistake of hunting solely for great radical inventions and we also look at developments within the limits of the traditional techniques. There was less—far less—if we avoid the reverse mistake and look not merely for the appearance of an invention, but also for the extent of its employment" (29).

Finley used the example of the watermill, a radical invention deployed to displace animate power, whose existence was clearly documented in a written source of the first century B.C.E. but that was used so sporadically during the next three centuries "that the total effect was very slight" (29). This claim was first challenged in a systematic manner by Wikander's (1981; 1983) studies of water power in antiquity, then in general terms by Greene (1990; 2000) and in a specific reappraisal of the waterwheel's history by Lewis (1997; see also Oleson 2008). Pleket (1990) even concluded that the Roman economy resembled in many aspects the situation that prevailed in northwestern Europe between the sixteenth and eighteenth centuries.

I demonstrate in the next section that Finley's interpretation is closer to the most likely reality than those of his critics. Here I look separately at the Greek and Roman achievements and then contrast the Roman record with the accomplishments of China's Han dynasty. Separate appraisals of the Greek and Roman contributions to a systematic, objective understanding of the world and to technical advances show a contrast that cannot be argued away. Lumping them together would be my gravest charge against Finley, but he followed the standard Western account of the history of science, which obscured the revolutionary nature of the Hellenistic contribution and conflated it with earlier Greek, and even Egyptian and Mesopotamian, achievements.

The Romans, while undoubtedly possessed of excellent organizational capability; proficient in large-scale planning, coordination and project execution; and successful in some fields of technical innovation, were oddly incurious in most fields of intellectual inquiry, content to live largely off the Greek legacy. Even the history of their venerated *imperium* found the most devoted and insightful chroniclers among the Greeks. How much poorer would be our knowledge of Roman history without the writings of Polybius (203–120 B.C.E.), Plutarch (46–125 C.E.), and Cassius Dio (c.150–c.235 C.E.). What would we know about the Roman *oikoumene* without Strabo (64 B.C.E.–24 C.E.) and Ptolemy (90–168 C.E.)?[10]

The most remarkable period of the Greek contribution to rational understanding—in Russo's (2004, 1) words "an explosion of objective knowledge about the external world"—did not take place during the height of classical Greek civilization (500–350 B.C.E.), when the citizens of small city-states perfected their architecture (e.g., Athenians built the Parthenon, 447–432 B.C.E.), art (e.g., Myron sculpted *Discobolos*, 450 B.C.E.), and philosophy (e.g., Socrates, 469–399 B.C.E.; Plato, 429–347 B.C.E.). That innovative burst came during what has become known as the Hellenistic period (Bugh 2006).

The Hellenistic period began in 323 B.C.E. with the death of Alexander the Great, and its preeminent inventive center was Alexandria, the newly established capital of Egypt (331 B.C.E.) ruled by the Ptolemaic dynasty. Famous scientists and engineers either lived or studied there or kept in contact with the city's thinkers, benefiting from the interest and approbation of the first two rulers of the Ptolemaic dynasty, Ptolemy I Soter (r. 323–283 B.C.E.), the founder of the city's famous *mouseion* and library (Erskine 1995), and Ptolemy II Philadelphus (r. 283–246 B.C.E.). Two names of Hellenic innovators stand out: Euclid (325–265 B.C.E.) and Archimedes (287–212 B.C.E.).

Euclid's writings on geometry served as a primary source of instruction for some 22 subsequent centuries (Glavas 1994). Both he and Archimedes were outstanding theoretical mathematicians, and Archimedes was also a great designer of practical war machines and mechanical devices. But to the public he is best known not for his approximations of π or for an early version of integral calculus but for a few of his reported sayings, especially, "Eureka!"[11]

There is a long list of lesser known but no less illustrious names; I introduce the leading ones in alphabetical order. Apollonius of Perga (262–190 B.C.E.) was the first master of conic sections. Aristarchos of Samos (325–255 B.C.E.) produced cogent arguments for the heliocentric system and the Earth's daily rotation about its axis. Ctesibius (285–222 B.C.E.) laid the foundation of pneumatics and hydraulics and built intricate machines, including an eponymous pump. Eratosthenes of Cyrene (276–194 B.C.E.) worked on prime numbers and established the circumference of the Earth along a meridian within less than 3% of its actual value.[12] Herophilus of Chalcedon (335–280 B.C.E.) was a pioneer of neuroscience, able to distinguish between sensory and motor nerves (Acar et al. 2005). Hipparchus of Nicaea (190–125 B.C.E.) assembled the first catalog of star positions and brightness, founded trigonometry, and explained a tricky matter of the precession of equinoxes.

Besides mathematics, the Hellenistic paradigm of science, the Hellenistic thinkers either made important advances or laid down new foundations of objective understanding in anatomy, astronomy, botany, geodesy, geometry, hydraulics, hydrostatics, instrumentation, linguistics, mechanics, optics, physiology, pneumatics, trigonometry, and zoology. They also designed the most famous lighthouse of all times (figure III.3), new military machines, steam-powered and water-lifting devices, and remarkably complicated automata, and left behind beautiful hexagonal tessellations in intricate mosaic floors and the astonishing Antikythera mechanism (named after a small island in whose waters the heavily corroded bronze object was found), whose 30 clockwork-like gears and differential turntable worked as a perpetual calendar.[13]

The efforts of these thinkers went beyond the mere accumulation of facts or purely speculative constructs. Theirs were deliberate inquiries into natural realities, including the formation of theories and application of abstract understanding to the solution of concrete challenges. If you think that what they practiced was not science, or that their technical innovations had nothing to do with scientific analyses, read Heath (1931), Fraser (1972), Irby-Massie and Keyser (2002), Bugh (2006) and, above all, Russo (2004). Particularly useful machines invented during the great Alexandrian era were two new devices for lifting water, welcome additions to the oldest and simplest water-lifting device of the pre-Hellenistic era, the counterpoise lift (swape; Arabic *shādūf*), first pictured on the Babylonian cylinder seal in 2000 B.C.E. (Molenaar 1956; Oleson 1984).

The Archimedean screw (Greek κοχλίας, Roman *cochlea*, Arabic *tanbur*), a wooden double helix inside a cylinder (150–250 cm long, 40–55 cm in diameter),

Figure III.3
Alexandria's lighthouse on the island of Pharos (built third century B.C.E.) in an imaginary depiction by an unknown nineteenth-century artist. It was one of the seven wonders of the ancient world and a symbol of the great Hellenistic city whose thinkers and experimenters contributed greatly to the genesis of scientific and technical innovation.

rotated by a crank, could deliver up to 15 m³/h with 75-cm lift when operated by two men.[14] A device powered by one or two animals walking in a circular path was called in Greek simply μηχανή (machine); it was known as the Roman *tympanum* and later as the Arabic *sāqīya*. It consisted of an endless chain of clay pots that was carried on two loops of rope on a wooden drum to fill at the lower end (from wells as deep as 9 m) and to discharge into a flume at the top. These two machines allowed for more efficient and more widespread irrigation throughout the eastern Mediterranean, and they remained in use in some of the region's areas well into the twentieth century.

What happened after the later Ptolemaic rulers showed little understanding for this great intellectual efflorescence (in 145 B.C.E. Ptolemy VIII actually expelled the scholars from the city) and after the Romans conquered Egypt in 30 B.C.E.? It is hard to disagree with Russo's (2004, 1) conclusion that "Rome borrowed what it was capable of from the Greeks and kept it for a little while yet, but created very little science of its own." Very little indeed; we do not know of any Roman Euclid or Herophilus, and no Roman city set up new museums and libraries that would have been worthy counterparts of those two institutions in Ptolemaic Alexandria. What has come down to us from the Roman writings that are broadly classifiable under the headings of science and engineering is disappointing.

Some of it is an interesting genre of literature (Lucretius's *Historia Naturalis* offers some memorable images), but even the most technically competent contributions (Vitruvius, Frontinus) are either highly derivative or lack clarity. Frontinus, the author of the only extant Roman work on the city's water supply, frustrated all subsequent students of his text by providing the discharge totals for individual aqueducts in terms of *quinaria,* a measure that is defined as the capacity of a pipe five *quandrantes* (quarter-fingers, or about 2.3 cm) in diameter. How does one translate a cross-section (an area) of a pipe to a fluctuating flow (volume) of water in an open aqueduct channel without knowing anything about the speed of flow through that standard pipe?[15]

The most detailed Roman work on the structure and dynamics of nature is the monumental *Historia Naturalis* by Pliny the Elder, whose 37 volumes cover everything from descriptions of distant lands and rare animals to notes on spices and gems and on the origins of ornamental stones for Rome's monumental buildings. But, as Fagan (2001, 249) noted in his review of a book about Pliny's life and work, science is a systematic and rational investigation of nature "through the proposal of hypotheses verified or falsified by experiment or observation; it is not an assemblage of stray facts, oddities and lore such as Pliny offers." And even one of his defenders concedes that "Pliny seems to have failed in his central purpose: Roman science never did take off. But is he to blame for that?" (Wallace-Hadrill 1990, 96). Of course not. How could he, singlehandedly, change the tenor of his time?

The Roman record of technical invention has been similarly sparse. The Romans are known for impressive water infrastructures, including aqueducts, siphons using metal pipes to cross deep valleys, cisterns, distribution *terracotta* pipes, and covered drains, but all these elements were used by the Greeks, some with true mastery.[16] Nor did the Romans invent other constructs and artifacts for which they are famous: tunneling, paved roads, large oared ships, and siege machines. Perhaps the most notable Roman inventions were large-scale deployment of hydraulic mining methods, including hushing and ground sluicing (Craddock 1995; Wilson 2002), and the only known agricultural machine of European antiquity, the Gallic grain reaper (*vallus*), a two-wheeled cart with tapered teeth (set at its front edge at a height a bit below the ears of a grain crop) that was pushed by an animal.[17]

Roman innovation has seen more substantial achievements; the empire's miners, manufacturers, and builders improved and diffused older Greek, Egyptian, and Persian structures, processes, and artifacts. These advances included complex arrangements for mine drainage; some relatively large-scale manufacturing—notably the firing of narrow Roman bricks (30 × 10 × 5 cm longer and slimmer than standard American bricks measuring 20.3 × 10.2 × 5.7 cm) and such quotidian objects as wine and olive amphorae (figure III.4), bowls, cups, and oil lamps—and concentrated food processing and preparation, particularly multipress enterprises producing olive oil in North Africa and large urban mills and bakeries (Bakker 1999). Roman large-scale engineering projects, above all aqueducts and roads, have been the empire's most widely admired innovation.

Impressive remnants of Roman aqueducts can be still seen in several Mediterranean countries, but Rome's system was particularly extensive (Evans 1994; Hodge 2002). Using technical details in Blackman and Hodge (2001), I calculated that Rome's 11 aqueducts (515 km, built between 312 B.C.E. and 226 C.E.) required as much stone for the water channels as did Khufu's pyramid (assuming nearly 6 m³ of stone were needed per meter of the conduit), and that total does not include an even larger volume of stone for about 58 km of elevated arches and of stone and soil that had to be removed for the sloping aqueduct ditches. Pliny (*Historia Naturalis* XXXVI) wrote that "there was never any design in the whole world . . . more admirable than this," and Frontinus (a practical engineer and a proud Roman) asked his readers to compare these structures with "the idle pyramids, or else the indolent but famous works of the Greeks."

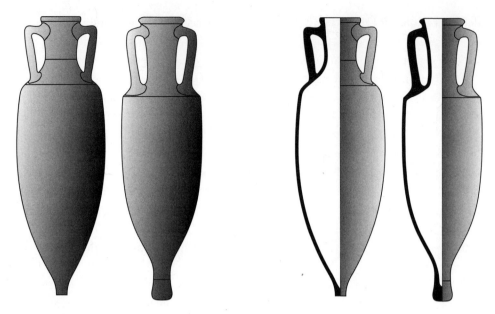

Figure III.4
These kinds of amphorae (designated Dressel 2–4) were perhaps the most mass-produced items of Roman antiquity.

The Romans did not invent any fundamentally new road construction techniques, but they applied and perfected a set of standardized procedures and invested an enormous amount of labor and organization into building and maintaining an extensive network of hard-top roads (Pekáry 1968; Sitwell 1981; van Tilburg 2007). The network began with the famous Via Appia between Rome and Capua (just north of Napoli) in 312 B.C.E. (figure III.5), and by the time of Diocletian's reign (285–305 C.E.) roads used by the *cursus publicus*, the Roman courier service, were extended to about 85,000 km. Principal Roman roads were 12 m wide, country roads less than 3 m (Forbes 1965). They were topped with gravel concrete, cobblestones, or slabs set in mortar. I have calculated that their construction would have required the emplacement of no less than 500 million m^3 of stone (for the base and the top *summa crusta*), gravel, sand, and lime after moving first some 750 million m^3 of earth and rock for the roadbed and earthen embankment (*agger*).[18]

But perhaps the most remarkable Roman innovation was the widespread use of *opus cementitium*, which made it possible to build large vaults and domed structures. This sturdy building material did not actually contain any cement, and it

Figure III.5
Interlocking paving stones of the Via Appia in an etching from Piranesi's *Le Antichità Romane* (1756), *left*, and a closeup of a wheel rut in that road (photo by V. Smil).

should not be called concrete. Modern cement is a carefully prepared and finely ground mixture of lime, clay, and metallic oxides, and modern concrete is a mixture of cement, aggregate (sand, pebbles), and water that is used, readymade, in construction. Roman *opus cementitium* was prepared on site by using lime mortar, aggregate (sand, gravel, stones, or even broken bricks or tiles), and water (Adam 1994). Slaked lime, the classic bonding agent for mortar, was already in use during the sixth millennium B.C.E., and according to Davidovits (2002), most of the blocks for Egypt's largest pyramids were cast *in situ* by mixing granular limestone aggregate with an alkali alumino-silicate-based binder.[19]

The Romans began to use mortar-stone mixtures by the end of the third century B.C.E., and the quality greatly improved once they discovered that volcanic sand found near Puteoli, north of the Bay of Naples and around Mount Vesuvius (*pulvere puteolano*, now commonly known as *pozzolana*), makes a superior material, one that will actually harden in a wet environment, even under water.[20] While still inferior compared to modern concrete, which is produced by firing limestone and clay at temperatures high enough to vitrify the alumina and silica, the pozzolanic aggregate and a high-quality lime were good enough to build highly durable walls and large vaults (M. W. Jones 2000).

Figure III.6
Four views of the Pantheon. *Clockwise from upper left*: north facade, massive bronze doorway, central oculus, and coffered dome ceiling. Photos by V. Smil.

The Pantheon, the pinnacle of Rome's "concrete" architecture—an inscription placed on its wall in 1632 by Urban VIII calls it *aedificium toto terrarum orbe celeberrimum* (the most celebrated building in the whole world)—was most likely built between 118 and 126 C.E., and it still stands in the heart of Rome (figure III.6). Its walls are a mortared aggregate inside a circular brick form, and the dome, spanning 43.2 m, consists of five rows of square coffers whose diminishing size converges on the stunning unglazed oculus (Lucchini 1966; MacDonald 1976). The dome's most intriguing property is the vertically decreasing specific density achieved by using progressively thinner layers of masonry with lighter aggregates (from travertine at the bottom to pumice at the top). No preindustrial builders ever topped this span, although Michelangelo came close with 41.75 m at St. Peter's Basilica.

This brief appraisal of Roman technical advances does not undermine the conclusion about Rome's relatively undistinguished record. It rightly shows that the

Romans were not as innovation-averse as has often been asserted and that they were skilled engineers and accomplished planners and managers of large projects. But the record is still one of only very modest inventive contributions and a near absence of new, incisive scientific inquiries. This relative weakness is best demonstrated by contrasting Roman science and engineering with those of its great Asian contemporary, China's Han dynasty (Hardy and Kinney 2005). By far the greatest concatenation of ancient Chinese inventions took place during that dynasty, whose duration (206 B.C.E.–220 C.E.) overlapped two centuries of the mature Roman Republic and slightly more than two centuries of the principate.

A list of engineering and scientific advances introduced or perfected during the Han years is even more impressive because many of these innovations and ideas were not adopted in practice or recognized in theory in the West for many centuries following their introduction in China (Needham 1965; 1971; Temple 1986). Chronologically, its basic engineering entries include routine casting of iron, steel production from cast iron, papermaking, crank handle, gimbal (Cardan) suspension (interlocking rings holding an object upright in the center of a sphere), efficient collar horse harness, multitube seed rill and rotary winnowing fan during the second century B.C.E., percussion drilling, belt drive and wheelbarrow during the first century B.C.E., chain pump, suspension bridge and rudder during the first century C.E., and watertight ship compartments, batten-strengthened lug sails and multiple masts (fore and aft rigging) during the second century C.E. During the third century C.E. the Chin inventors added the stirrup and porcelain.

Fundamental scientific advances of the era included the recognition of circadian rhythms in human body, introduction of negative numbers and decimal fractions, the first simple seismographs (by Zhang Heng in 130 C.E., who also invented the armillary sphere and a celestial globe), and a spreading reliance on the magnetic compass, as well as such esthetic accomplishments like the introduction of tuned drums and the recognition of the hexagonal structure of snowflakes. Graduates of the Han's state academy produced books on mathematics (*Jiuzhang suanshu*), clinical medicine and acupuncture (*Huangdi neijing*), and pharmacology (*Shennong bencaojing*), and agriculture benefited from proposed rationalizations, summarized in Fan Shengzhi's writings, which included recommendations for crop rotations, selection of crops according to soil quality, irrigation, and transplantation of seedlings.

This is a stunning list of accomplishments; it contains items whose later diffusion and worldwide adoption have helped—a cliché is the most appropriate choice in this context—to change the world. Without the three fundamental Chinese shipping inventions—stern-post rudder (it appeared in Europe only a millennium later), multiple masts, and magnetic compass—there could have been no reasonably accurate and relatively fast long-distance navigation whose exploits later helped to create modern Europe (Cipolla 1966; McNeill 1989). The Han's metallurgical accomplishments were even more important. Han iron furnaces were charged with nearly 1 t of iron ore and produced liquid cast iron in two tappings a day, a relatively large-scale production.[21]

Iron casting into interchangeable molds was used to mass-produce iron tools, thin-walled cooking pots and pans, and statues (Hua 1983). Coins were also cast rather than minted, and nonbrittle metal was used to mass-produce iron moldboard plows, which were naturally heavier than wooden plows but created much less friction and could be pulled by a single animal even in water-logged clay soils.[22] Decarburization, the removal of carbon from brittle cast iron by oxygenation, yields strong steel, and this Han invention made it possible to produce heavy chains for suspension bridges as well as excellent weapons.

Coal, not just charcoal, was used in iron smelting during the Han dynasty. Another great pioneering use of a fossil fuel was the extraction of natural gas in the landlocked Sichuan to produce salt by evaporating brines (Adshead 1992). Chinese gas extraction relied on percussion drilling, using heavy iron bits that were attached to long bamboo cables from bamboo derricks and were raised rhythmically by men jumping on a lever (figure III.7).[23] Natural gas was distributed by bamboo pipelines to evaporate brines in huge cast iron pans (Needham 1964). This was undoubtedly one of the most consequential inventions of all times; 19 centuries later, when percussion drilling was used to develop the modern oil and gas industry, the only key difference was that small steam engines rather than jumping men powered the drilling (Smil 2008c). The deepest percussion-drilled wells eventually reached more than 2.3 km, and even in the United States the cable tool rigs outnumbered rotary drills (patented by Howard Hughes in 1909) until the early 1950s.

As far objects of everyday use, there is hardly any need to extol the essential role of paper in civilization or the admirable combination of utility and beauty that is porcelain. In agriculture the advantage of iron moldboard plows was greatly potentiated by the introduction of a superior collar horse harness. The ancient throat harness was not suited for heavy draft, and the breastband harness (introduced during the early Han Period) had its point of traction too far away from the animal's powerful pectoral muscles. The evolution of the most efficient as well as the most comfortable harness began in China during the first century B.C.E. as

Figure III.7
Percussion drilling was one of the most important technical advances introduced during the Han dynasty (206 B.C.E.–220 C.E.). This woodcut is reproduced from a survey of China's techniques published during the Qing dynasty.

a soft support for the wooden yoke; by the fifth century C.E. it evolved into a single piece.[24]

This brief account suffices to demonstrate how superior were the technical and proto-scientific achievements of the Han dynasty in comparison with Roman records. The Romans did little to advance the scientific and inventive accomplishments of the Hellenistic era, and on both of these counts they come as distant seconds to their great Asian counterpart. But some historians have argued for a reappraisal of the empire's technical innovation and have made much of new archaeological finds of Roman watermills, claiming not only their relatively widespread use in flour milling but also in other applications. But were the Romans vigorous innovators at least as far as the introduction of the first inanimate prime mover was concerned?

Answering this specific question, and appraising the dependence on machines in the Roman world in contrast with machine-dominated America makes us understand a critical factor in the functioning of the two societies. We take this reality entirely for granted and rarely comment on it, but most of the functional differences between these two worlds—impossible to grasp in their totality and in their depth and reach of everyday impact on modern populations—are due to our reliance on machines. This dependence has evolved from the use of a widening variety of mechanical arrangements (some used since antiquity), to a rapid diffusion (starting in the 1880s) of machines powered by electricity and since the early 1950s, to the now universal reliance on ever more complex micromachinery of electronic assemblies.

There is little need to dwell on the ubiquity, affordability, versatility, and reliability of modern machines. I introduce only some key numbers to emphasize their importance. But I do review more extensively the Roman use of machines that were not powered by people or animals (leaving sailing ships aside, only waterwheels are in that category), offer some order-of-magnitude calculations to underscore their relative unimportance, and look briefly at flour mills, the most common of all Roman mechanical devices that were energized by human and animal labor.

Power of Machines

The ideal aim of historical understanding—multifaceted, balanced, and credible interpretation of the past—is commonly an extraordinary challenge because the available evidence is often too fragmentary to allow for any confident conclusions. Nearly every aspect of Roman studies is subject to this fundamental limitation, and one of the most prominent weaknesses in our understanding—our unsatisfactory knowledge about Roman demography—is taken up in some detail in chapter IV. Modern conclusions regarding the Roman use of mechanical devices illustrate another commonly encountered problem of historical interpretations: misleading conclusions based on insufficient (or selective use of) evidence that acquire the power of standard accounts.

The slow adoption of waterwheels throughout the Roman Empire is often cited as an example of prolonged technical stagnation (innovation blockage). The water-driven flour mill was only the second instance of harnessing inanimate energy to perform mechanical work (preceded only by the use of sails on boats and ships) and the first instance of using inanimate energy for stationary tasks with potentially widespread applications for other tasks. In these simple wooden machines, attested to in literary sources since the first century B.C.E. (by Antipater of Thessalonica), water turned paddles fitted to a hub that rotated on a sturdy shaft, which was usually directly attached to a millstone above.[25]

Soon afterward more efficient vertical wheels turned the millstones by right-angle gears, and depending on the point of water impact, they could be built as undershots, breast wheels, or (the most efficient) overshots. Their first clear description, by Vitruvius, comes from 27 B.C.E., but it was generally assumed that they were not in widespread use until the fifth century C.E. This conclusion was first challenged by Wikander (1981; 1983), who refuted the commonly given reasons for neglect or at best a slow diffusion of these machines (availability of slave labor; lack of interest in mechanization among the ruling classes; radical nature of a new design; high cost of the needed investment; few opportunities to locate watermills in towns; scarcity of suitable streams in the Mediterranean; difficulties of land transport), and proposed the late second century C.E. as the time of the breakthrough for the technique.

By 1985 new evidence came up, with about 30 Roman or early Byzantine watermills; by the year 2000 this list of ancient watermills had grown to nearly 60 items, and new additions are being made every year (Wilson 2002). Lewis (1997) concluded that the invention of the watermill took place during the first half of the third century B.C.E. (most likely in Alexandria) and that by the first century C.E. water power was used not only for the milling of grain but also for some industrial tasks, above all, to drive ore-crushing hammers. Greene (2000), refuting Finley's ideas of economic stagnation and technical blockage, argued that economic historians "approaching the classical period from more recent perspectives, need to rid themselves of the notion that it was any less complex than later centuries, even if the pace of change was not remarkable" (56).

These new arguments on behalf of a more machine-dependent Rome rest on some irrefutable foundations. The paucity of references to water-powered machines in the surviving written record is not a reliable measure of their actual adoption and diffusion, and neither is the relatively low number of archaeological finds. There are fewer than 20 clearly identified watermill sites dating from the early medieval England, whereas the Domesday Book lists about 6,500 (Holt 1988). But I feel that the new-found enthusiasm regarding the early diffusion of Roman waterwheels has carried the evidence too far. The key questions—how common these mills were; how powerful and how efficient; what were their typical utilization rates; how much were they used for tasks other than milling—cannot be answered with high certainty, but revealing approximations based on other evidence argue for a rather subdued overall assessment.

To conclude that the Romans took a crucial step in deploying water power beyond grain milling may be factually correct, but except for a few anecdotal (and uncertain) cases, we have no basis to estimate how far this process had progressed.[26] But we know that the great panoply of water power uses, including sawing, paper making, cloth fulling, extracting tannin from bark, oil pressing, ore crushing, wire pulling, stamping, metal grinding, majolica glazing, and polishing, came only about 1,000 years after the demise of the Western Roman Empire (A. R. Lucas 2005). To conclude, as Wilson (2002, 12) did, that "developments in the last 1,800 years of water-milling largely constituted refinements of an already mature technology" is a clearly indefensible statement.

He based this claim on the fact that a pair of stones at a Roman mill at Barbegal (near Arles, Roman *Arelate*) produced 24 kg of flour per hour, the rate virtually identical with the output of traditional small mills in Sweden or an old wooden mill that still works in Livno (Bosnia). This comparison neglects to note that the few surviving small mills are outdated curiosities whose performance was greatly surpassed after 1800 when designs of iron waterwheels with superior gearing and high conversion efficiency resulted in wheels with capacities as high as 200 kW (J. Reynolds 1970; F. P. Woodall 1982) and with even more powerful multiple assemblies.[27] And yet Barbegal was called by Greene (2000, 39) "the greatest known concentration of mechanical power in the ancient world" and by Hodge (1990, 106) "something that, according to all the textbooks, never existed at all—an authentic, ancient Roman, power-driven, mass-production, assembly-line factory." Such claims demand a closer look at the installation.

Water for the Barbegal mill was diverted from an aqueduct, and it flowed in two parallel channels (partly hewn from the underlying rock, partly built in stone) down a steep slope and turned 16 overshot wheels (figure III.8). Stony remnants of this large installation were identified as a multiple watermill and excavated during the 1930s (Benoit 1940), and subsequent reconstructions of the most likely performance produced widely differing results.[28] Conservative assumptions of water flow (240 L/s) and conversion efficiency (55%) give unit power of about 1.5 kW, equal to that of three small horses.[29] Other remnants of Roman mills with multiple wheels have been found in Israel and Tunisia and in Rome itself, on a slope of the Janiculum on the right bank of the river (fed by water from *Aqua Traiana*), hinting at a much larger number of original installations.

Figure III.8
A reconstruction of a large Roman flour mill powered by 16 overshot waterwheels at Barbegal, near Arles in Provence (Roman *Narbonensis*). Reproduced from Sagui (1948).

The most revealing thought experiment attempting to quantify the importance of Roman water power is to assume both a very high average power rating and a fairly high number of wheels. Even when applying the roughly 1:500 ratio of identified to documented Domesday watermills to the Roman situation of nearly a millennium earlier, we get a very high total of some 25,000 watermills; and even when assuming that an average wheel was capable of 1.5 kW of useful power, their combined output would reach (with a high load factor around 50%) about 300 trillion joules of useful energy per year. In contrast, the exertions of some 30 million working adults and 6 million draft and pack animals add up to at least 100 times as much useful energy per year.[30] This means that even with the high assumptions regarding unit power and the total number of wheels, water power would have equaled just 1% of useful kinetic energy supplied by people and animals.

The real share was most likely just a fraction of 1%. As there were no windmills in antiquity, this share indicates the likely maximum of all useful energy supplied by machines driven by inanimate power, and it makes clear that even exceedingly liberal assumptions concerning the Roman adoption of waterwheels do not change the fundamental conclusion that inanimately powered mechanical devices were of marginal importance in the empire's economy. As a result, the empire's most ubiquitous machines, flour mills and dough-kneading assemblies, continued to be powered by animals and slaves.

Distribution of free grain required milling and baking on a relatively large scale because neither process could be done in urban apartments; city *pistores* were both millers and bakers (Bakker 1999). In order to meet large-scale demand for bread they had to replace laborious grinding with rotary *mola manualis* (yielding between less than 1 kg and 2.5 kg of very coarse flour per hour), which had been used since the third century B.C.E., by installing larger and more efficient rotary *mola asinalis* (although in locations with limited space, slaves were used to turn them). Commercial bakeries are documented in Rome at least since the middle of the second century B.C.E. (Moritz 1958). Millstones of the typical Roman design (often called the Pompeian mill, confined to cities and towns) were fashioned from rough volcanic rock, the lower part (*meta*) was cylindrical, covered by the hourglass bell-shaped *catillus*, which was supplied by grain from a hopper and had horizontal beams inserted in the middle.[31]

Animals (donkeys and mules) walked in a small circle, rotating the *catillus*. Grain was usually ground twice (in order to achieve good separation of bran), followed by sieving. Large bakeries had dough-kneading machines (round stone reservoirs where the dough was kneaded between stationary and moving blades) that were powered by people or animals pushing against a crossbeam. Working conditions were abominable, and as Lucius Apuleius attests, the slaves suffered terribly.[32] Because the capacity of animal-powered mills ranged from less than 10 kg/h to 25 kg/h (Forbes 1965), because their average hours of operation were necessarily variable, and most important, because we have no good basis on which to estimate the shares of grain ground by households and by commercial bakeries, we can calculate the number of the empire's most commonly used mechanical device only to the nearest order of magnitude. If a quarter of all grain was processed commercially by *mola asinalis* and if millstones produced on average just 10–15 kg/h, then the empire of the second century C.E. had most likely 150,000–200,000 animal-powered mills (figure III.9).

In contrast, the ubiquity and power of machines in modern U.S. society has reached levels unequaled in history and unmatched by any other large economy; their numbers are in the hundreds of millions, their aggregate power in trillions of watts (for individual data categories, see USDOT 2008; EIA 2008a). In 2005 there were nearly 250 million registered road vehicles, including about 137 million cars, 95 million vans, pickup trucks, and SUVs, and more than 6 million trucks. To these

Figure III.9
Hourglass flour mill was the most common animal-powered machine of the late Roman Empire. This marble relief, in Museo Chiaramonti (Vatican Museums), shows a horse-powered mill. Photo courtesy of Barbara F. McManus.

must be added more than 100 million other internal combustion engines, ranging from small units in lawnmowers (about 50 million) to much more powerful units in snowmobiles (about 2 million), motorcycles (about 6 million), and powerboats (about 13 million in- and outboard engines) (USDOT 2008). Finally, there were also about 225,000 small planes and more than 8,000 commercial jet planes.

In aggregate these internal combustion engines had about 30 trillion watts of installed power.[33] This aggregate prorates to 100 kW per capita, whereas the useful adult labor rate cannot be sustained at more than 100 W. The installed power of machines serving an average American is thus more than 1,000 times greater than the labor rate that can be sustained by an average person, whereas in the Roman Empire the reverse was true: inanimate power harnessed by waterwheels and sails added to no more than 1/1000 of animate (somatic) power supplied by human and animal labor. *This is a stunning difference of 6 orders of magnitude. An average American is now served by machines whose capacity is about 1 million times greater than that of inanimately energized machines serving an average Roman.*

These realities make it easy to conclude that today's America is more a society of machines than people. I have argued that an extraterrestrial observer who knows nothing of the history of technical advances on Earth the resulting intricate relations between humans and machines could easily conclude—judging simply by the magnitude and intensity of carbon metabolism (carbon oxidation through digestion by humans, carbon oxidation through high-temperature combustion by fuel-powered machines)—that machines are the planet's dominant creatures, with humans as their servants (Smil 2006).

An illustration of this reality is the servitude that underlies car ownership, a quotidian reality whose surprisingly demanding (yet voluntarily assumed) obligations were explained by Illich (1974, 18–19), who calculated that the time required to earn money for the purchase, operation, and maintenance of a car adds up to about 1600 hs; with 12,000 km of travel this prorates to a car travel speed of 7.5 km/h, equivalent to a very fast walk. More than 30 years after Illich's calculations matters are even worse; my calculation for 2005 puts the average effective speed of U.S. car travel at only 5 km/h, a pace that could be matched by millions of sprightly walking retirees, and convincing testimony of a counterintuitive (but all too real) human servitude to the most commonly owned transportation machine.

Such musings and comparative notions have no place in appraising Roman society, where more complicated mechanical devices were uncommon and all machines, except for a limited number of just-described waterwheels, were powered by repetitive, often exhausting and painful animal and human exertions. The two societies are thus fundamentally incomparable. In Rome, as in every other ancient polity, animate labor, including heavy human exertion, often under abominable conditions, was (marginal exceptions aside) the energizer of every productive activity.

In contrast, in modern America there are virtually no working animals (except those used in shows and sports), and an overwhelming majority of people work in occupations where they are just controllers of inanimate energy flows. Physically demanding tasks are reserved for leisure and sports activities, and heavy human exertions have become the shrinking preserve of a few physically demanding occupations, including logging, mining, and fishing. But even there human labor is dwarfed by enormous inputs of inanimate energies used to power a variety of machines (chain saws, continuous mining assemblies, high-tech trawlers). These enormous differences in the dependence on machines must be reflected in overall rates of energy consumption.

Energy Sources

Much like many reasons have been proposed for the demise of the Western Roman Empire, America's unique position in the modern world has been ascribed to many different factors. Matters are less complicated when we search for the physical foundations of the country's success; here its energy use—its pattern, level, and efficiency—provides the single most important factor that explains the differences between standards of living and the overall power of states (Smil 1994; 2008a). America could have its unique constitution, its melting-pot population, and its sovereignty over a continent-sized territory, but it is its high energy consumption that transforms these desirable attributes into a unique reality.

Yet it is precisely this critical factor that makes the two societies fundamentally incomparable. America is an unequaled example of a large modern economy that derives most of its power from the combustion of fossil fuels, supplemented by generation of primary electricity (hydro, nuclear, wind, solar) that converts it to useful tasks (heat, motion, light) with high efficiency and that consumes energy at a very high per capita rate. In contrast, Rome's energetic foundations, much like those of every ancient society, rested on the low-efficiency combustion of wood and the muscular exertions of people and animals, with overall per capita energy use being a small fraction of modern rates. These limits constrained every aspect of Roman society, much as America's high energy use creates opportunities (and problems) for the country's economy, environment, and global standing.

Most important, the energy sources of traditional societies were renewable and hence, at least theoretically, sustainable on a time scale far surpassing that of recorded history. Of course, in practice this was often not the case because extensive deforestation led to excessive erosion, which made reforestation of such damaged ecosystems impossible or very difficult. But with a modicum of careful management a society energized by phytomass fuels and animate muscles could undoubtedly be perpetuated on a civilizational time scale of thousands of years; its energy sources would limit its accomplishments but not its durability.

Dynastic China offers the best example of this reality. The centralized state that emerged during the short-lived Qin dynasty (221–206 B.C.E.) and that was consolidated and greatly expanded under the Han dynasty (Rome's contemporary) was then perpetuated in a remarkably stable manner (with gradual improvements and after successfully coping with external threats) for nearly another two millennia.[34] In contrast, a society energized largely by fossil fuels would not be able to match the combined duration of the Roman Republic and the Roman Empire (more than a thousand years) without a profound transformation of its current energy foundation. If there is to be a powerful American state two or five centuries in the future, it will have to derive the bulk of its primary energy either from renewable energies or from nuclear power (Smil 2003; 2008b).

While we cannot estimate with a high degree of reliability the mass of fossil fuels that will ultimately be recovered from the Earth's crust, we know that it is final and that even if future demand were to stay at the current level, we would not have enough coal, crude oil, and natural gas to run a modern civilization for even one millennium.[35] Moreover, extraction and conversion of these fuels create enormous environmental problems that, too, were unknown in traditional societies. Deforestation was locally, even regionally, crippling, and inefficient charcoaling, smelting, and wood burning were sources of local air pollution, but none of these impacts were global, and none had the potential to change the Earth's climate as does today's combustion of fossil fuels. Besides these fundamental qualitative differences (renewable versus nonrenewable energy sources, local versus global) there are truly stunning quantitative contrasts between the levels of prevailing energy use in ancient Rome and in modern America and, even more so, between their net (useful) energy supplies.

There was nothing very remarkable to set apart Rome's energy use from that of other ancient societies, wheras America clearly stands, together with Canada, at the top rung of energy use among all large modern economies.[36] Today's global average of primary energy use—all fossil fuels, wood, hydro, nuclear, wind, and solar electricity—is equivalent to just over 1.5 t of oil equivalent (toe) per capita.[37] India uses about 0.35 toe, China roughly 1.5 toe, the poorest EU countries just over 2.5 toe, the richest ones and Japan over 4 toe. But the U.S. average is more than 7.5 toe per capita, nearly twice the German, French, or Japanese rate. The only countries whose average annual per capita energy consumption is even higher than that of the United States (and Canada) are small states whose high rate of energy use reflects their dependence on fuel extraction or processing destined largely for exports; hydrocarbon-rich Kuwait, Qatar, and United Arab Emirates (UAE) are the foremost examples of this category (BP 2008; EIA 2008a).[38]

But gross energy consumption is not the best indicator of a society's energy use; most of that flux is converted with low efficiencies, leaving a relatively small amount of useful energy to provide heat or motion. Gasoline-fueled internal combustion engines are inherently less efficient than diesel engines, which are widely used in Europe, and U.S. cars are more massive than Europe's or Japan's. America's conversion of gasoline to kinetic energy is thus less efficient than in the EU and Japan, but its transportation techniques are identical to those used in other affluent countries, and its industrial processes and household heating are highly energy-efficient. The U.S. economy now converts about 40% of its gross energy input into useful energies, including motion, heat for industrial processes, indoor heating and cooling, and light (EIA 2008b). This prorates to an annual equivalent of just over 3 toe per capita, a total nearly twice as high as in any other major economy.

In contrast, there was nothing exceptional or superior about Rome's average per capita energy use when compared to levels that prevailed among the empire's contemporaries. Much like the other ancient economies, Rome derived most of its kinetic energy human and animal labor and its thermal energy from combustion of phytomass fuels, the burning of wood, crop residues, and charcoal (Smil 1994; Wilson 2002). Inevitably, any quantification of these energy uses requires a number of assumptions, but despite many inherent uncertainties it is possible to come up with the right order of magnitude to represent the typical level of consumption.

Primary inputs needed for animate kinetic energies are established by making liberal assumptions about average food and feed intakes. Average daily food consumption of about 2400 kcal is a good mean to calculate the total per capita food demand, but daily rates had to be as much as 40%–50% higher for many slaves engaged in such hard labor as quarrying, tree cutting, or mining.[39] In order to estimate the energy value of feed needed for the Roman draft animals it is necessary to establish first their overall numbers. In the fields oxen were the dominant draft animals; horses and mules were too expensive to keep, and given their small stature and the absence of proper harness, they would not provide superior power. A pair of oxen was needed for about 180–200 h to plow, harrow, and harvest 1 ha of wheat yielding about 500 kg of grain (Smil 1994), so it can be calculated that the Romans had perhaps as many as 5 million oxen for field and farmyard work.[40]

Local and long-distance transport needed at least 500,000 animals, including about 200,000 horses (the rest were mules, donkeys, and oxen).[41] Roman armies were dominated by infantry forces; descriptions by Livius and Varro make it clear that a *legio* of between 3,000 and 5,000 foot soldiers had a regular complement (*justus equitatus*) of 300–400 horses, and this ratio was similar in allied units. The empire's entire cavalry during the early centuries C.E. thus had a maximum of 50,000–70,000 horses. Mules—used to carry food rations, tents, and weapons, to pull heavy carts with siege equipment, and to take home the spoils of war after conquests in distant territories—were present in larger numbers. Peddie (1994) calculated that 8,750 animals accompanied an army consisting of six legions.

A defensible order-of-magnitude estimate thus puts the total of Roman draft and pack animals at about 6 million during the second century C.E., and given their relatively small size and limited power, their annual feed requirements (secured overwhelmingly by grazing) prorate to about 0.1 toe of feed energy per every inhabitant of the empire.[42] The empire's annual primary biomass energy inputs of food and feed thus add up to about 0.2 toe per capita. Given the inevitable approximations used in calculating these means, the very minor contribution of kinetic energy harnessed by waterwheels (the Romans had no windmills) can be easily disregarded.

Estimating Roman fuel consumption is an exceedingly difficult task. The most reliable estimate that is closest in time to the Roman era dates only to the year 1300 for annual wood consumption in London. That average, including all heating and cooking needs and a multitude of uses in small manufactures, amounted to more than 1.5 t of air-dried wood per capita, (Galloway, Keene, and Murphy 1996). My calculations of Roman fuel needs add up to at least 0.25 toe per capita.[43] Consequently, the grand total of inputs to generate animate kinetic power and thermal power from combustion of phytomass add to no less than 0.4 toe and very unlikely to more than 0.5 toe of food, feed, and fuel per capita. Today's gross U.S. rate is 18 times higher, but the contrast between energy flows that were actually controlled by individuals in large Roman cities and that are commanded by the quotidian actions of today's average urban consumers is even greater.

A poor citizen of Rome who was clothed and ate adequately, worked as an artisan, had to walk everywhere (only the most privileged individuals could travel in litters or ride horses), and owned just a few pieces of simple furniture would control only his own labor exertion, his purchases of food and necessities, and an occasional use of one of the city's hundreds of baths. His decisions thus led to annual per capita consumption of no more than 0.10–0.15 toe of primary energy. In contrast, in the United States at the beginning of the twenty-first century the combined share of annual energy used by the residential sector approached 45% of total primary energy demand (EIA 2008b). This total is composed of three principal inputs: electricity for household uses; gasoline for transportation fuel; and fuels for heating.

An average American owning a suburban house in a large city lives in a dwelling that draws upward of 30 kW; because the efficiency of U.S. electricity generation averages about 33%, this means that about 1 toe per capita is needed to generate household electricity consumed annually (EIA 2008b). Much more power commanded by that suburban American household (on the order of 200 kW) is installed in the family's two vehicles, whose annual fuel consumption amounts to about 1.5 toe per capita (EIA 2008a). Adding the fuels used for house heating brings the total of primary energy flows directly commanded by a household to an equivalent of roughly 3.5 toe per capita.

This is about 30 times the Roman urban mean, and it represents a constant power rate of nearly 5 kW per capita. Equivalent power would have been available to a Roman citizen only if about 50 strong slaves had labored continuously (24 hours per day for 365 days) on his behalf, or if about 200 slaves had worked eight hours per day for 300 days, making every Roman citizen (whether a busy seamstress or a drunkard eating free bread) equal to a sizable *latifundium* owner. But there is an even better way to contrast the two levels of use, one that is most revealing because it compares average per capita rates of useful energy that are calculated by taking into account prevailing conversion efficiencies of all major energy transformations.

As in all traditional agricultural societies, only the most demanding tasks (plowing, pulling out stumps) were done by animals, and field and farmyard activities were energized overwhelmingly by human labor. Healthy adult men convert no more than 15%–20% of metabolized food to kinetic energy (useful energy at rates of just 15–30 W per capita), and the rates for women would commonly be 10%–20% lower. A relatively limited use of animal draft is explained by the absence of efficient harnessing and by the shortage of good forage. As in all ancient societies, Roman horses were overwhelmingly destined for battle and as carriers of messages along the *cursus publicus* (Hyland 1990). Light weight and a limited draft of horses produced average power of just 400–500 W, but poor harnessing could not take full advantage of even that low rate; inherently less powerful oxen could sustain just 250–350 W, donkeys just 100–200 W (Smil 2008a).

Roman metal smelting was, like all ancient metallurgies, very inefficient. To begin with, charcoal production was inefficient, requiring at least 5–6 kg of wood to produce 1 kg of charcoal; in energy terms this represents a loss of about 70% of the primary energy. Roman metal smelting was a leading cause of Mediterranean deforestation. Cooking also wasted a great deal of energy. Typical cooking arrangements—a raised masonry hearth with wood or charcoal burning underneath clay or metal vessels sitting on iron tripods or grid irons—let most of the heat escape and had conversion efficiencies no higher than 10%–15%.

Large pieces of meat were cooked less efficiently in cauldrons suspended over wood fires or roasted on spits. Bread dough was placed in heated brick ovens after the ashes were raked out, and the oven was sealed for baking. Energy waste would have been even greater if families had cooked for themselves. That was not the case in larger slave-owning establishments, which had communal cooking, and in Rome itself the poorer inhabitants never cooked; they were crammed into multi-storied *insulae* (houses) subdivided into *coenacula* (apartments)[44] that had no cooking or heating arrangements (nor any running water or toilets), and unless they were given their food, they had to buy bread from *pistrinae* and cooked food from *tabernae*.

In contrast, Roman heating in large private houses, in *thermae*, and in some public buildings was relatively efficient because of the hypocaust, a simple but effective arrangement that used combustion gases to heat raised floors before escaping through a chimney.[45] This Greek invention whose oldest remains, found both in Greece and in *Magna Graecia*, date to the third century B.C.E. (Ginouvès 1962). It was first used by the Romans in the *caldaria* of their public baths, then in stone houses in colder provinces (figure III.10). Trials with a preserved hypocaust showed that just 1 kg of charcoal per hour could maintain 22°C in a room 5 × 4 × 3 m when the outside temperature was 0°C (Forbes 1966).

My estimate of the most likely grand total of useful energy—kinetic (animate) and thermal (fuel wood and charcoal)—thus amounts to an equivalent of no more than about 180–200 kg of wood per capita (that is, 0.07 toe) or no more than 15% of initial energy inputs. Compared to the mean U.S. equivalents of about 3.5 t of oil (or at least 8.5 t of wood), this means that on average an American benefits every year from useful energy flows that are nearly 50 times higher than those accruing to an average Roman in the early centuries C.E. When differences get this large, it is difficult to realize their import and their consequences. We are intuitively comfort-

Figure III.10
Part of a hypocaust, an ancient Roman central heating system, with skeleton of a dog killed by fumes. Displayed at Homburg-Schwarzenacker Roman Museum (Saarland). Photo courtesy of Barbara F. McManus.

able with a world of human proportions, with doubling, tripling, and quadrupling, with halving of quantities or dividing them into three or four parts.

Consequently, it is not difficult to imagine the implications and consequences of somebody being twice or three times as well off or living with half of an income, but none of us can truly grasp what it would mean to live with 1/50th of the useful energy we now consume, that is, with 1/50th of the amenities, services, goods and opportunities that we enjoy today. An average Roman might perhaps have an easier task comprehending a life with 50 times as many amenities because he might imagine leading a life of the richest senators or an emperor, but even if he could do that, the comparison would be still fall short because modern energy services are incomparably more convenient, reliable, and (almost magically) flexible compared to those that were available even to the most profligate emperors.

Even an emperor had to ride a horse if he wanted to accomplish his journey in the fastest possible time; riding in a saddle for many hours is hard, whether on hard-top *viae* or some barbaric terrain, and some emperors rode thousands of kilometers during their lives. Traveling in Roman litters (*lecticae*, common since the time of the late republic) would have been much slower; these containers were often furnished with soft bedding, but prolonged lying in a swaying litter was not very comfortable for long journeys. And even an emperor had his rooms lit by oil lamps or candles, both rather inconvenient and grossly inefficient sources of illumination, converting less than 0.01% of the chemical energy of fuels into light.[46]

And a Roman imagining a life with 200 personal slaves would still get a grossly inadequate impression of modern advantages because even those scores of servants and laborers could not provide energy services comparable in terms of convenience, versatility, flexibility, and reliability with those delivered by electricity and fossil fuels: no filling of oil lamps, no fiddling with wicks, no preparation of kindling. No lighting of charcoal, no frequent stoking of a wood fire, no heavy smoke from insufficiently air-dried wood, no scraping out of ashes from a bread oven, no carrying of heavy shoulder loads, no dragging of a recalcitrant mule or donkey—just a flip of a switch, a turn of a key, numbers punched into a thermostat are enough to start flows of perfectly regulated and amazingly reliable light, heat, or kinetic power. The only way for a modern American to get a taste of typical Roman conditions would be to try out for a week some key realities of common Roman life, an experience that would not actually be easy to arrange.

Here are the basic conditions of energy supply that would resemble that of a typical Roman household: either no source of heat in a room (no stove, no chimney) or perhaps just a couple of small charcoal-fueled braziers; no glass windows, just rough shutters or a small latticed opening; an entirely dark room once the doors were closed; no arrangement to cook anything inside; no water piped in and no waste led out; no elevator (some *insulae* had five floors); and essentially no privacy, with the constant noise and presence of other people.

Outside of a dwelling, one would first walk to a communal toilet with a brush (wetted in a shallow runnel in front of the toilets and then, without the least privacy, stuck backward through a frontal opening of the seat for cleansing); once in a while a visit to a communal bath; getting loaves of bread from a nearby bakery (the cheapest *panis primis* made from grains other than wheat; even wheat breads contained ground beans or lentils) and some hard cheese (easy to keep), the two staples of the common diet that often provided as much as 80%–90% of all food energy; an occasional indulgence in a small portion of *puls* (wheat porridge, prepared from bulgur-like *alica*) with pieces of meat;[47] walking everywhere in streets choked with people, dust, mud, and waste; and after a day's work having no comfortable place to sit or to relax, no adequate light for manual work.

This brief recounting of some essential aspects of everyday life in the ancient cosmopolis is a fitting bridge to the next chapter, to a closer look at matters of life and death, the patterns of Roman fertility, births, abandonments, diseases, mortality, and life expectancies (including hygiene, food supply, prevailing diet, and whatever passed for medical care) as well as at the sources of the empire's riches, the magnitude of Roman economic activity, its temporal changes and spatial variations, and its distribution of wealth, both in terms of typical earnings and net accumulated worth.

IV

Life, Death, Wealth

Brevis ipsa vita, sed malis fit longior.

Our life is short but is made longer by misfortunes.

—Publilius Syrus, *Sententiae*

Recent comparisons of imperial Rome and modern America have taken place mostly on the elevated planes of grand strategy, armed conflicts, public policies, foreign relations, and cultural appeal, as if to descend to the level of private lives, to inquire into the enormous differences in the population dynamics of the two societies, and to assess the extent of economic growth and the distribution of wealth were irrelevant and unworthy choices. The very opposite is true. Much like the proper understanding of inventiveness, reliance on machines, and levels of energy use, these matters are essential for any revealing historical comparisons.

The reasons for this are fundamental because so many socioeconomic variables, and hence the long-term fortunes, of every society are strongly determined or greatly influenced by complex demographic patterns of fertility, birth, and death rates; the age and sex structure of populations; the participation in labor force; the cohorts available for recruitment into armies; the length of typical life expectancy; and the composition and levels of morbidity, that is, the prevalence of quotidian sufferings and maladies, the extent of chronic diseases, and the frequency of periodic health crises brought by widespread epidemics.

And the key demographic variables—total populations (traditionally determined by a census); prevailing fertilities (total births per female); infant mortalities (numbers of children deceased during the first year of life per 1,000 newborn); specific morbidities (frequencies of different illnesses); vulnerability to epidemics and overall death rate (expressed per 100,000 people); age and gender composition (usually summed up graphically in age-sex pyramids); and average life expectancies—also co-determine (or at least heavily influence) family structure, women's position in society, attitudes to life and death, and the economic fortunes of a society.

High fertility is highly correlated with the low status of women; childhood experiences have profound influence on the perception of our place in society and our adult behavior; different frequencies of fatal illnesses and premature deaths create different attitudes and expectations regarding family life, education, and economic progress; and specific age-sex distributions and average life expectancies leave a complex imprint on virtually all social and economical processes, ranging from the propensity for violence (it rises with a higher share of young males) to the length of economically active life, and from marriage patterns to the structure of families.

Appraising these demographic and economic contrasts should be based on the best available physical, quantitative evidence rather than on arguable impressions derived from a sparse documentary record or from generalized interpretations of anecdotal bits. For modern America we can describe and analyze all these variables and their long-term dynamics with a great deal of quantitative detail, if not always with the desired precision (e.g., the total number of illegal immigrants resident in the United States is not known with accuracy better than ±5 million, and we have no idea if the available estimates of their annual influx are becoming more or less accurate).[1]

In contrast, Roman demography is a realm of vast ignorance, ubiquitous uncertainties, and endless conjectures where assumptions are the norm and the vigor of arguments can only rarely be matched by the solidity of available evidence. Still, enough is known and more can be deduced by careful and conservative reasoning and analysis (and by resorting to appropriate analogies) to have at least a semiquantitative impression of that ancient population, its constant acquaintance with death, its suffering owing to disease, its truncated lifespans, and its labor.

Assessing Rome's macroeconomic situation—the size of its total annual output (in modern terms, expressed as GDP, gross domestic product, the aggregate value of all goods and services); its typical growth rate; its composition (shares of the total contributed by agriculture, manufacturing, trade, and services); its degree of dependence on foreign trade (expressed as a share of GDP)—is no less challenging than offering even the simplest, heavily approximated demographic indicators. And given the major uncertainties regarding the size and the dynamics of Roman population, any economic indicators expressed in per capita terms—the equivalents of such modern favorites as annual GDP per capita, average per capita income, and average net worth—must be even more suspect.[2]

But none of these tasks is hopeless: our understanding of the Roman population and economy will always remain severely limited, but the best available information can be mined to fix the relative magnitudes, frequencies, and per capita rates. I first appraise what we know about Roman population dynamics—the best available estimates of population totals, long-term growth rates, vital (birth and death) rates, life expectancies, age-sex structure, and participation in economic and military activities—and contrast these with the modern U.S. experience. Then I assess the toll of major illnesses (including chronic diseases and epidemics), poor nutrition and periodic famines, specific morbidities and mortalities and life expectancies, and compare them to current U.S. patterns. I close the chapter with approximate quantifications of Rome's wealth (an exceedingly skewed distribution) compared to America's economic achievements and its pattern of personal riches.

Population Dynamics

Our understanding of the Roman population (aggregate numbers, vital indicators, structural changes in time) is hardly better than our knowledge of the empire's energy uses and its reliance on machines—overwhelmingly qualitative, with only fragmentary quantitative evidence whose relevance for representing more general structures and trends is rightly questionable. The best preserved information on Roman population comes from the early imperial censuses in Egypt (they were taken every 14 years), but even those data add up to only a tiny set of demographic information and raise the obvious questions of wider applicability. Egypt's population at that time was estimated at about 4.5 million, but the detailed analysis of census declarations for the period between 12 C.E. and 259 C.E. rests on information for 487 females and 540 males (Bagnall and Frier 1994).

This means that the analyzed set (we cannot call it a sample because we have no idea how representative of the general population these people were) amounted to just 0.02% of the province's population. And even if it were perfectly representative of the Egyptian situation, it is virtually certain, given the extent of the Roman Empire and its heterogeneity, that these data could not be entirely representative of the empire's entire population. No less important, that record includes some hard-to-reconcile numbers, for instance, the claim that Egypt's population was 3 million near the end of the first century B.C.E. but 7.5 million (exclusive of Alexandria) less than a century later. This implies a growth rate that is improbably high for any ancient population.[3]

And this is the best-known segment of the Roman population. Other approaches are even more problematic (Parkin 1992). Tombstone inscriptions are relatively plentiful, but they have the obvious bias of representing only a subpopulation of the commemorated people. Burials usually come in small lots, the evidence is frequently biased (graves contain too few children, in garrison towns too many young men), the sexing and age determination of skeletons are subject to uncertainties and individual bias (error margins of two to eight years), and even if everything were optimal, skeletal analysis in a growing population overestimates mortality and underestimates life expectancy (the reverse is true in a declining population).

Consequently, as Walter Scheidel, the most incisive analyst of Roman society, put it, "our ignorance of ancient population is one of the biggest obstacles to our understanding of Roman history" (2007, 2). The most rudimentary uncertainty concerns the total number of inhabitants of the Roman Empire at any stage of its history, and it is symptomatic of the poor state of our understanding that a population estimate more than a century old is still debated vigorously in modern writings. Beloch's (1886) estimate, an outgrowth of his regional studies of the history of population and an extension of his total of 6 million people in Augustan Italy, was 54 million people in 14 C.E. (the year Augustus died).

Lo Cascio (1994) criticized Beloch's reasoning because of a flawed explanation of a large gap between the census counts of the free Italian population during the last decades of the Roman Republic and the first decades of the empire. The last republican total (70–69 B.C.E.) was 910,000; the first Augustan total (28 B.C.E.) was 4.063 million and the last one (14 C.E.) 4.937 million. Beloch explained that large difference by arguing that the republican total referred only to adult males (aged 17 and over), whereas the Augustan totals encompassed the entire population, including women and children. Brunt (1987) agreed with this explanation. Others suggested that a combination of strong underregistration during the republican censuses, natural increase, the extension of citizenship to the Transpadana (north of the Po) (49 B.C.E.), and colonization yields a better explanation. There are nontrivial problems with all of these assumptions (Lo Cascio 1994; Scheidel 2007), but none of the arguments and counterarguments brings us closer to a more confidently estimated population total.[4]

A second estimate, by McEvedy and Jones (1978), was a part of their ambitious attempt to estimate all of the ancient world's populations at 200-year intervals between 400 B.C.E. and 1000 C.E.. Their total for the beginning of the first century C.E. was 40.25 million. A third estimate for the beginning of the first century C.E. was prepared by Frier (2000), who put the Roman Empire's population at 45.5

million (and Italy's at 7 million). Maddison (2007) used all these estimates to offer a compromise figure of 44 million. As for later totals, Beloch (1886) thought that the empire's population was as high as 100 million people in the second century C.E.; McEvedy and Jones (1978) offered (within the Augustan boundaries) 45 million in 200 C.E. and 37 million in 400 C.E.; and Frier (2000) put the total at 61.4 million in 164 C.E.

A similar challenge is presented by estimates of the empire's urban population. All we know for certain is that Rome's population was exceptionally large in relation to other towns, but we do not know their average or modal size (Scheidel 2007). Available reconstructions of the shares of Roman urban population imply urbanization levels that were reached by European countries only during the course of the nineteenth century, and hence these may be seen as implausibly high: 25% for Italy excluding Rome (whose population is commonly set at 1 million during Augustan times) and almost 40% including Rome (Scheidel 2001). A total of 800,000 to 1 million people in Augustan Rome would mean that the city's population size had remained unsurpassed in Europe until the beginning of the nineteenth century, when London reached that number, and that even allowing the total area of some 15 km² (assuming settlement extending beyond the later fortifications), its density was on the order of 60,000 people/km², very high even by modern standards (figure IV.1).[5]

But arguments can go both ways. Rome's population could have been exaggerated but, on the other hand, Rome's extraordinarily large size could have been due to its ability to ensure the transfers of food and materials from the entire empire (Scheidel 2001). Moreover, high urban estimates are not limited to Italy. Bagnall and Frier (1994) put the urban population of Roman Egypt at about 35% of the total, a share not matched by any other preindustrial society and not reached by the United States until the mid-1890s.

Classical historians have engaged in two additional debates related to the uncertain Roman population number: the total number of slaves, and the military recruitment ratios. Roman mobilization rates were very high during the Punic Wars, with up to 12.6% of all citizen males serving in 212 B.C.E. (Lo Cascio 2001). Although the share declined to less than 9% in 43 B.C.E., it would still mean that in the case of a low population count at least 50% of all *iuniores* (males aged 17–45) had to serve (Scheidel 2007). Similarly high rates of mobilization have been supported only briefly during conflicts of the past two centuries (12% for the United States during WW II, including 56% of all eligible males), and today's active standing armies range from a high of 2.8% in Israel to less than 0.5% in most of the EU nations;

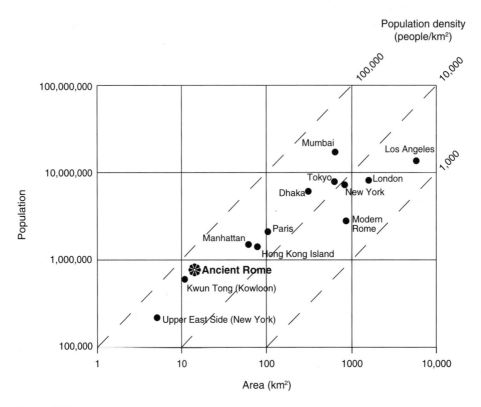

Figure IV.1
Population density of ancient Rome compared with that of selected large modern cities at the beginning of the twenty-first century. Plotted mostly from data at *Demographia* Web site. Area of Rome (within the Aurelian walls) was 15 km².

the U.S. share is 0.46% (and 0.95% with the reserves).[6] As for the total number of slaves, estimates have ranged from an indefensibly large number of some 20 million to just 1.2 million in the Augustan times.[7]

Regardless of the actual urban, slave, and recruitment shares, unless the Romans followed a trajectory unmatched by any other preindustrial society, we must assume that the annual growth of the Roman population was slow, on the order of 0.1% (that was also the French rate during the seventeenth and eighteenth centuries) and most likely no more than 0.2%, although at least for Egypt the available data allow a possible annual growth rate as high as 0.5%. The first growth rate would double the population in 350 years, the other in 140 years. In contrast, natural growth (excluding immigration) of the U.S. population was as high as 1.5% during the peak years of the baby boom generation (1946–1964), its average was 0.6% during the first half decade of the twenty-first century, and it reached 0.89% in 2007, whereas most European populations have either stagnated or declined except for immigration.

But even with very low population numbers and natural growth rates it is possible to argue that parts of the Roman Empire were actually overpopulated; Braudel (1972) thought the Mediterranean circa 1600, with 60–70 million people, definitely was. Excess population gain would have been possible even with very low annual growth rates due to low and very slowly increasing capacity to feed the population. There is some evidence that such a trend might have led to higher food and land prices in the Roman Egypt (Duncan-Jones 1990), but the record is unclear because there are no obvious price trends in the extant record. On the other hand, the record is ambiguous enough that it is possible to argue that there was a long-term population decline (starting in the late second century C.E. and severe in some regions) that was manifested in manpower shortages and recruitment problems (Parkin 1992). Or, even more direly, should we see a protracted population decline as one of the principal reasons for the weakening of the Western Empire and its eventual subjugation by migrants from distant places?

These fundamental uncertainties regarding the long-term dynamics of Roman population are a consequence of a complete lack of direct quantitative information about ancient vital statistics, birth and death rates and total fertility rates, as well as about the course of what was at times undoubtedly heavy immigration. What follows is thus a recounting of the best available information that has been gathered from very limited and fragmentary textual and archaeological evidence or that has been derived from the application of (more or less) suitable models of population dynamics based inevitably on much more recent data from population censuses in some of the poorer regions of the modern world.

As in all traditional societies, very few Roman women remained unmarried, but the best evidence we have indicates that the mean age of marriage was not exceptionally early. Bagnall, Frier, and Rutheford (1997) used the Egyptian census declarations to set the average age of Roman marriage at about 20 years for women (starting as early as 12 years, with more than 60% of all women married by age 20 and more than 85% by age 25), and a similar situation applied in the western part of the empire (Frier 2001). There is no surprise in these numbers: if anything, they appear to be somewhat conservative when compared to the nuptiality pattern of some premodern societies. For example, the average marriage age of Indian women was just 14.3 years during the early 1950s; it only rose above 18 years during the 1970s.

An average age of marriage at 20 years clearly indicates that the Romans did not regulate their numbers by postponing marriage (and thereby reducing the chances of conception and lowering overall fertility), as has been the case in many modern societies, particularly in Europe (Sobotka 2004) and Japan. The Romans were monogamous (but marital infidelity was common), most marriages were virilocal, divorce in the empire was legally possible but uncommon, remarriage after the death of a spouse was common (Rawson 1991).[8] The average age of females getting married in modern America is about five years higher than the Roman mean, but contrary to a common belief about younger marriage ages in the past, it has not changed dramatically during the twentieth century. In 1900 it was about 26 years for men and 22 years for women; by 2005 it was nearly 27 years for men and 25 years for women (USCB 1976; 2008).

Although the Roman term *familia* was at once broader and narrower than the English noun we use to describe the principal subunit of society (Saller 1984; Martin 1996), a broad consensus among classical historians has come to see the Roman family as a nuclear one (Kertzer and Saller 1991) and hence fundamentally akin to contemporary configurations; despite its modifications and fraying, the nuclear family remains the modal unit of modern American society. What is different— indeed so different that the very comparison of the two sets of conditions demonstrates how fundamentally incomparable they are—is the overall dynamics of these two populations, their vital statistics, their structure, growth, and long-term change.

America's demographic transition, a gradual shift from the premodern combination of high birth rates and high death rates eventually resulting in relatively slow population growth, began in the early 1800s, when the mean total fertility rate (the average number of children born to a woman during her lifetime) was seven children, and it was basically completed during the 1930s (Greenwood and Seshadri 2002). At the beginning of the twentieth century the U.S. total fertility rate was still well above 3.0 and the birth rate was a bit above 30/1,000 (USCB 1976). By the late 1930s total fertility approached the replacement level (2.3 in 1940, as birth rates fell well below 30/1,000), and after a temporary postwar rise (baby boom generation) to as high as 3.76 in 1957, it fell gradually so that by 2000 its mean rate was just a bit below the replacement rate of 2.1 births (figure IV.2).[9]

The best Roman evidence (once again, from the Egyptian census declarations during the first three centuries of the empire) points to a classic premodern high-high combination; high fertility (averaging about six children per woman) and hence a high birth rate, on the order of 44/1,000, were needed to compensate for a high

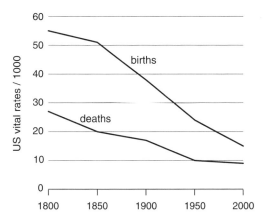

Figure IV.2
U.S. fertility transition, 1800–2000. Plotted from data in USCB (1976) and subsequent editions of the *Statistical Abstract of the United States*.

death rate on the order of 42/1,000 (Bagnall and Frier 1994). These conclusions (in line with informed expectations) invalidate Riddle's (1999) arguments that married Roman women had access to a variety of efficacious oral contraceptive (as well as abortifacients) and that they used them commonly in order to limit their fertility. Riddle's work has been criticized for a variety of reasons, and the best documentary evidence concerning women's ages at conception does not support the existence of any conscious, widespread effort to limit births among married women.

The combination of Roman vital rates has no close counterpart in the modern world. Today an analogue of these Roman values exists only in terms of continuing high birth rates and total fertility rates in Western, Eastern, and Central Africa; in 2007 these regions had average birth rates of, respectively, 42, 41, and 46/1,000, and average total fertilities of their countries ranged between 5.5 and 6.3 (UN 2006). But even in these sub-Saharan countries, where the demographic transition has yet to run its full course, death rates have been already reduced quite significantly, to between 15 and 18/1,000, still nearly twice the current global mean of 9/1,000 but only about 35%–40% of the high Roman value.

In order to find the most recent combination of such high birth and death rates we would have to go at least three generation back to the worst-off regions of sub-Saharan Africa, but we have no reliable demographic data for those populations. The earliest fairly well documented populations that fit the dismal demographic pattern are Chile and Taiwan at the beginning of the twentieth century (Preston, Keyfitz, and Schoen 1972). The last decade that America had a birth rate between

40 and 45/1,000 was during the 1860s, and we have to go back to colonial times of the seventeenth century in order to encounter any U.S. population whose vital statistics bore a close resemblance to the Roman-like combination of high birth and death rates. Some European countries had death rates in excess of 40/1,000 well into the eighteenth century but only during years of famines or epidemics.

Estimates of mean Roman life expectancy based on limited quantitative information may be no more reliable than the averages derived from theoretical models. The so-called Ulpianic life table is not what it is commonly claimed to be: it does not give actual figures for life expectancy but is merely a rough guide used to calculate the tax value of annuities over a course of estimated lifetime. Although it shows (in a simplified stepwise manner) an expected decline of life expectancy with advancing age (30 years at age 20, 25 years at age 30, 10 years at age 50), it also sets a constant value of 5 years for every year above 60, a demographic impossibility.[10] But the average life expectancy of just over 20 years that is implied by this schedule falls within the range of the best estimates advanced by recent demographic studies.

Hopkins (1966) was the first historian to argue that the average Roman life expectancy at birth was no greater than 20–30 years, and Bagnall and Frier (1994) used the only preserved record of Roman age composition from Egyptian censuses to estimate the mean life expectancy of 22.5 years for females and 25 years for males. Their female life expectancy pattern is close to the high-mortality life tables of the Model West by Coale and Demeny (1983), with life expectancy just 20–25 years and very high infant mortality, but the fit is not so good for the assumed male life expectancy. Uncertainties and problems of these reconstructions were reviewed in detail by Scheidel (2001; 2007). The main questions concern the representativeness of those ancient Egyptian data and the relevance of comparisons with model populations.[11]

Woods (2007) argued that he had better models in two life tables that he derived from the Chilean and the Taiwanese standards of the early twentieth century. When compared to the Coale-Demeny model they show generally lower infant mortality rates and higher mortalities in adulthood, but for comparisons with modern survival patterns these differences are basically irrelevant: the survival probabilities of the two populations trace two very different curves (figure IV.3). In any case, these high mortality patterns would mean that only about half (46%–51%) of girls would have survived to the age 20 and just over one-fifth (21%–24%) of women would make it to the age 50. And even if average life expectancy were as high as 30 years,

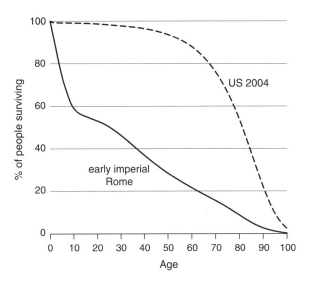

Figure IV.3
Percentage of population surviving, by age, in early imperial Rome and in the United States in 2004. Plotted from a model life table in Woods (2007) and a life table for total U.S. population (CDC 2007b).

the survival share goes up to only 51%–55% for age 20 and to 29%–31% for age 50.

There is virtually no chance that actual Roman life expectancy fell outside the range of 20–30 years—a conclusion strongly supported by much better Chinese data that show life expectancy at birth of 27–30 years after 1300 (Lee and Wang (1999)—and for the comparison at hand it does not make a fundamental difference if the actual mean was 22.5, 25, or 27.5 years. Scheidel's (1999) analysis of the extant records on the life expectancy of Roman emperors and senators shows that these elite populations did not live significantly longer and that they, too, could expect average lifespans no longer than 30 years. That the first emperor lived and reigned for so long (76 and 40 years, respectively) was such a rare event that the length of his reign was surpassed only four centuries later.[12]

In contrast to Rome's truncated lives, the latest life tables for the United States indicate a female life expectancy of 80.4 years at birth, with 98.5% of girls alive at age 20 and 92% of women alive at age 50 (CDC 2007b). Most of the difference is obviously attributable to very high infant and childhood mortalities that were the norm during the Roman era, but large differences exist even when comparing life expectancies at mature ages. A Roman woman aged 20 could expect to live approximately another 30 (27–35) years, but an American woman aged 20 could look forward to 61 more years of life; by age 50 the difference remains roughly twofold, 15 versus 33 years.

The extraordinarily low Roman life expectancy resulted in a very young population in which about 35% of all people were younger than 15 years, nearly half were between the ages of 15 and 44, and only about 3% were older than 65 years. In contrast, the U.S. population seems old (although still considerably younger and much better reproducing than the European populations), and it will be aging rapidly in the decades ahead. Average life expectancy is expected to increase from the 2005 combined mean of 77.9 years (nearly 76 years for males and almost 81 years for females) to 80 years by 2025 and 83 years by 2050, and whereas in 2005 only about 20% of people were younger than 15 years, and people 65 years and older made up 12%, by 2025 people 65 and older will be about 18% of the total, roughly the same as that of children aged 0–14.[13]

These fundamental realities should always be kept in mind when speaking about the grandeur of the Roman Empire, its admirable accomplishments, and its irresistible attraction as a basis for comparisons with modern powerful states. There is no modern population—even among the worst-off countries of sub-Saharan Africa—whose growth, longevity, and age structure would even remotely resemble the ancient Roman pattern. Perhaps the best contemporary analogy would be to imagine a population that is even more destitute and desperate than those of Sierra Leone or Bourkina Faso and then to contrast it with the long-lived, formerly fast growing and now rapidly aging U.S. population, whose mean life expectancy at birth is more than three times as high as the Roman Empire's. Extraordinarily high infant and childhood mortality was the main cause of the dismal Roman situation, but a closer look reveals that ill health and death were parts of the quotidian Roman experience for every citizen, free man or slave.

Illness and Death

Demographic realities like high death rates of infants and children in ancient populations are easily stated, but can we truly imagine and understand their mental and behavioral consequences? Roman infant mortality (deaths during the first year of life per 1,000 newborn) ranged between 225 and 290, that is, roughly one-quarter of all babies did not survive the first year. Early childhood mortality (deaths between 1 and 4 years of life) ranged most likely between 180 and 220: one out of five children who made it through the first year died by age 4. In contrast, U.S. infant mortality in 2005 was 6.9/1,000, less than 3% of the Roman rate.[14]

In our society few events are as feared and few are perceived to be as traumatic as the death of a child. Did the ubiquity of ancient infant death (or, for that matter, medieval or early modern infant death, because major gains did not take place before the eighteenth century) make a child's death an almost expected event; did it blunt the parents' sense of loss? Moreover, in ancient Rome, death, or at least deliberate attempts to induce it, came even when a newborn child was healthy. As in many traditional agrarian societies (Dickeman 1975)—despite some arguments to minimize its importance (Engels 1980)—infanticide was not an uncommon Roman practice, and its impact was not certainly negligible (Harris 1982).

This practice had three principal causes. Removal of defective newborns ended the lives of infants with such easily recognizable congenital defects as harelip–cleft palate, hunchback, club foot, or blindness. Manipulation of the sex ratio was most commonly seen in female infanticide, a cruel bias that has persisted in some cultures for millennia and that can be still encountered today.[15] By far the most common reason for infanticide was the regulation of overall population numbers owing to environmental or socioeconomic circumstances. We have no basis to estimate the relative frequency of outright killings and child exposure caused by food shortages or economic hardship. The distinction is important because exposure often did not result in death but rather in a rescue followed by enslavement.

Exposure of children continued throughout the entire history of Roman Empire, and while we cannot quantify the practice even in approximate terms, abundant literary sources leave no doubt about its rather high frequency and general acceptance as an unavoidable course of action (Harris 1994). Rescue of abandoned infants was not uncommon; its primary motive was to turn the children into slaves. There is no doubt that this practice was a significant means of transferring potentially free labor to slavery. Matters changed only slowly as disapproval of the practice increased even before Christianity emerged as the state religion. In 313 C.E. (the same year he issued the Edict of Milan tolerating Christianity) Constantine removed the long-standing ban of putting a price on the head of a free person to allow the sale of free children into slavery, a change that should have lessened the frequency of child exposure in exchange for another moral dilemma: Was not the selling of children even more immoral than exposing them?

The legislative end to child exposure came only in 374 C.E. with an edict of the three emperors Valentinian, Valens, and Gratian: *Unusquisque subolem suam nutriat. Quod si exponendam putaverit, animadversioni quae constituta est subiacebit.* (Let everyone nourish his own progeny. But if anyone thinks about exposing it, he will be subject to the declared punishment.) Naturally, the criminalization of child exposure could not stop the practice, whose frequency was more dependent on adverse economic conditions and general attitudes (particularly those fashioned by an increasing role of Christian churches) than on imperial laws. That is why child abandonment continued in medieval and early modern Europe, but quantifying it reliably is as elusive for the year 1300 or 1600 as it is for 300.

The health of those who belonged to the lower economic strata (that is, most Romans) was commonly undermined by inadequate diet and periodic famines. Often cited or surmised, figures of Roman grain supply and free grain distribution in the capital indicate average per capita rates that should have been quite sufficient to ensure an adequate supply of food energy. What is usually forgotten is that these totals do not represent actual food intakes. They must first be corrected for high rates of transportation losses, grain spoilage and diversion, and typical milling extraction.[16] Perhaps a better way than trying to reconstruct a typical diet (an impossible goal if it were to be done within narrow constraints) is to turn to anthropometric evidence.

Studies of dental enamel hypoplasia based on 1,465 permanent teeth provide indisputable physical evidence of systemic metabolic stress during the time of tooth and bone development, both in a small rural town (inhabited largely by slaves and veterans) and in a more affluent residential area of Rome (Manzi, Santandrea, and Passarello 1997). The best explanation of this unexpected result is the combined effect of urban crowding, epidemics, and periodic famines. Another dental analysis, a study of Wilson bands (microstructural growth markers) in infant teeth, points to two periods of particular metabolic vulnerability, around three months, when unsuitable supplementary food was first introduced, and around nine months, when weaned infants did not receive enough solid food (FitzGerald et al. 2006).

Koepke and Baten (2005) used mostly skeleton-based height measurements of 9,477 European individuals who lived in the central and western parts of the continent between the first and eighteenth centuries as a proxy for what they call the biological standard of living, a variable subsuming such essential elements as quality of nutrition, overall health, and longevity. They found that during the entire period of Roman imperial rule, male and female heights did not increase at all (figure IV.4). This conclusion "stands in contrast to the common view that living standards and especially purchasing power increased during the Roman Empire, due to economic growth and protection of the *pax Romana*" (2005, 76). They also found that

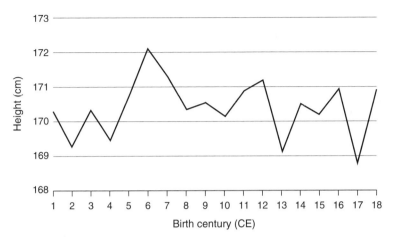

Figure IV.4
Body height development (male and female) in Western and Central Europe from the first to the eighteenth century shows no increase over the period of the Roman Empire (Koepke and Baten 2005). This physical evidence contradicts the commonly held view about the beneficial effects of the protracted *pax Romana* (27 B.C.E.–c. 180 C.E.).

Roman migrants from the Mediterranean region to Central Europe (soldiers, officers, administrators) were on average 4 cm shorter than the local populations.[17]

Low rates of average consumption of high-quality animal proteins are the best explanation for this significant height difference. In the seasonally arid Mediterranean extensive cattle grazing was only a limited option, and as in all traditional agricultures, low (and highly fluctuating) cereal and legume yields made it impossible to divert a significant share of grains to animal feeding. As a result, cow's milk, one of the best sources of protein for human growth and a staple of many tribes in Germania, was not commonly consumed throughout the Roman Mediterranean (Peters 1998). In common with the region's other agricultural societies, the typical Roman diet was heavily dominated by grains (cereals and legumes) and vegetables. Low crop yields did not allow for any substantial diversion of harvests to animal feeding, and the semi-arid and arid environments of the Mediterranean would not support large herds of big grazers.

In Rome's case the intakes of meat were further reduced by the need to feed the densely inhabited megacity of the imperial era. Excavation of animal bones at different locations in Rome show a cattle share falling from 28% during the first century B.C.E. to about 8% in the first and the second centuries C.E. and to zero in the second and third centuries, returning to a substantial share only during the fifth century with the Germanic invaders (Koepke and Baten 2005). Excavations in Napoli and Ostia show similar trends. No less remarkably, the skeletal evidence indicates a significant height increase during the fifth and sixth centuries; clearly, the breakdown of Roman rule in the West had no deleterious effect on human growth. This impressive change can best be explained by lower population density and urbanization rates (in response to invasions and epidemics) as more rural populations benefited from better (locally produced) nutrition.

As for food shortages, Garnsey (1988) concluded that major famines were not common but that inadequate supply was a recurrent problem. Food shortages were often handled by distribution of money or grain from emperor's own funds, and the government responded with measures ranging from short-term relief (grain rationing and temporary expulsions of some groups, including gladiators, foreigners, and unsold slaves, from Rome) to better long-term arrangements (above all, increased imports of Egyptian and North African grain). But Garnsey's detailed survey of known famines during the principate makes it clear that they were not rare either.

The first one, in 23–22 B.C.E. ("great numbers perished," according to Cassius Dio), required Augustus to use his own money to buy rations for at least 250,000 people. The next food crises came in 5–9 C.E., a particularly severe one in 6 C.E. High food prices caused protests and riots in 19 C.E. and again in 32 C.E., and "destruction and famine" returned in 40–41 C.E. and again ten years later. The famous great fire of 64 C.E. destroyed Rome's grain stocks, and the hardships of civil war of 68–70 C.E. were made worse by a major flood in the spring 69 C.E. Undatable famines took place during the reigns of Hadrian, Antoninus Pius, and Marcus Aurelius, including "a most severe food crisis" caused by another major flood. The next documented food crises in Rome date to 189 C.E. (caused by epidemics and corruption) and 193 C.E.

Roman health was also compromised by appalling hygienic conditions. References to Rome's extraordinarily high rate of average per capita water supply carried by aqueducts, monumental ruins of Rome's imperial baths (Caracalla's and Diocletian's), archaeological confirmation of marble-clad public *foricae* (public toilets), and admiring comments on the splendid construction and large dimensions of the *Cloaca Maxima* (figure IV.5), which sluiced the city's human waste into the Tiber, have created an image of ancient Rome as place of remarkably advanced sanitation.[18] In reality, the capital was a fetid and filthy congested city, one of the least salubrious places of antiquity.

Figure IV.5
Stone arch outlet of the *Cloaca Maxima*, Rome's ancient principal sewer. Etching from Piranesi's *Le Antichità Romane* (1756).

The reasons for this range from quotidian matters of urban hygiene to endemic parasitic diseases (Scobie 1986; Sallares 2002; Scheidel 2003). The city had no regular garbage removal or street cleaning, and individual property owners were responsible for keeping the streets in front of their properties clean. This was no small task given common urination and defecation in streets, doorways, and other public places and frequent emptying of chamber pots (*matellae* or *lasana*) from the windows of *insulae* into the streets below. The sick and dying were left in the streets, and *egeni* (destitutes) lived out in the open or in improvised shanties and lean-tos (*parapetasia*) and under stairs in cellars and vaults.

Dogs (including rabid ones) ran around, ate excrement, and gnawed on dumped corpses. Suetonius (*Vita Divi Vespasiani* V:4) relates how a street dog brought a human hand into the room where the emperor was dining and set it underneath his table (*canis extrarius e trivio manum humanam intulit mensaeque subiecit*). With no centralized slaughter houses, animals were driven through the narrow streets and killed in or in front of the butcher shops, spilling blood and guts. Fortunately, necrophagous vultures were around, but so were myriads of flies.

There was no legal obligation to connect houses to a public sewer, and archaeological explorations in Rome have confirmed that most of the houses were not connected (Lanciani 1888). Latrines were dry pits (*sterquilinia*) dug into porous rock; liquids percolated underground, putrefying solids had to be emptied periodically; the latrines were a constant source of smell and infections, particularly because they were often located near the kitchen. Public latrines (records of the fourth century C.E. list 144 *foricae* but not the typical number of seats per facility) were hardly cleaned daily, and baths functioned in ways that were conducive to the spread of diseases.[19]

There were no disinfectants and no water chlorination, and both healthy and sick people soaked in the same hot baths where, unlike in the cold water pools, water did not circulate and the high cost of heating precluded frequent changes and thorough repetitive pool cleaning. Overflow from fountains and public basins flushed the major sewers, but these backed up whenever the Tiber flooded. Scobie (1986, 417) rightly concluded that "the inhabitants of Rome lived in an extremely insanitary environment" and added that such conditions were similar to these prevailing in Europe's large cities until the middle of the nineteenth century, when modern sanitation efforts began to change urban waste management.

Water from all but two Roman aqueducts was potable, but it became contaminated during its distribution from open water basins; a single *lacus* (according to Frontinus, there were 591 open basins in the city) served about 1,000 people jostling for the supply. Toxicity of lead (used for conduit lining, aqueduct siphons, and pipes) has been cited among the causes responsible for the demise of the Western Empire, but the effect is difficult to assess because alkaline waters can lay down protective mineral deposits and prevent the leaching of the metal, but acidic waters are plumbosolvent (Hodge 1981). In any case, the common simmering of wine and food in leaden cauldrons would have been a greater source of contamination.

That the contamination of water and food (due to unhygienic handling and vegetables fertilized with improperly fermented feces) was common is best attested by the fact that intestinal disorders were endemic. And, needless to say, urban population density higher than 500 people per hectare provided ideal conditions for the spread of communicable diseases. The list of ubiquitous afflictions ran from diarrhea (to which undernourished infants succumbed rapidly), gastroenteritis, dysentery, infectious hepatitis, typhoid, and cholera to parasites (tapeworms, roundworms, pinworms, amoebae), chronic bronchial infections (exacerbated by poor ventilation), infected wounds and ulcers, tuberculosis (to which undernourished and weakened people were more susceptible), and rabies from packs of stray dogs.

But Roman epitaphs also indicate a strong seasonality of the highest frequency of deaths among teenagers and adults during the late summer and early fall (August to October). As these population groups are usually the least affected by recurrent epidemics (infants, young children, and elderly are most susceptible), this phenomenon is best explained by endemic falciparian malaria (commencing in July and lasting until October), more precisely by its synergistic interaction with hot-season infections, above all, with gastrointestinal disorders (Scheidel 2001). Primary symptoms of malaria include high quotidian fevers, spleen enlargement, jaundice, anemia, hemoglobinuria, renal dysfunction, and pulmonary edema. Malaria also makes all gastrointestinal illnesses and respiratory diseases (including tuberculosis, pneumonia, asthma, and bronchitis) more dangerous; its coexistence with diarrhea leads to particularly high infant and childhood mortality.

Sallares (2002) used the historical record and modern medical approaches to detail the ubiquity, spatial extent, and population consequences of this debilitating and often fatal illness, which was contracted by most small children and common among adult men. The most virulent of the four malaria-causing parasitic species, *Plasmodium falciparum*, diffused from the south to central Italy during the fifth century B.C.E., and its presence in the imperial Rome was convincingly proved by isolating its DNA from an infant skeleton in a cemetery in Teverina in Umbria, some 110 km north of the city (Sallares, Bouwman, and Anderung 2004). Malaria became hyperendemic in the valley of the lower Tiber and in the adjoining coastal Latium, and judging by the nineteenth-century evidence from similarly afflicted Italian locales, its presence could have shortened life expectancies by more than one-third. Ironically, an opulent *domus* of a rich Roman actually facilitated the spread of the disease to affluent classes; its courtyard *impluvium* provided a perfect breeding ground for mosquitoes and their *P. falciparum* parasites.

Rome's extraordinarily high residential density made it easier for recurrent epidemics to claim an unusually high share of victims. Suetonius (*Vita Neronis* XXXIX:1) noted that during Nero's time "in a single autumn 30,000 deaths from plague were registered at the Temple of Libitina" (*pestilentia unius autumni, quo triginta funerum milia in rationem Libitinae venerunt*). According to Cassius Dio (Romaika LXXII:14.3), 2,000 people per day died in 189 C.E., and in 166 C.E. during what was most likely a smallpox pandemic (but it is impossible to exclude anthrax) one-third of the city's population could have died (Littman and Littman 1973; Fears 2004).[20] Other major epidemics are recorded during the third century C.E. Roman stonemasons making funerary marbles were never idle (figure IV.6).

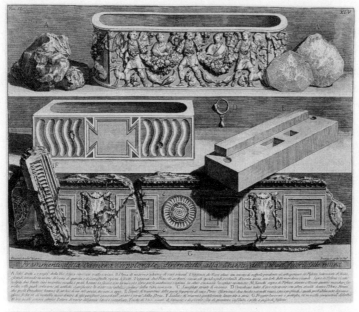

Figure IV.6
Funerary marbles found in sepulchral chambers of rich Roman families, *top,* and funerary inscriptions with the names of freedmen and slaves from the family of Augustus. Etchings from Piranesi's *Le Antichità Romane* (1756).

How to end this recital of illnesses and premature deaths? Perhaps by noting that the inhabitants of *insulae*, who were defenseless against numerous diseases, were also nearly defenseless against robberies and violence, had hardly any privacy, and lived in darkness and cold in winter and heat in summer. There can be only one conclusion: "a short, often violent, life" was "the common lot of the millions of people in the Roman world who lived on or below the subsistence level" (Scobie 1986, 433). Deaths surpassed births by such a large margin—Rome's mortality could have surpassed 50/1,000 or even 60/1,000, cutting down the mean life expectancy at birth to less than 20 years—that the city required a constant and massive influx of immigrants who were ignorant of the city's grim conditions, desperate enough not to be deterred by them, or attracted by free food and cash handouts.[21]

For an ordinary Roman citizen the city was not a stunning cosmopolis of marble temples and showy *fora*; it was a squalid, fetid, unsanitary, noisy, and dangerous amalgam of people, animals, wastes, germs, diseases, and suffering. The city's filthy, grossly unhygienic environment deserves to be called appalling when measured by modern standards, and the consequences of this reality were profound: the Rome of hyperbolic praise was a *caput mundi*, but to most of its inhabitants it was (in Scheidel's apt phrase) *vorax populorum*, a devourer of people.

Wealth and Misery

The Roman economy is no easier to understand or quantify than the Roman population. We know it was monetized (coins were used for transactions in cities and rural areas, in Italy and on the fringes of the empire and beyond), and we also know that farm products, particularly grains, were used in paying taxes, rents, and wages (Howgego 1992). But was it powered by a combination of taxes and wealth transfers from military conquests, or was it a version of a market economy? What was its approximate GDP and the distribution of its wealth? All these uncertainties have an important common denominator, the role of trade in Rome's economy.

Trade within the empire, most famously the regular imports of Egyptian and North African grain to Rome (Erdkamp 2005; Kessler and Temin 2007) and across its borders has been long recognized as a notable feature of Roman imperial expansion. The Romans also traded with their two great perennial enemies, the Parthian/Sasanid empire in the east (Thorley 1969; Young 2001; Dignas and Winter 2007) and the free Germans in the north (Brogan 1936). But how important was Roman trade for the economy? Was there a largely cellular arrangement with a high degree of local and regional autarky in which long-distance trade had only a modest role (even after the Augustan peace made it safer to trade), or was there truly a Roman economy with trade integrating the empire's far-flung regions?

Garnsey and Saller (1987) and Duncan-Jones (1990) argued the first case. Similarly, Woolf (1992, 289) used the archaeological evidence of wine and oil amphorae (some of them mass-produced on a Mediterranean-wide scale; see figure III.4) to conclude that while some empire-wide distributions appeared during the last generations of the republic, "for the most part exchange within the empire was rarely integrated above the regional level." And Bang (2007) thought that it is not enough to notice the existence of prices but that we must ask if the system depended on realizing the gains of trade: his answer was negative.

But the arguments in favor of a more integrated economy have been gaining some ground. Temin (2001) concluded that the early Roman Empire was a market economy and that market exchange was the modal form of Roman economic integration. He conceded that there was no single empire-wide market for all goods but argued that there were many connections among local markets throughout the Mediterranean, including even far-flung parts of the empire. Levick (2004) concluded that trade was really important for some regions, particularly in Asia Minor. And Geraghty (2007) went a step further and constructed a simplified general equilibrium model for the entire Roman Italy. The title of his article makes his intent clear: "The impact of globalization in the Roman Empire."[22]

In contrast (and notwithstanding increasing governmental intervention and participation), there can be no doubt about the market nature of the U.S. economy and the importance of trade, in both intrastate and international terms, for the American way of life. While it is true that all other major Western economies derive a larger share of their GDP from trade, in absolute terms the United States is by far the world's largest importer, with more than 15% of the total annual value of traded goods and services, and the second largest (having been recently overtaken by Germany) exporter (WTO 2008).[23]

The second fundamental difference that needs to be pointed out is the structure of the two economies. In 2005 only about 1.5% of the U.S. labor force was engaged in agriculture, about 11% in manufacturing, 9% in extraction, construction, and transportation, and the rest (78.5%) in a multitude of largely urban-based services (BLS 2008). The Roman economy, like those of its ancient contemporaries, was fundamentally different. Classical writers left a record in which urban and military affairs take center place, and this strong urban bias has been perpetuated by popular modern histories of Rome, fictional writings about the empire, and movies and TV series. An untutored consumer of these products might think that most Romans were either affluent or reasonably well-off city dwellers spending their time in feasts, plots, and quarrels in their villas or cheering the death of gladiators in arenas.

The truth is much less exalting. Given the low productivity of traditional agriculture, it was inevitable that most Romans spent their lives in fields and yards and along seashores, cultivating crops, threshing grains, pressing olives, producing wine, taking care of domestic animals, and harvesting marine foods. A single key example illustrates why it had to be so. An American grain farmer growing bread wheat in one of the Great Plains states needs less than 2 h of labor to produce 1 t of grain (Smil 2008a).[24] But even the best-organized Roman farmer in one of the most productive regions of Italy would, even in a year with excellent weather, need about 350 h of labor to produce that amount of wheat (Smil 1994).[25] Using the standard Roman monthly *anona* rations (5 *modii* of grain per adult, 4 *modii* per slave), a day's work of an American farmer could provide a gross grain supply for 180 adult Romans for a month, whereas a day's work by a Latium peasant could barely supply a monthly ration for a single household slave.[26]

The third key difference that must be stressed before addressing the matters of per capita income and wealth distribution is Roman slavery. It formed a fundamental substructure of the Roman economy, and animalizing slaves was the norm (Raymer 1940; Bradley 2000). This attitude was, of course, just a continuation from the Greeks, whose dehumanizing term for slave, *andrapodon* (man-footed creature), derives from the common name for cattle, *tetrapodon* (four-footed creature), and whose hallowed philosopher, Aristotle, opined that "Indeed, the use made of slaves and of tame animals is not very different" (*Politics*, V; Benjamin Jowett translation, 1885).

And so for the Romans the law treated equally slaves and quadrupeds kept in herds, defined the slave as *res* (a thing) or as a talking tool (*instrumentum vocale*). Cato, ever a frugal manager of his estate, had helpful advice for his fellow landowners: "When the slaves were sick, such large rations should not have been issued. . . . Sell worn-out oxen, blemished cattle, blemished sheep, wool, hides, an old wagon, old tools, an old slave, a sickly slave, and whatever else is superfluous" (*De re rustica*, ii; W.D. Hooper translation, 1934). Inevitably, and all the dehumanizing attitudes notwithstanding, the Romans had to be aware of the essential humanity of slaves, and this makes it even more remarkable "that for a thousand years and more slavery never produced any serious moral crisis in the classical world at all" (Bradley 2000, 124). Hostility between slave owners and slaves was an ever-present undercurrent of the Roman world, a situation that was not helped by the fact that not a few Roman slaves were better educated than their masters and held considerable responsibilities as secretaries, physicians, or architects (K. Hopkins 1993).[27]

Now, finally, some rough appraisals of Roman economic product, income, and wealth distribution. Estimates of gross domestic product (GDP) are a challenge even for early modern economies where many relevant income, expenditure, budget, and investment figures are available and only in very few cases we have fairly reliable reconstructions going back for more than a century.[28] Inevitably, any attempt to calculate per capita GDP typical of the early period of the Roman Empire is an exercise in rough approximation whose value rests more in affirming the right order of magnitude (and perhaps placing the value within its lower or higher range) than in pretending that we can ever get a real rate. The boldest attempt to estimate the size and structure of the economic product of the early Roman Empire was made by Goldsmith (1984).

He used approximation for annual per capita expenditures as well as for income. The former data included living allowances (*alimenta*) from government regulations and relatively abundant information on food rations and the cost of grains. His conclusion was that overall consumer expenditures were well above 300 *sestercii* (HS) in Italy and a bit lower for the entire empire (Goldsmith 1984); after adding relatively small central government and gross private capital expenditures, he ended up with an annual per capita mean of 380 *sestercii*.[29] On the income side, the quotes on daily wages for free male labor range mostly between HS 2.5 and HS 4, but converting them to annual values rests on a critical assumption of the total of working days.

Goldsmith assumed 200–250 working days, resulting in income aggregates of HS 500–1,000 and a mean of close to HS 800 per worker. Upward adjustment of 20% (to account for nonwage income) ends up with about HS 1,000 per worker, and downward adjustment (assuming average dependency ratio of 2.5) yields about HS 380, a total identical with the mean derived from expenditures. For 55 million people (Goldsmith's total for 14 C.E.) this would yield about HS 21 billion. K. Hopkins's (1995/6) estimate is lower, a GDP of HS 13.5 billion (minimum of HS 9 billion) for 60 million people, with government budget of HS 700–900 million per year and 55%–65% of it spent on the army.

An entirely different approach to the challenge yielded a per capita rate that supports Goldsmith's reasoning. Frier (1993) analyzed all of the extant evidence from the Roman jurists regarding the small subsistence annuities left by testators to their freedmen or to their foster children. He concluded that most of these annuities ranged from about HS 380 to HS 600, not substantially above Goldsmith's calculation of average annual per capita income of HS 320–440. Yet another confirmation comes from the values of alimentary annuities in Italy that benefited children: HS 120–240, representing the lower limit of subsistence.

Maddison (2007) accepted Goldsmith's estimate of mean annual total expenditures, but because he assumed a smaller population total (44 million) he ended up with an aggregate GDP of about HS 17 billion. With HS 380 equal to about 30 g of gold, comparisons in gold indicate that Roman income of 14 c.e. was about 38% of the English and Welsh annual income for 1688, and comparisons in terms of average cereal units give a somewhat higher share of about 42%. Maddison also made separate estimates for peninsular Italy; modified estimates of elite income share and separate values for free and slave labor; offered a rough quantification of tax and transfers from the rest of the empire to Italy; and provided what he called "stylized conjectures" of per capita income in different provinces.

Finally, Scheidel and Friesen (2008) built on all these exercises by the means of "controlled conjecture" constrained by the available evidence and by the interdependence of different assumptions. They put the total economic product during the middle of the second century c.e. at nearly 50 million t of wheat equivalent consumption, or almost HS 20 billion, of which no more than 5% was claimed by state and local government. With a maximum population of about 70 million the totals would prorate to an average annual per capita wheat supply of about 700 kg and a mean economic product of about HS 290 per person.

While we have no reliable way to ascertain the long-term change of Roman per capita GDP, we can be quite sure that it did not double even during the empire's most prosperous century. K. Hopkins (1995/6) ventured a rough trend estimate that showed economic growth during the last two centuries of the republic (roughly a 20% increase over 200 years) followed by a plateau during the first century of the empire and then a gradual decline of per capita productivity during the second and third centuries c.e. The modern trend is dramatically different; the relentless growth of modern economies (albeit at fluctuating rates) can double average per capita GDP in a single generation.[30] In the United States the 2005 rate was nearly 1.9 times the 1975 level, almost 3.5 times the mean in 1950, about 7 times the average of 1900, and nearly 30 times the mean at the beginning of the nineteenth century (Maddison 2007; USCB 2008).

Translating those annual per capita approximations in *sestercii* to modern monetary units requires yet more conjecture. Maddison (2007) used the following procedure. He assumed that Roman per capita income averaged about 40% of the

English and Welsh rate for 1688 and related it to the value of $1,411—in international dollars in purchasing power parity (PPP) terms for the year 1990—that he had previously established (Maddison 2001) as the equivalent of the English and Welsh income of nearly 80 g gold per capita in 1688. This conversion yields Roman per capita GDP of about $570 in 14 c.e.[31] Making one more adjustment, from 1990 to 2005 dollars (in order to account for the intervening inflation), we get Roman per capita GDP (in PPP terms) at about $850 and an aggregate of about $40 billion for a population of roughly 50 million. Using a lower per capita mean estimated by Scheidel and Friesen (2008) would yield, following the same conversion procedure, a per capita average of about $650 and an aggregate of about $45 billion.

In 2005 America's per capita GDP was about $41,700, or roughly 50 times (using Maddison's account) or nearly 65 times (using Scheidel-Friesen's rate) the Roman mean. America's total economic product reached roughly $12.5 trillion in 2005, or approximately 275–300 times the Roman aggregate. An aggregate Roman GDP of $40–$50 billion would be inconsequential in today's world: in 2005 goods and services in that range were produced in Europe by Lithuania or Slovenia (among the smallest of all EU countries), in Africa by Ethiopia or Kenya (World Bank 2008). This is a terribly deflating comparison, and the overall value is so low that even its doubling would turn the Roman Empire into only a very modest economic powerhouse in today's world; even at $100 billion a year its GDP would be equal only to the economies of New Zealand or Morocco.

In per capita terms the countries that come closest to the Roman rate ($650–$850) are among the world's poorest nations in the sub-Saharan Africa. Using the latest World Bank (2008) data with the rates calculated in PPP values, their ranking is as follows: Ethiopia ($591), Niger ($613), Central African Republic ($675), Malawi ($691), Gambia ($726), Sierra Leone ($790), Rwanda ($813), and Togo ($888). But even this bleak comparison exaggerates the Roman achievement. Most of these impoverished countries have infant mortality below 100/1,000 (Rome's was well above 200/1,000), their low life expectancies are 40–55 years (Rome's was well below 30 years), in all of them most children attend grade school, and most children are protected by inoculation against such common contagious diseases as tuberculosis and measles (UNDP 2008).

Allen (2007) chose a different approach to Roman per capita income, one that obviates the problems with GDP calculation, by attempting to find the purchasing power of an unskilled free male laborer. First he calculated a basic daily wage, and then he contrasted it with the cost of a basic consumption basket, an aggregate of food and goods needed to sustain a family for a year, with both the wages and prices derived from Diocletian's edict (*edictum de pretiis*) of 301 C.E. Unskilled labor earned about 36 *denarii* a day (including the value of grain allowance), and in 250 days of work the laborer would earn an equivalent of 289 g of silver. A Mediterranean consumption basket that would give a family of three a respectable level of food, fuel, and clothes came to about 516 g of silver, and hence the worker earned only 56% of its cost.[32]

Allen (2007) argued that the most common way out of this predicament was to cut expenditures, and he constructed a bare-bones consumption basket that a laborer's family could afford and that captures minimal subsistence needs; it was worth about 249 g of silver, leaving a tiny sum for discretionary spending and indicating a hard life for families in such circumstances.[33] Comparisons with incomes and consumption of a few other preindustrial societies showed that the standard of living of a laborer's family surviving on a bare subsistence income resembled most closely the situation of unskilled labor in Delhi or Beijing in the mid-eighteenth century, and that workers in late medieval (1475) London or Amsterdam were better off by more than a factor of 4.

Another interesting comparison is provided by Scheidel's (2008) list of real daily wages of unskilled workers in ancient and medieval economies between 2000 B.C.E. and 1300 C.E. Expressed in volume of wheat, the most trustworthy Roman rate (for the early fourth century C.E.) is 4.7 L/day (and 4.9 L/day in Egypt) compared to 5.3–6.4 L/day in ancient (twentieth–sixteenth centuries B.C.E.) southern Mesopotamia, 8.7 L/day in late fifth-century B.C.E. Athens, and 7.7–13.4 L/day for early medieval Egypt (seventh–eighth centuries C.E.). Clearly, Roman wages do not indicate any superior performance, and the comparison confirms that the empire's economy was able to offer little beyond basic subsistence to the great majority of its workers.

Wealth and imperial legislation divided the Romans into two starkly unequal categories. *Honestiores* included senators, knights (*equites*), municipal *decuriones*, and army veterans; they and their families numbered at least 350,000 and perhaps as many as 500,000 people, or no more than 0.5%–1% of the empire's entire population. *Humiliores* (better known under another collective name, *plebs*) made up the vast remainder. This social division was closely replicated in a deep divide between wealth and poverty with no middle class. This widely accepted conclusion was challenged by Morley (2006) and Scheidel (2006b). Morley (2006) even asked if there were any poor in the city of Rome (although, to be fair, it was at least partly a rhetorical question, posed in the context of discussing problematic definitions of poverty). More important, he argued (dubiously, I think) that the poor could not be a significant social group and that economic poverty in Rome was not a state that could be endured for long because it was usually rapidly fatal.

Scheidel (2006b) made a more nuanced point, arguing that not all *humiliores* should be lumped into a homogeneous economic class because there were sufficient opportunities for many of them to reach what we would see today as a middle-class status. In other words, there was no stark cleavage between opulence and destitution but rather a graduated economic stratification. This is undoubtedly true, but it is the size of the middle class that makes it of such a special import in modern societies. Scheidel's own estimate posits some 225,000 households in Roman Italy who were fairly well-off; even if that were true, fewer than 20% of citizens in Italy would be in that class, compared to well over 50% in modern economies.[34]

Maddison (2007) assessed the distribution of Roman wealth in the following way. The emperor's annual income was at least HS 15 million, that of 600 senators averaged about HS 150,000, and some 40,000 *equites* were assumed to earn about HS 30,000 per year. In aggregate, the elite income (including some 240,000 *decuriones*, municipal councilors in the cities, and 50,000 other rich people) amounted to about 26% of the empire's aggregate income for a group that made up less than 0.7% of the population; in contrast, Milanovic, Lindert, and Williamson (2007) put the income of the richest 1% of Romans at "just" 16%.

Scheidel and Friesen (2008) argued that the Pareto ratio does not apply to Roman elite wealth and that the actual income distribution had to be even steeper (if it was applicable at all). That is why they favored a revision of the published estimates and concluded that the Roman elite (the top 1.5% percent of households) claimed about 20% of total income; better-off non-elite groups (about 10% of the population) got perhaps another 20%; and most of the remaining population survived at near-subsistence levels while generating more than half of total economic output. This distribution results in a Gini coefficient of income inequality at about 0.6, much higher than the mean of 0.38 proposed by Milanovic, Lindert, and Williamson (2007) and similar to some of the highest modern inequalities that prevail, above all, in Latin America: Bolivia with 0.60, Brazil with 0.58, Peru with 0.55 (UNDP 2008). The approximate band of likely Roman income inequality is contrasted with the Lorenz curve for the United States (Gini index of 0.40) (figure IV.7).[35]

Another revealing indicator of inequality is the cutoff point (in terms of mean income) that puts people into the top income percentile. In the United States it takes less than five times the mean income level in order to get into that top category; in seventeenth- and eighteenth-century England it was about six times; but in early imperial Rome it was at least 12–15 times. Roman wealth distribution was thus

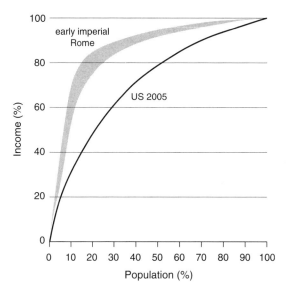

Figure IV.7
Lorenz curves of income distribution in early imperial Rome and in the United States in 2005. A diagonal line would indicate perfect income equality. Roman curve plotted from estimates by Maddison (2007), Milanovic, Lindert, and Williamson (2007), and Scheidel and Friesen (2008); U.S. curve from data in USCB (2007).

clearly emblematic of a traditional society without a substantial middle class, the group whose wealth ranges typically between the mean and rates that are three to four times higher. Bastomsky (1990) calculated the typical differences between a poor man's income and the annual incomes of moderately and extremely rich Romans: the first multiple was just over 700, the other about 17,100, substantially higher than inequalities in Victorian England, where the analogical multiples were 24 and about 6,000.

Statistics on the share of America's household income received by each quintile and by the top 5% have been available annually since 1947, and they indicate a relatively stable pattern until the early 1990s followed by a slight (but still significant) rise of inequality (USCB 2008). In 1950 the lowest quintile received 4.5% of all income, the highest 42.7%; a quarter century later these shares were, respectively, 4.3% and 43.6%; by 2005 they deteriorated noticeably to 3.4% and 50.4% (USCB 2008).[36] During that time the income received by the richest 5% of the U. S. population first fell slightly from 17.3% in 1950 to 16.5% in 1975 and then rose appreciably to 22.2% in 2005 (see figure IV.7). Despite this recent worsening of income equality it took only 3.6 times the average U.S. household income of about $46,300 in 2005 to put a family into the top 5% of income earners, and the mean income of the highest quintile was only 2.2 times that of the fourth quintile (USCB 2008).

Another approach to comparing ancient Roman and modern American inequality, and one that is perhaps more meaningful that the inherently uncertain monetary values, is to contrast typical urban housing conditions. The *insulae* to *domus* ratio in Rome was 26:1, so there is not the slightest doubt that only a very small fraction of Romans enjoyed the quiet opulence and spaciousness of their walled dwellings. Records of the fourth century c.e. put the total of *insulae* at 46,000, but Hermansen (1978) argued that 25,000 was a more realistic figure.[37] Absence of sound structural engineering (load-bearing walls no thicker than many room partitions), hasty construction, shoddy workmanship, substandard building materials, and poor foundations weakened by the Tiber's periodic flooding were the reasons for their frequent structural collapse (*ruina*). Moreover, the height restrictions of 70 Roman feet (the Augustan limit of 20.65 m was lowered to 17.7 m by Trajan) were often ignored.

And poor construction was not redeemed by adequate space. Wealthier freedmen lived on the lower floors of *insulae*; the upper floors were for the poor; rooms were let long-term or on a daily basis; some poor also lived in *tabernae* or rooming houses (*cauponae* or *hospitia*). Overcrowding in the *insulae* was the norm, but we have no reliable information about the number of people living in an *insula*. Estimates range from 12–30 people per floor, and numbers from one of the very few surviving structures—48 tenants per 138 m^2 on the fourth and fifth floors—prorate to less than 3 m^2/person (Hermansen 1978). Many families lived in rooms of 10 m^2 that provided as little space as 2 m^2 per capita. Taking a relatively generous rate of 3 m^2 per capita as Rome's modal living space in *insulae* and contrasting it with the dwellings of the city's richest inhabitants sets the extreme space differences.

I am ignoring Domus Aurea, Nero's short-lived superresidence, which occupied perhaps as much as 400,000 m^2 in the center of Rome.[38] My maximum is the Palatium, the imperial residence on the Palatine Hill whose construction began under Augustus and that was enlarged by Domitian between 81 c.e. and 96 c.e. and then used by the Roman emperors for some 300 years. Its two sections—Domus Flavia reserved for public functions, and the residence of Domus Augustana—had about 40,000 m^2 of opulently finished, furnished, and decorated space (figure IV.8).[39] Large villas could have more than 2000 or 3000 m^2, a large *domus* was easily 1000 m^2 and Hermansen (1978) assumes 675 m^2 to be its average Roman area, and

Figure IV.8
A plan of Rome's imperial palace, *upper left*; and photographs of the peristyle (with a shallow water basin) at the lower level of the Domus Augustana, *upper right*, and the remnants of its brick walls towering above Circus Maximus. Photos by V. Smil.

(judging by the floor plans in Pompeii) houses of well-off families ranged between 175 m^2 and 345 m^2 (Wallace-Hadrill 1994).

Comparisons of habitation density are less prone to major error when done per household rather than per capita because of the highly variable number of inhabitants, particularly in a large *domus* with many slaves. A large *villa* household had 10^2 (150–300) times more space than a family living in an *insula*, and the differences between average *domus* and *insula* dwellings were 10–40-fold.

In contrast, in 2005 the average size of American dwellings (apartments and houses, owned and rented) was 158 m^2, the mean area of newly built houses reached 220 m^2 (that is 12% larger than a tennis court), and that of custom-built houses rose to 450 m^2 (USCB 2008). Houses in excess of 600 m^2 were not uncommon in exurban areas, many estates of billionaires had a central structure of 2000–3000 m^2, and Bill Gates (at that time still the world's richest man) owned a 4600-m^2 house on the shore of Lake Washington in Medina near Seattle. This means that the largest private houses were mostly no more than 20–25 times the size of an average dwelling and that a typical custom-built house (the equivalent of a *domus*) was less than three times as large as the mean of all dwellings. Consequently, Roman housing disparities were easily 1 order of magnitude greater than the differences prevailing in the United States at the beginning of the twentieth century.

Given all this evidence of average income, affordable consumption, wealth distribution, and housing space, it is clear that we are encountering yet again the same degree of disparity as in many previous comparisons, be it energy use, reliance on inanimate prime movers, infant mortality, or common morbidity. The differences between the two societies are not just two- or threefold (and hence easily imaginable and intuitively understandable) but span at least 1 order of magnitude, reaching levels with which our normal experience cannot easily cope. I have assiduously avoided any use of hyperboles in these comparisons, but the following labels are fully justified: by any comparative measure, an average Roman lived in misery, and an average American enjoys a level of affluence unprecedented in human history.

3
Why Comparisons Fail

Neque enim conferendum esse Gallium cum Germanorum agro, neque hanc consuetudinem victus cum illa comparandum.

For neither must the land of Gaul be compared with the land of the Germans, nor must the habit of living of the latter be put on a level with that of the former.

—Gaius Julius Caesar, *De bello Gallico* I:xxxi (W.A. McDevitte and W.S. Bohn translation, 1851)

Caeasar's command should be taken as a universal admonition, as a warning to all those eager to rush even into what appear to be simple comparisons of two contemporaneous societies in order to draw hard conclusions based on seemingly revealing contrasts or parallels. Obviously, the task becomes even more questionable if the societies are separated by two millennia of history. But the temptation to compare cannot be stilled, and the impulse is particularly irresistible where ancient Rome is concerned. As I showed in chapter I, admiration and exaltation of that long-lived empire has itself become a part of Western history. Hyperbolic statements concerning the Roman Empire's extent and achievements abound (see chapter II), and some make similarly exorbitant claims on behalf of its capital city.[1]

Superficial comparisons are easy to make, and not all of them are merely rhetorical devices or tools of essayist craft; some of them do read well and make interesting connections. Besides, making them may also feel at least a bit ennobling because the author can display some classicist training and follow in the footsteps of numerous literati who could not resist Roman allusions and references.[2] Fascination with Rome's decline and fall has been as alive during recent generations as it was when Gibbon penned his masterpiece or when the savants of the Renaissance were intent on reclaiming the antique understanding. And given the extent of today's graphomania, which finds its expression in outlets ranging from newspaper editorials to memoirs of superannuated politicians, and from books where reality is hard to disentangle from fiction to undisciplined blogs, it is hardly surprising that looking for comparisons, analogies, and parallels between ancient Roman and modern America has become so common, and commonly so misleading and misinformed, so superficial and so emotional.

In the preceding chapters I have offered a systematic appraisal of a large number of specific and fundamental differences between Roman and American ways of wielding power and living everyday lives. This final chapter reinforces this message of incomparable differences by recapitulating the principal conclusions of my inquiry and by illustrating with specific Roman and American examples the most common weaknesses and failings of historical comparisons. I close the chapter (and the book) by stressing yet again the differences between the circumstances (and hence consequences) that prevailed at the time of the formal dissolution of the Western Roman Empire and those that characterize today's highly interdependent, interconnected global civilization. Whatever lessons can be drawn from the demise of the Western Roman Empire are of little avail in illuminating the global reverberations of any dramatic weakening of America's standing in the modern world.

V

Historical Analogies and Their (Lack of) Meaning

... one of the major tasks of large-scale history is to develop the grounds for criticizing historical comparisons. It must criticize above all the units valid for various sorts of historical comparison, and the context in terms of which comparison can be relevant.
—M.G.S. Hodgson, *Rethinking World History* (1993)

Giardina's (1993) reminder should be kept in mind even before starting any comparative exercises: "Whatever noun we place with the adjective "Roman" (the Roman world, Roman man, etc.), the result is the same: what we are constructing is an abstract and totalizing, thus a partial, category. . . . The same is of course true in all complex civilizations" (5). Modern America, despite its relatively short history and high degree of economic and social homogenization, is an old state (older than most in today's world). It encompasses diverse environments and values liberty and free speech, and its ideal of *ex pluribus unum* has been no obstacle for its uncommon heterogeneity. These are self-evident, yet repeatedly overlooked, caveats.

Most of the historical allusions and analogies to ancient Rome are either off the mark or bring no great revelations because the comparisons fit into one of the following three undesirable categories. First, they entail only superficial realities and hence can yield only questionable insights. Second, they deal with universal human attributes and hence there is no particular insight to be gained by contrasting Rome with Washington; many other combinations of two societies or two capitals would serve as well. Third, they use simple quantitative contrasts without attention to vastly different qualities and hence end up with very misleading conclusions. I illustrate each of these failings with a few examples.

Common Shortcomings

Perhaps no other inappropriate comparison based on the existence of a superficially similar feature is as overworked as are the references to Rome's Capitoline Hill and

Washington's Capitol Hill and, even more so, to Rome's *senatus* and the U.S. Senate. When Cullen Murphy, the author of *Are We Rome?*, gave a tour of "imperial" Washington to a newspaper reporter, he pointed out "numerous physical manifestations of the Rome-Washington link" (Thompson 2007, 1), including the obelisk to memorialize the first president and a triple Roman triumphal arch at Union Station, its "vaulted ceilings taken from the Baths of Diocletian." Using such criteria, just about every major Western city and scores of smaller places have the Roman link, and implicitly, imperial pretensions or aspirations.[1]

America's invasion of Iraq in 2003 provided yet another analogy for those who draw simplistic parallels between the two states based on outwardly similar actions. That comparison is deeply flawed because Rome's extended presence in Mesopotamia—the provinces of Osrhoene, created in 195 C.E., and Mesopotamia, created in 198–199 C.E. (Millar 1993)—was limited to the territory between the Euphrates and the Chaboras rivers, which is entirely in today's eastern Syria, and Rome's small temporary easternmost extensions (from Sophēnēnē to Zabdikēnē) reached just east of the Tigris (northeast of Mosul) in what is today the northernmost Kurdish part of Iraq near the border with Turkey (northern parts of Nīnawā and Dahūk provinces). The Roman Empire never had any lasting presence in the heart of Mesopotamia (centered on Baghdad) or in today's southern Iraq (figure V.1).

Another approach favored by eager comparison makers is to point out the parallels concerning the style of government of the two countries and its obvious structural weaknesses and operational failures. This is a particularly appealing method because there was no shortage of keen critics, devoted moralizers, and busy gossipers among Roman politicians, historians, diarists, and letter writers, and they left behind many pithy observations and memorable quotes that expose and condemn everything from ambition and avarice to corruption and sexual misconduct. All that is needed in order to draw the parallels is to juxtapose such narratives or statements with similar (indeed often nearly identical) sentiments regarding public affairs and condemnations of actions and morals in contemporary America.

This is where Murphy's (2007) six great parallels between ancient Roman and modern American ways of governance come in. According to Murphy, the two states share the self-centered behavior of ruling elites who see the world as revolving around their capitals; a widening divide between military and civilian society, and recruitment difficulties; privatization of public services, leading to greater corruption; a myopic view of the world; porous borders; and the complexity parallel, the impossibility of managing their sprawling affairs and powers. All this is interesting and thoughtfully presented without being contrived. But do we have to go back

Figure V.1
Roman Mesopotamia, its frontier with the Sasanid Empire, and the current boundary of Iraq. Names of the Roman border provinces are according to the Verona List (early fourth century C.E.). Based on maps in Talbert (2000) and Dignas and Winter (2007).

to Roman antiquity to encounter these nearly universal weaknesses, ineptitudes, delusions, and complications?

Parading Roman quotes and stories, and contrasting them with relevant American situations or dilemmas, does not yield any special insights into Roman or American affairs. Although such contrasts refer to people and events of particular times and places, they illuminate universal human attributes because they illustrate the expected range of human pretensions, propensities, misjudgments, and foibles. Consequently, we could get similarly evocative pairings by using Greek and Renaissance sources of moral discourse, by contrasting modern Italian and Russian business practices, or by borrowing from the Chinese classics for comparisons with today's East Asian mores and transgressions. Aggrandizing behavior of capital elites, corruption of bloated bureaucracies and privatization of services, an unrealistic view of the world, and overly complex decision making—all these could be studied (where relevant archives, memoirs, and histories are accessible) with nearly identical conclusions in many societies, be they ancient, premodern, or contemporary.

For the self-centered, secretive, and dishonest behavior of capital elites we could mine evidence from the ten centuries of the Byzantine Empire; after all, their way of governing gave us the adjective *byzantine*, meaning devious and surreptitious. Or we could dissect the two centuries of decay of the Ottoman powers (roughly from 1700 to 1922), whose inept rulers presided over a crumbling empire from the same capital as the eastern rulers of the *imperium Romanum* (Finkel 2005; Quataert 2005). Or we could look at the rulers of the Manchu Qing dynasty in Beijing (1644–1911), who transformed the world's largest economy into a decrepit shell of a state open to foreign dismemberment and civil war (Rawski 1998). Most recently such grand lessons could be taught by studying the delusions held and decisions made in the Kremlin of Lenin and Stalin and by the politburos of Stalin's less lethal successors, who were in charge of the "superpower" USSR until its dissolution in 1991.

A great divide between military and civilian society is an inevitable consequence of having a professional army. Most Americans do not now directly encounter anything military, much as they go through life without having anything directly to do with structural engineers or organic chemists (to name at random two other self-selected professions that are indispensable for any modern civilization). And the endlessly highlighted similarities of "imperial overstretch" tell us nothing specific either about Roman or American military power. Major powers projecting their might far beyond their borders found themselves overextended long before the Romans embarked on their conquests, and ever since.

The most spectacular demonstration in antiquity of this universal phenomenon took place when Alexander the Great pushed his Macedonian troops all the way to the Indian Punjab. The overreach syndrome can be identified in every bold expansionist foray ever since, be it the Umayyad dynasty's (660–750 C.E.) push into central France; the Mongol thrust, led by Batu, Genghis Khan's grandson, to the heart of Europe (1222–1242); the Chinese conquest of Central Asia (1644–1759) by the Qing dynasty (Perdue 2005); or Napoleon's or Hitler's mad attempts to subdue Russia (1812 and 1941, respectively) (figure V.2). Again, what insight is gained by singling out Pompey or Trajan, especially when one can recall (in a

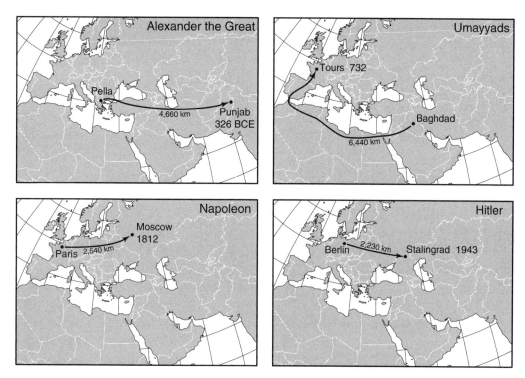

Figure V.2
Four classic cases of strategic overextension: Alexander the Great's advance to Punjab, the Umayyad dynasty's expansion into Atlantic Europe, Napoleon's march to Russia, and Hitler's attempt to subdue the USSR. Eventual checks are indicated by place and year, and approximate maximum distances of the armed reach from the national core are shown in kilometers.

complete antithesis of the Roman military ethos) the voices of some of America's most eminent military leaders speaking against war and warning the country about the dangers of the military-industrial complex.[2]

As far as corruption is concerned, I do not see why we have to search for prominent examples of corrupt political and business behavior in ancient Rome in order to contrast them with current American practices. The Romans were surely far from being the only ancients whose *honestiores* (*potentes, magni, maximi viri*) possessed and expected *dignitas, licentia* (authority), and *potestas*, acted as *patrones* for numerous suppliants, and were ready to bestow *beneficia* and exercise their *suffragium* (influence) in exchange for assorted promises or payments. MacMullen (1988) is an excellent guide to these intricacies of Roman power for sale and the price of privatizing government. But if we had a similarly extensive record of ancient

Persian or Indian corruption and malfeasance, we could draw very similar conclusions, and we can do so on the basis of abundant evidence for Japan, a society that is in many other respects as unlike ancient Rome or modern America as can be imagined.[3]

We have abundant evidence—as attested by publications like *EU Corruption News* or the Global Policy Forum's *Corruption and Money Laundering*—that today's American politicians and entrepreneurs are hardly alone among the elites resorting to corruption. And we have an objective gauge of worldwide corruption in the annual surveys of Transparency International (headquartered in Berlin), which show that modern America is actually among the less corrupt societies (TI 2008b).[4] In 2008, Denmark, Sweden, and New Zealand were ranked as the least corrupt of 180 countries (score 9.3 out of a possible 10). The United States was eighteenth (7.3), scoring much like Japan (7.3) or France (6.9). In contrast, Italy ranked fifty-fifth (4.8), China seventy-second (3.6), India eighty-fifth (3.4), Russia one hundred and forty-seventh (2.1), and Myanmar (1.3) and Somalia (1.0) most corrupt.

The Bribe Payers Index (BPI) explores commercial bribery by assessing the likelihood of companies from 22 leading exporting countries to bribe abroad (TI 2008a). In 2008, Belgian and Canadian companies bribed abroad least frequently (score 8.8 out of a possible 10), the Netherlands and Switzerland ranked third (8.7), and the United Kingdom, Japan, and Germany fifth (8.6). The United States and France shared ninth place (8.1), and Italy ranked seventeenth (7.4). Firms headquartered in India (6.8), China (6.5), and Russia (5.9) were most likely to bribe abroad. The laws of some countries have actually allowed companies operating abroad to claim bribes as tax write-offs.

Myopic views of the world were surely no Roman preserve, and today they are not America's prerogative. Many words were written about a rather extreme variety of China's ethnocentrism as a ruling ethos of the country that has always considered itself the center of the world (*zhong guo*) and whose emperors so haughtily dismissed any need for material or intellectual interaction with the barbarians from a distant island without having the least understanding of the vastly superior technical powers that the island nation had come to possess.[5] And *myopic* perfectly describes the foreign policy of the Tokugawa shōguns who naively assumed that virtually complete isolation of Japan could be maintained indefinitely (Totman 1980; Jansen 2002), or the ideologically blinded Soviet Communist leaders with their endless boasts of economic and technical superiority (recall Khrushchev's "We will bury you!") that could not prevent the dissolution of their empire.

As for porous borders, a decidedly anti-imperial European Union has borders no less porous than those of supposedly imperial America or those that the Romans tried to maintain along the Rhine and the Danube. This comparison shows that the reality of porous borders has nothing to do with imperial intentions but everything to do with a well-appreciated and universal combination of pull-push migration factors. Economic opportunities in much richer (and aging) nations pull in migrants; war and misery at home pushes them out; and it does not matter if the actors were Tervingi and Greuthungi fleeing the Huns along Rome's Danubian border of the late fourth century C.E., or if they are poor peasants from Chiapas crossing into Arizona or young males from the sub-Saharan countries crowded into small boats trying to reach the Canary Islands, the southernmost territory of the promised Euroland, by a perilous voyage from Senegal or Cape Verde.

The complexity argument—making decisions that create rather than solve many problems "because the very act of managing has unpredictable ripple effects . . . which in turn become part of the environment that needs to be managed" (Murphy 2007, 20)—is about as universal a phenomenon as one can imagine. As such it can be applied not only to strategic and political changes faced by the expanding and contracting Roman Empire and by America in a new multipolar world but also to just about every large-scale business decision, every fundamental technical choice (e.g., nuclear versus solar energy), and all major scientific advances that we make, support, and promote as societies and as individuals.[6]

The category of human universalities from which examples can be selected for any society or any historical period also includes all matters concerning marital and sexual affairs and enthusiasm for spectacularly staged events. On the first score, there are no indicators to attest that American mores are grossly out of line with behavior in other affluent countries, and nothing unexpected or shocking is revealed when they are contrasted with the Roman descriptions of human sexuality.[7] As for the staged events, Americans are, if anything, rather disciplined and well-behaved spectators in comparison with many European or Latin American crowds. Their inexplicable fondness for baseball (a boring, sluggish game fueled by steroid-infused muscles) and their distinctly déclassé passion for fake wrestling matches are innocuous when compared to the violence-prone behavior of modern European and Latin American soccer crowds (Reilly and Williams 2003).

And even though the Romans did not stage gladiatorial contests with the frequency implied by modern popular accounts of that horrid pastime, there is simply no meaningful comparison between modern spectator sports and the callousness, brutality, and casual killing that were on display in Roman amphitheaters.[8]

Figure V.3
Detail of the Arch of Titus (81 C.E.) on the Via Sacra in Rome, showing Romans carrying the menorah and trumpets taken from the Second Temple after the Jewish defeat and the conquest of Jerusalem in 70 C.E. The triumphal arch was dedicated by the Roman senate jointly to the emperors Vespasian and his son Titus. Photo by V. Smil.

Similarly, America's spectacular parades—ranging from a newly elected president's walk (or ride) to the White House to processions of garish floats preceding various football contests (Rose Bowl, Orange Bowl)—are nothing but wholesome and child-friendly displays compared to the triumphal marches that victorious magistrates and emperors staged in Rome for the benefit of the city's *plebs* (Beard 2007). It was one thing to display looted military standards and precious gems or to parade such exotic animals as elephants or giraffes through the center of Rome, and quite another to exhibit caged (and soon to be executed) leaders of defeated adversaries and manacled (and soon to be sold into slavery) prisoners of war (figure V.3).[9]

Comparisons of America's top leaders with Roman emperors, senators, and generals will show (unsurprisingly) many kindred characteristics that are almost expected of powerful men in virtually all socially stratified societies: having a temper or a low tolerance for dissent, conducting extramarital affairs, and doing favors for friends. But, once again, American realities are, thankfully, so much more mundane compared to the stories emanating from Asia, Latin America, and the Middle East. Many U.S. presidents have been anything but paragons of virtue, humility, and consensus, but even those who have been accused (by their adversaries or by the media) of scheming and indulging in imperial tendencies (Schlesinger 1973; *New York Times* 2007) hardly behave like emperors. Curiously enough, the obvious but nontrivial fact that the Roman Empire was a monarchy, and the United States is not, is casually ignored by those determined to see the country as a great new imperial power.

Finally, there is a class of comparisons where superficially similar realities are used to draw or imply misleading conclusions by simply contrasting two aggregate numbers and ignoring (often profound) qualitative differences. For example, admiration has been lavished on the Roman hard-topped roads that served the empire's courier service (*cursus publicus*) and whose total length eventually reached about 85,000 km, or (as we are triumphantly reminded) about 10,000 km (13%) longer than the U.S. interstate highway system.

Such a comparison cannot be taken seriously by anyone familiar with even the first-class Roman *viae* with their fitted stones and deep wheel ruts and America's multilane freeways. It is rendered totally ineffective when one considers the enormous differences between the dominant prime movers used on the two road systems: in the first instance, courier horses, draft mules, and donkeys delivering useful power of 100–500 W at speeds of 4–5 km/h for cargo transport and 10–15 km/h for the fastest messengers, and in the second instance, cars and trucks powered by internal combustion engines mostly capable of 100–200 kW at speeds of 60–120 km/h.

Although it was also used for military transport, the Roman *cursus publicus* served primarily as a means of rapid communication, and on this score the Romans did not come up with anything radically new. The *cursus* could not claim any speed records because a system of long-distance horse riders had already been optimized long before. After Cyrus the Great became the ruler of Persia (550 B.C.E.), he established a fast messenger service between Susa and Sardis, which Xenophon thought to be "undeniably the fastest travel by land possible by humans." Given the biophysical constraints on horses (as modern anatomy and physiology understands them today), he was right; nobody (not even the Mongols or the Overland Pony Express) could optimize daily staging better than did the ancient Persians.[10]

Another often admired Roman feat was the capital's food supply. Rome's population of 1 million people required about 30 million *modii*, or 200,000 t, of grain every year (Garnsey 1988), nearly all of it shipped from Egypt and North Africa (Temin 2001). Add to this olive oil and wine, and we have annual shipments of comestibles easily as massive as 250,000 t. Undoubtedly, their procurement required a great deal of planning and coordination in order to produce the requisite quantities of grain, olives, and grapes, to press the oil and ferment the wine, and to gather all these commodities and ship them overseas.[11]

But in modern terms this amounts to only a mundane bulk cargo transportation enterprise. Even small grain ships used for regional transfers now carry 30,000–40,000 t per vessel, large ocean-going bulk cargo carriers load 80,000–100,000 t of grain, and a large wine tanker can carry 40,000,000 liters. Consequently, two large dry bulk carriers and a single tanker could bring Rome's entire annual grain and wine requirements from Africa, Asia Minor, or other parts of Europe, yet another example of truly incomparable technical differences between the two societies: the empire's greatest logistic accomplishment is today's unremarkable minor shipping transaction.

Fundamental Differences

In this book I have tried to follow a dispassionate, scientific approach. I eschewed hyperbolic pronouncements, stayed away from sentimental arguments, and avoided comparing specific displays of universal human behavior, a choice that I criticized in the preceding section. My approach is guided by a firm belief that there is no need to add to facile, superficial comparisons that end with prophetic pronouncements or dire warnings. My aim is not only to subject the latest wave of imperial parallels to critical appraisal but to redo the comparisons as if words and realities mattered, by using rigorous criteria and (whenever possible) quantifiable variables in order to focus on the most fundamental differences between the two societies.

Surprisingly, I had to conclude that the most notable commonality between ancient Rome and modern America is the (vastly exaggerated) perception of their respective powers, be they judged in terms of territorial extent, effective political influence, or convincing military superiority. If words are to retain their meaning, then I am far from alone in concluding that America is not an empire, but I believe that even America's undoubted global hegemony is of a very peculiar kind, much less effective and much more fragile than commonly thought. In all other aspects

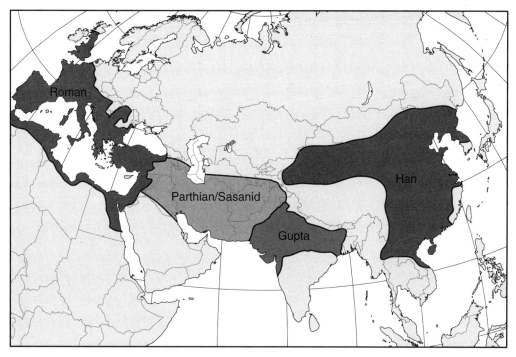

Figure V.4
Non-Eurocentric view of the world of late antiquity, showing the Roman (27 B.C.E.–476 C.E.), Parthian/Sasanid (247 B.C.E.–651 C.E.), Gupta (320–550 C.E.), and Han (206 B.C.E.–220 C.E.) empires in their greatest territorial extent.

my inquiry found two fundamentally different worlds. A short recapitulation of these conclusions are in order.

I have demonstrated that Rome was never as powerful as implied by the hyperbolic claims of contemporary observers.[12] At the peak of its imperial power the Roman Empire controlled no more than 15% of the inhabited world as it was then known and a mere 3% of what we now know to be the entire continental surface. The Romans were aware that the easternmost provinces of their empire did not even reach the midpoint of the *oikoumene* depicted in Greek maps, yet they boasted (and some Greeks eagerly agreed) that they controlled the entire world. Inexplicably, an uncritical acceptance of this claim and the persistently Eurocentric point of view of modern Western inquiries helped to perpetuate this impression through four kinds of distortion (figure V.4).

First, proper attention has not been paid to India, a subcontinent whose GDP in the first century C.E. was perhaps larger than that of the Roman Empire and about whose affairs the Romans were fairly well informed because of constant trade and a periodic reception of embassies.[13] Second, the very existence of China's Han Empire, Rome's powerful and inventive contemporary, has basically been ignored. Third, Rome's accomplished eastern neighbors, the Parthian and Sasanid empires, have been portrayed merely as armed adversaries rather than as accomplished empire builders. Finally, hyperbolic claims of Rome's greatness have been repeated uncritically instead of with critical deconstruction.

Similarly, America has never been as powerful as implied by the repeated use of such terms as "only remaining superpower," "new empire," "virtual empire," or "unprecedented hyperpower" (Howe 2003, 5). The country's outsize power reputation rests to a large extent on irrationally exaggerated appraisals of uninformed foreigners.[14] I find this gap between exaggerated perceptions and mundane realities perhaps the strongest parallel between the two states. But as a broad range of comparisons shows, many fundamental differences are encompassed in the key fact that America has never been an empire and has not pursued any overtly imperial policy (see chapter II).

In order to assert this there is no need to weigh or reaffirm arguments concerning America's exceptionalism, what Lipset (1996) called a set of dogmas about the nature of a society (liberty, egalitarianism, individualism, populism, laissez faire) that make the country unique. Those who are committed to the notion of American empire will remain unpersuaded (in addition to sources noted in chapter II, see also Ferguson 2004 and Go 2007). Those who believe that words should have clear meanings have little problem with stating simply that "for better or worse, the American hegemony will continue . . . but 'American Empire' will remain a misnomer" (Robinson 2005, 50).

Parting with the traditional preoccupation with social, political, and strategic comparisons, I then turned to the technical underpinnings and biophysical fundamentals of the two societies in order to demonstrate the profound differences. In chapter III, looking first at the intellectual foundations of the economic and technical achievements of the two states, I showed how incomparable was the Roman mode of action with America's enormously inventive and innovative drive. The Romans were relatively incurious, a trait that is evident when their technical and scientific achievements are contrasted with the accomplishments of their two inquisitive contemporaries, the Hellenistic world (above all, new knowledge associated with Ptolemaic Alexandria's museum and library) and China's Han dynasty.[15]

What was accomplished by the Hellenistic thinkers and practitioners mostly between the late third and the late second centuries B.C.E. provided an essential foundation for the flowering of medieval Arabic science and served as one of the intellectual foundations of the European Renaissance. Even more remarkably, some of the great Han dynasty inventions (including the iron moldboard plow and percussion drilling of deep wells) were adopted by the Europeans only during the early modern era. Although the Romans were not as averse to introducing technical improvements as has been commonly claimed, their only inanimate prime mover, the vertical waterwheel, remained limited in both numbers and capacity, and all wheels contributed most likely less than 0.5% of the empire's total power capacity dominated by human and animal muscles. After all, we must keep in mind that the empire's by far most commonly encountered large machine was a donkey- or mule-powered grain mill.[16]

In contrast, America's enormous power capacity resides in hundreds of millions of machines, and a large share of this power is directly controlled by individual families. In all cases where these disparities can be quantified they illustrate conditions in two very different worlds, and as some gaps span 1 or 2 orders of magnitude, they signify realities that are basically beyond the comprehension of the inhabitants of either world. Energy use is a key physical determinant of overall economic ability, per capita wealth, and quality of life, but in Roman society it was no different from that of its neighbors, dominated by wood for heat and human and animal muscles for labor.

Could an average Roman citizen imagine a society where every person enjoyed effortless access to roughly 50 times more useful energy (heat, motion, light) than was the Roman norm (figure V.5)? Could a Roman citizen conceive living in a society where every person is attended (in power terms) by an equivalent of 50 strong and continuously hard-working slaves? How could an average American grasp the real import of the fact that on average inanimate prime movers that power the machines that serve him have a 1,000 times larger capacity than the power of his muscles, whereas for the Romans the ratio was reversed, with human and animal exertions providing in aggregate 1,000 times more power than the nascent waterwheels? Similarly incomprehensible comparisons can be made by contrasting the basic demographic and economic variables whose quantification I presented in chapter IV.

Could an average American truly imagine a family life where one out of four newborns would not live to see the first birthday and average life expectancy would be only 20–25 years (see figure V.5)? Could a young American family contemplate with equanimity the prospect of a life whose physical quality would be inferior to that in the most desperate countries of today's sub-Saharan Africa? Could a young

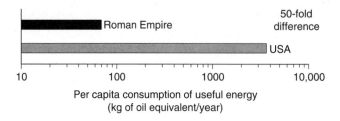

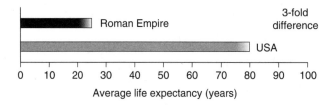

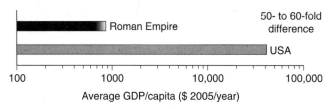

Figure V.5
Comparing two incomparable worlds: per capita consumption of useful energy, average life expectancy, and average per capita GDP in the mature Roman Empire (early centuries C.E.) and in the United States (2005). Horizontal axes in first and third comparisons are logarithmic to accommodate 50-fold differences.

Roman woman, whose prospects of survival at age 20 were no better than to live to her late 40s, imagine a society where women lived on average past their eightieth birthday? And could an ordinary Roman family grasp the full reality of an economy whose annual average income would be 50, 80, or 100 times its own (see figure V.5)? Negative answers, in every case, are all too obvious. And how would today's families cope with severe recurrent food shortages, with the prospect of regular annual spikes in malaria-caused mortality killing their children, or with an ever-present possibility of famine?[17]

But those bent on finding great meaningful analogies between Rome and America might argue that the biophysical fundamentals whose extensive comparisons I have presented are irrelevant, even as they maintain that comparisons of such universal weaknesses as corruption or problems with social cohesion provide valuable and unique insights. There is nothing else I can do to change their mind; after all, even much less rational positions have been advocated by dueling intellectuals. And those critics might also ask why I avoided contrasting the grand national strategies of the two states in order to uncover rewarding parallels between the rise and fall of Rome and of America. Definitional and semantic pitfalls of *rise* and *fall* aside, I could say this might be a profitable approach if there *were* any national strategies.

One World

The best way to deal with the question of a grand Roman strategy is to acknowledge many semantic, methodological, and interpretational problems with the term *strategy*, elaborate the modes of operation of the process (particularly important for such a long-lived state), and recognize that this leads inevitably to a range of irreconcilable conclusions (Luttwak 1976; E. Wheeler 1993; Isaac 1992; K. Kagan 2006). Was Rome an accidental power, reluctant to expand and forced to extend its influence, diplomatically and militarily, in a primarily defensive manner? Or was its empire a product of a deliberate, long-term strategy of expansion whose extent was limited only by its internal resources and external resistance? Complex and yet highly fragmentary and debatable evidence makes it possible to advance arguments for either case and to see Rome as an accidental empire or as a deliberately created superpower of the antique world.[18]

For example, Millar (1993, 80) concluded that the development of the Roman provincial system and the transformation of military dispositions in the Middle East during the latter part of the first century C.E. "give every impression of representing an integrated plan, conceived in Rome and thought out with the aid of a map." This formulation conveys an image on a par with the high command of the *Wehrmacht* (OKW) fashioning the infamous Barbarossa plan and penciling their arrows toward the Volga and the Caucasus.[19] But the Romans never had any class of high career army officers with permanent commissions; we have no indications that their armies had good maps of the frontier areas; and there is no evidence that they engaged in a systematic collection of information on topographic, economic, and political conditions of the areas beyond their control (something that OKW excelled at).

Similarly incompatible arguments have been advanced with regard to the principal motives of Roman expansion, ranging from crude Marxist-materialistic interpretations to ennobling images of a high civilization subduing barbarians. When the ancient sources actually give the reasons for fighting, they often refer to the glory or dignity of empire or to the desire to subjugate tribes or nations, reasons that may not support economic gains but bring prolonged losses. As Isaac (1992) noted, the Romans did not try to rationalize their actions even after a conquest.

In my reading of the evidence I join those who argue that the Romans had no grand imperial strategy, unless exploiting opportunities or reacting to new circumstances could be seen as having one, and that most great powers have always followed a similar course of action. So, yet again, there is nothing uniquely Roman or American in this. A critical reading of modern American history shows foreign policies that were overwhelmingly reactive rather than deliberately transformative and actions that were embodiments of calculated self-interest rather than demonstrations of ideological fervor.[20] This conclusion applies even to America's key foreign policy objective, one shared by all post–WW II administrations, the desirability of spreading democracy abroad. Self-interest has made it easy for the United States to make monumental exceptions for Saudi Arabia, Egypt, Pakistan, or China.[21]

Even the attempt at a major democratic transformation, the U.S. invasion of Iraq in 2003, whose aim was political reform of the Middle East, had its obviously reactive origins; its proximate trigger was the fear of weapons of mass destruction in Saddam Hussein's hands, a fear engendered by the attacks of 9/11. During the summer of 2001 the new Bush administration had no grand plans for such action. In fact, as a candidate and after accession to power in the spring and summer of 2001, George W. Bush explicitly disavowed any nation-building enterprises and advocated inward-oriented policies.[22] And despite bold public announcements matters have not really changed since 9/11.

In his West Point graduation address in June 2002, President Bush enunciated a doctrine of permanent superiority: "America has, and intends to keep, military strengths beyond challenge—thereby making the destabilizing arms races of other areas pointless—and limiting rivalries to trade and other pursuits of peace" (4). That is easy to say but impossible to do. Achieving superior power temporarily without a peer competitor has been done many times on a regional scale but never globally.

As demonstrated in chapter II, America's considerable post-1945 power has always been limited in a number of ways, some amounting only to temporary complications that can be addressed by technical fixes, others presenting more fundamental challenges that have no rapid or tolerably affordable solutions. Biased perceptions keep seeing the United States as a military hyperpower, but impartial assessments tell a different story. Of course, the United States may have more (and more sophisticated) military hardware than anyone else, but repeated experiences (Korea, Vietnam, Iraq) have demonstrated the limits of material superiority, particularly when nuclear warheads, the ultimate weapons, can be used only as a strategic deterrent, not as a battlefield option.

Moreover, since the Spanish-American War of 1898 all major engagements of U.S. forces have been fought overseas, and the requisite projection of U.S. power— now epitomized by aircraft carrier groups, intercontinental stealth bombers, refueling tankers, and pre-positioned armor—is expensive, making it more difficult for the United States to fight wars in Europe and Asia than it would be for the Russians or the Chinese to be engaged in their own backyards. Even so, the limits on the U.S. military have not been (so far) primarily economic. During the 1990s U.S. military spending averaged 3.8% of the country's GDP, compared to 5.6% for Russia and 2.7% for France (Chamberlin 2004). And even with the costly engagements in Iraq and Afghanistan, the 2005 share was equal to 4.1%, much lower than during the decades of the Cold War (even during the 1980s it averaged 5.8%) and lower than in 1992 and 1993, after the collapse of the USSR and the quickly concluded Gulf War (SIPRI 2008; figure V.6).[23]

The limits have been thus less a matter of expenditures (although the recent extraordinary expansion of debt may change that) and more a matter of public commitment, a willingness to stay the course and to sacrifice, however modestly. And in this very respect there are profound differences between Roman determination and current U.S. sentiments. If the Romans had no grand imperial strategy, they certainly did not lack what Harris (1979, 107) called "a strong continuing drive to expand" and a remarkable persistence in confronting a powerful neighboring empire ruled first by Parthian Arsacids and then by Persian Sasanids (Greatrex and Lieu 2007; Dignas and Winter 2007).

The two states first came into contact when Parthia extended its rule to Armenia and Mesopotamia during the first century B.C.E. In 64 B.C.E. Pompey brought Syria under Roman rule, and in 53 B.C.E. the Romans (under Crassus) suffered their first major defeat, at Carrhae. As noted in chapter II, Trajan made it all the way to the shores of the Persian Gulf, and he was the first leader of a military expedition to enter (but not occupy) Ktēsiphōn, the Parthian (and later Sasanid) capital located about 30 km southeast of Baghdad on the Tigris, in 116 C.E. The Romans plundered

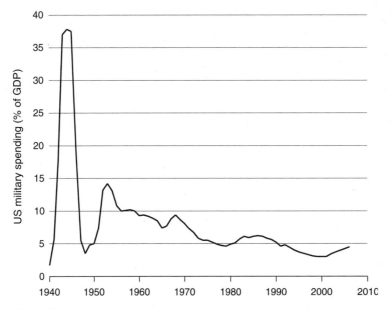

Figure V.6
U.S. military spending as a percentage of GDP, 1940–2008. Plotted from data available at Office of Management and Budget, the White House.

the city again in 165 C.E., then once more under Septimius Severus in 197 C.E., and in 216 C.E. Caracalla was the last Roman emperor to fight Parthia.

The first Sasanid ruler, Šāpūr I, fought three emperors, Gordian III (whom he killed in 244 C.E.), Philip the Arab, and Valerian I, whom he captured in 260 C.E. (figure V.7). Between 262 and 264 C.E. Rome's Palmyrian ally Odaenathus entered Ktēsiphōn twice; in 298 C.E. Šāpūr's grandson Narsé defeated Galerius, only to be beaten by him two years later. In 338 C.E. Constantius II fought Šāpūr II, and the conflict continued long after the Western Empire's demise. The Eastern Empire waged wars with Sasanids in 421–422, 439–442, 502–532, 540–562, 572–590, and 627–629 C.E.; soon afterward the Arab conquest of the region finally put the end to this nearly 700-year-old enmity. America has never had (and almost surely will never have) such a closely matched enemy at its borders, and although I always abstain from any long-term forecasts, it is a very safe bet that Americans will have neither the tenacity nor the resources to match the Roman record and be engaged for another 600 years in one of the overseas regions where they previously fought (Europe, Japan, Middle East).

Figure V.7
Triumphal rock relief of Šāpūr I at Bīšāpūr (about 20 km north of Kazerun in Fars province, southwestern Iran) sums up the period of the greatest Roman defeats: Gordian III lies dead under the horse, and Valerian I kneels before the Sasanid ruler. Photo courtesy of H. Lotfi-Azad.

More important, in the long run (meaning just decades in this context), there has been nothing implacable in America's foreign policy. For instance, the country rushed to resurrect defeated Germany and Japan; took no advantage of the post-1990 malaise of Japan's economy or the post-1991 economic downfall of Russia; and worked for reconciliation with its former ideological and combat enemies in Maoist China, Vietnam, and North Korea. The grand lineaments of American policy are fundamentally different from those of ancient Rome. This leaves me with a last comparison addressing the most provocative analogy—that the fall of the Roman Empire will be mirrored by the imminent "fall" of the superpower America.

This popular vision is easily deconstructed. To begin with, the prevailing Euro-centrism inevitably sees the decapitation of Rome by the barbarians before the end of the fifth century C.E. as the end of the Roman Empire, whereas the empire not only continued but often prospered in the East. The most accurate description, then, is not *fall* but *partial demise*. Gibbon agreed; his history of decline chronicled nearly another millennium after the end of the Western Empire.

And even with respect to its Western domains, one can argue that the empire did not fall but was transformed through more flexible, more suitable, more dynamic arrangements.[24] Gunderson (1976) went so far as to argue that its inhabitants came rationally (on economic grounds) to prefer barbarian rule to the continuation of the Roman *imperium*. Others strongly disagree (for example, see a rebuttal by Anderson and Lewit 1992), but reviewing these arguments would lead us into the maze of causes of the Western Roman decline and fall (assuming there was one).

What should be done instead is to contrast the enormous differences between the fall (end, demise, transformation) of the Western Roman Empire and a similar set of events (processes, actions, consequences) that is forecast (anticipated, feared, seen as inevitable) for the superpower America. What will actually take place in coming decades can be outlined in broad terms but cannot be forecast with any accuracy. There is only one trajectory the United States will follow during the coming generations: a gradual retreat encompassing all parameters that make a nation a great power. There will be nothing surprising about this because it will merely be a continuation of a trend that began right after WW II (figure V.8).

America's population weight has been diminishing even with largely unrestricted immigration, from 6.2% of the global total in 1950 to 5.4% in 1975 and 4.6% in 2005: by 2050 it may be no greater than 4%. In the long run America's economy will continue to grow (albeit at a much slower pace than during the second half of the twentieth century), but its share of the global economic product will be further reduced. The U.S. dollar will not remain the unchallenged global currency, and America's capacity to solve problems with military intervention will further weaken. I must stress the importance of the gradual nature of this retreat. Unless America sustains a massive unanswered nuclear attack (an event of a negligibly low probability because its nuclear triad guarantees a devastating retaliation), there is no way its power could vanish instantly. Nor is it easy to come up with rational scenarios (large-scale urban terrorist attacks, collapse of the country's economy that would leave other major players entirely unaffected) that would see America's power completely drained away in a matter of years.[25]

America's retreat is a process that will continue, at varying speeds and very much in a nonlinear fashion, for decades. Being more definitive, or making appropriate Roman analogies, is impossible. America is not yet definitely at a point akin to the

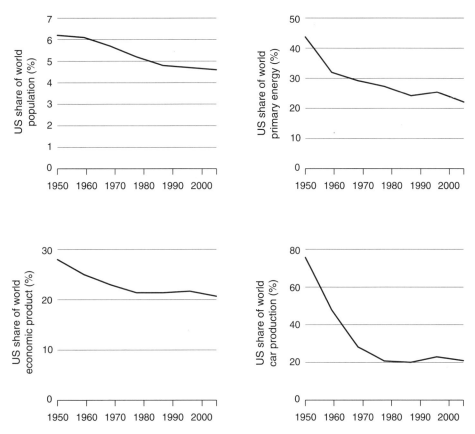

Figure V.8
Decline of the relative importance of the United States in the global order, 1950–2005, is illustrated by trends of four key variables: U.S. share of world population (25% decline); U.S. share of world primary energy consumption (50% decline); U.S. share of world economic product (25% decline); U.S. share of world car production (75% decline). Plotted from various U.S. and UN statistical sources.

time when the Roman legions began withdrawing from England (383 C.E.), but it is surely past the point akin to the peak of imperial power under Trajan (117 C.E.). This is a safe bracketing, but one that leaves us with a time span of more than 250 years, and, in any case, such analogies must be suspect because today's international situation is profoundly different from the relations that prevailed two millennia ago. Undoubtedly, America shows undeniable signs of economic malaise and public ennui, and historians and political commentators have noted some unmistakable evidence of power overstretch (Nye 2002b; Ferguson 2004; Johnson 2004; Cohen 2004). But America's gradual retreat, unlike Rome's long loss of power, takes place in a historically unprecedented setting, in a world that is, in many important ways, truly one world.

The demise of a state, even one as expansive as the Western Roman Empire, had a very limited impact outside of its boundaries in a world without any highly productive and tightly integrated economies and without instant communications. Generations of the Western Empire's progressive weakening and eventual dismemberment by the invaders had no lasting crippling effect on the Eastern Empire. In fact, under Justinian (527–565 C.E.) the empire was much enlarged by temporarily regaining control of large parts of North Africa (conquered by Belisarius in 534 C.E.), Italy (535 C.E.), and southeastern Spain (554 C.E.). At the same time, the disappearance of the Western Empire had no consequences at all for temporarily partitioned China of the northern and southern dynasties (indeed Rome's takeover by invaders was most likely completely unknown at those courts) or for the first Japanese state that was forming at that time on the Yamato Plain. And for the rulers and people of Teotihuacán (America's first metropolis, perhaps as populous as Rome) the world of the Eastern Hemisphere simply did not exist.

In contrast, there is little need to belabor the manifold implications of America's economic and military retreat; just a few key reminders of the country's unique role will suffice. The country still produces more than one-fifth of the global economic product, and it is by far the world's leading importer of manufactured goods as well as the world's largest exporter of both grain and sophisticated aerospace designs. Its largest corporations dominate (or co-dominate) entire industrial or service segments and operate in virtually every state on all continents. More important, the country still has a great edge in basic and applied scientific research and in high-tech design and manufacturing, including such key sectors as aerospace, microprocessors, software, telecommunications, and biotech.

Despite its enormous economic problems, no other assets are held by as many countries and in such quantities as U.S. Treasury bills. America's annual defense budget is more than three times as large as the combined military outlays of China, Russia, Germany, and Japan. Its strategic forces contain a superior combination of nuclear weapons that can be delivered by long-distance bombers, launched from nuclear submarines and from land-based silos, and its conventional forces are better trained, better equipped, and at a higher state of combat readiness than any army of a major power, and it can be projected worldwide to distant conflict zones. And while its military power (or the mere possibility of its deployment) may be much criticized and often feared, it is also perceived as a great stabilizing factor and is relied on to prevent new conflicts and to solve situations that others are unwilling to tackle.[26]

A specific look at modern countries whose predecessors were unaffected by the demise of the Western Roman Empire reveals very different consequences. The Middle Eastern balance of power (countries in the territories once ruled by the Eastern Roman Empire) would change profoundly with America in retreat. Israel's very existence might be in even greater peril, and the ascendance of fundamentalist regimes would continue unchecked. In Asia the economic reforms of post-Mao China have been closely tied to free trade on a massive scale with the United States. Japan, a former enemy, has become America's pivotal Asian ally with very close economic and strategies ties. And, of course, America's retreat (including a drastic economic weakening) would reverberate in Mexico in countless ways. And the global economy would lose its greatest champion of free trade and free information flows.

A new post–WW II global economic regime built with America's inspiration, support, and guarantees has created an unprecedented set of international arrangements. The emergence of global markets for all fundamental resources and the trading of all products and services on a global scale have transformed the traditional meanings of sovereignty, independence, and power. New trading rules have led to a partial but significant surrender of national sovereignty; interdependence is a key economic reality; even countries possessing large territories cannot be autarkic, and even the most powerful nations have their power curbed by a multitude of new social, political, and environmental considerations.

America's position in the modern world of global interdependence is thus fundamentally different from Rome's importance in antiquity. Any significant shift in the country's power, performance, and influence would bring profound changes to the entire world civilization, changes whose extent and magnitude would be simply incomparable with those that followed the cessation of Roman rule over the Western Mediterranean and Atlantic Europe. Once again, studying the particulars of the

Roman demise does little to illuminate the consequences of America's retreat from global affairs.

I should give Polybius, that perceptive Greek historian of ancient Rome who also had an intimate knowledge of the Romans of his age, the last word. At the outset of his great opus, *The Histories*, he remarked that those studying isolated histories—as we do when we compare Roman corruption or Roman military affairs with their American counterparts—are like a man who "after having looked at the dissevered limbs of an animal once alive and beautiful, fancies he has been as good as an eyewitness of the [living] creature itself in all its action and grace" (I:IV.7). Undoubtedly, "we can get some idea of a whole from a part, but never knowledge or exact opinion." That is why Polybius maintained that only "study of the inter-connection of all the particulars, their resemblances and differences" makes it possible to "derive both benefit and pleasure from history" (I:IV.11).

That many Roman and American particulars are similar, some even nearly identical in their general features, is inevitable. It would be surprising if they were not, because basic human qualities, failures, and propensities have not undergone any cosmic shift in the last two millennia of human evolution. But paying closer attention to those fundamental particulars that have been repeatedly ignored in the comparisons of the two societies—their real territorial and political control, the nature of their relations with other nations, their energetic foundations and power capacities, and their population dynamics and wealth—leads us to conclude that the two societies are so profoundly different that the experiences of the ancient one do not offer any profound, unique, and specific lessons for the modern one.

That is why, if they are to be successful, American solutions to America's immense challenges will have to fit the unique imperatives of a new global civilization. Polybius concluded that the Roman ascent was "an event completely without precedent in the past," and America's ascent surely merits the same description. When seen in its requisite complexity, it is this very similarity that makes the two societies fundamentally so different. Comparisons uncover some fascinating parallels derived from shared imperatives of human behavior and from recurrent modes of social dynamics, but, above all, they illuminate two incomparable worlds.

Notes

Chapter I

1. Edward Gibbon (1737–1794) published his incomparable *opus* in six volumes over a period of 12 years (Gibbon 1776–1788). The work has never been out of print, and in addition to many complete editions there are abridgments, including those of Saunders in 1952, Low in 1960, and Mueller in 2003. All my citations come from the three-volume edition originally published by the Modern Library (Random House) in 1932 and reprinted thereafter.

2. This line must have been the origin of an often-repeated quip about Japan's Liberal Democratic Party during its interminable years in power: it was neither liberal (its pedigree was unquestionably conservative), nor democratic (not with the famous smoke-filled-room decisions taken by its gerontocratic leadership), nor a party (being a conglomerate of many jockeying and horse-trading factions spanning a considerable political spectrum).

3. Paradoxically, this exclusion was one of my first encounters with the Roman Empire. When I was between 10 and 17 years of age, we lived in the Bohemian Forest (Romans knew it as *Gabreta Silva*; Germans as *Böhmerwald*), on the Czech-Bavarian border. The border of the Roman Empire used to be less than 50 km away along the Ister (Danube), with the closest fortified settlement at Regina Castra (today's Regensburg, built by legionnaires in 179 c.e.). I always wondered if the history of *Boiohaemum* (Bohemia, the western part of the Czech kingdom) would been different if Marcus Aurelius could have realized his intended north-ward expansion and made it into a province of the empire.

4. Most of them read large chunks of the Roman historians and poets in the original and were keenly aware of many historical (political and military) precedents; some of them could qualify as classical scholars. But perhaps none of them was such a brilliant linguist as an officer who never got much chance of ruling anything: Richard Burton's restless nature and unorthodox manners were not suited for that. See Farwell (1963) and Rice (1990).

5. Inaccurately because in such overseas possessions as Canada and Australia the empire was nearly as Greek as it was in the homeland.

6. The range is due largely to the assumptions regarding the southward extent of the Roman penetration from the coastal regions of provinces in North Africa. I return to the comparisons of territorial extent and control in a much greater detail in chapter II.

7. An important caveat: An argument could be made that a complete decolonization of the former British possessions in Africa was accomplished only with the establishment of Zimbabwe in 1980 (replacing the white-ruled Southern Rhodesia, which declared a unilateral independence in 1965) and with majority rule in South Africa (National African Congress electoral victory in 1994).

8. The mausoleum—long ago stripped of its marble cladding, as is every ancient Roman structure—is but an unsightly heap of inner brickwork overgrown with weeds, a *ruina* contrasting with the modernistic structure built across the street to display the reconstructed Augustan *Ara Pacis*.

9. *Adlocutio cohortium* was traditionally given either before a battle or before a parade of victorious legions. On the Arch of Constantine (315 C.E.) in Rome there is a well-preserved older sculpture of Marcus Aurelius giving an *adlocutio* to a gathering of soldiers.

10. That building is now the headquarters of the UN's Food and Agriculture Organization. The Axum obelisk (one of seven from that ancient site) is 24 m tall and weighs 180 t; in 1937 it was reconstructed from broken pieces. Its return to Ethiopia began, after decades of postponed promises, in 2003, when it had to be cut into three sections. Finally, in 2005 the sections were flown to Axum by a Russian giant cargo plane Antonov An-124.

11. Stalin gave explicit approval to Kim Il Sung's attack on the United States and South Korean armies on June 25, 1950. On the origins of the Korean War, see Goncharov, Lewis, and Litai (1993) and Thornton (2001).

12. The final dissolution meeting of Russian, Ukrainian, and Belorussian leaders was held in, of all places, a wooden hunting lodge at the Belovezhskaya Pushcha, a forest reserve near the Polish border known for containing the last remaining herd of European bison.

13. The term was used by the field officers when they informed General Schwarzkopf about the route of the retreating Iraqi Army, and the prospect of additional destruction contributed to the decision to end the war. See Norman Schwarzkopf's interview with *Frontline* (PBS 1996).

14. Persistence of Japan's economic difficulties is illustrated by the fact that during the year 2008 the Nikkei index was still below 15,000, or more than 60% below its 1989 peak.

15. The label soft power may be new—Nye (1991; 2004) has been the concept's most enthusiastic proponent—but the practice is ancient: the Romans were masters at using soft power, for instance, granting Roman citizenship to distinguished barbarians and constructing luxurious *thermae* in distant outposts of the empire.

16. Although it must be said that China, with its tens of thousands of censors and blocking of Web sites has had considerable success (helped by the reprehensible cooperation by Yahoo and Google) in stoppering the bottles containing those heady vapors.

17. The average size of Japan's dwellings is now almost exactly 95 m^2 (Statistics Bureau 2008).

18. Some of America's most notable excesses (absolute and relative) are addressed briefly in chapter II.

19. Vidal's musings on the decline and fall of the American empire appeared as early as 1992. He published the latest edition of his *Imperial America* in 2005. I examine the validity of his assertions in some detail in chapter II.

20. A collection of *Krokodil's* cartoons of "enemies and friends" was published for the journal's sixtieth anniversary (Semenov 1983); there is also a volume in English (*Krokodil* 1989).

21. Deficit spending by the Bush administration can be only partly justified by the exigencies of the post-9/11 world, including the funding for wars in Afghanistan and Iraq and the creation of a dysfunctional Department of Homeland Security. The two most important reasons for rising trade deficits were the continuing decline of U.S. manufacturing and, after 2004, the sharply higher cost of energy imports. Deficit statistics are available at USDT (2008), trade statistics at USCB (2008).

22. A Swede, Rudolf Kjellén, and an Englishman, Halford Mackinder, were the early proponents of geopolitical thinking at the beginning of the twentieth century, but the ideas were most eagerly embraced and developed in post–WW I Germany, with Karl Haushofer (founder of *Zeitschrift für Geopolitik*) as the leading theorist. For details, see Laack-Michel (1974).

23. A study in *Lancet*, criticized for its methodology, claimed that as of July 2006 there were about 655,000 excess Iraqi deaths as a consequence of war (Burnham et al. 2006). Iraq Body Count (2007), an impartial human security project, counted about 85,000 casualties by the end of 2007.

24. As with any Google search, these numbers offer only relative impressions because many only marginally related or unrelated entries are swept in by the simple (frequency-based) search algorithm.

25. A fine corrective of Napoleon's image as a heroic creator of united Europe is now available in a book by Ribbe (2005) that details the crimes against humanity committed by *le petit caporal*.

26. The percentage comes from a Gallup poll (Newport 2007) of Americans' perception of biblical accuracy. The 1991–2007 share of 31% of true believers is actually down from 38%, the rate that prevailed during 1978–1984, and there is also a high inverse correlation between education and belief in a literal Bible: 42% of people with a high school education or less believe so, but only 11% of people with postgraduate education do.

27. There is a rich literature on U.S.-European (mis)perceptions and mutual accusations. Some of the best insights have been offered by Revel (2003), Levy (2003), and Cox (2008).

28. This mispronunciation has become so common that I get startled when I hear a correct "et" coming from my TV.

29. Here is Lucretius (*De rerum natura* VI), first on Etna and then on Egyptian gales (Charles E. Bennett translation):

Earth may be moved, and over sea and land
May sweep the rapid whirlwind, and the fire
Of Aetna bursts its bounds, till all the heavens
Are bright with flame.

. . . .
The Nile alone of all the streams of earth
Doth rise at summer's advent and o'erflow
The plains of all the land of Egypt . . .
In summer's prime, those northern gales, which now

Men name etesian winds, pursue their course
Set dead against its mouth, and with their blasts,
Breasting high tides they check and stem his flow . . .

30. Augusta Treverorum is Trier on the Moselle in Germany, once a capital of the Roman province Gallia Belgica and a residence of Western Roman emperors; the great imperial audience hall where Valentinian I was crowned in 369 C.E. still stands. Dura Europos was a great multinational outpost on a high escarpment above the Euphrates (close to today's Syrian-Iraqi border) that was captured by the Romans in 165 C.E. and abandoned less than 100 years later, only to disappear under sands until 1920, when an accidental discovery led to its excavation (C. Hopkins 1979).

31. Tarraconensis was a prosperous part of northeastern Hispania, but during Roman times Barcino (today's Barcelona) was a smaller town than Tarraco (today's Tarragona), its capital. Fields in Paphlagonia (today's Sinop and Samsun provinces in Turkey on the southern shore of the Black Sea) still produce stone fruits (apricots, peaches, plums), and the sands of Syrtica (in today's northern Libya) still hide buried Roman structures.

Part 2   Introduction

1. The Roman universe (courtesy of the myth-loving Greeks) was full of triads: there were three graces (Gratiae), three Sirens, and three Gorgons; the entrance to the underworld was guarded by a three-headed dog (Cerberus); and Chimera was made up of three beasts (to mention just a few of the most famous examples). Lemprière's *Classical Dictionary of Proper Names Mentioned in Ancient Authors Writ Large* (originally published in 1788) is a standard guide to the exceedingly complex Graeco-Roman mythology.

2. Reasons advanced for the fall of the Roman Empire have ranged from such overarching causes as moral decay, military overextension, and barbarian invasions to more specific factors, including the influence of Christianity, the debasement of the currency, and the effects of chronic lead poisoning. Singling out a sole factor and arguing strongly in its favor is akin to those misguided, futile modern attempts at isolating individual micronutrients (vitamins, minerals, antioxidants) that supposedly hold the key to longevity.

Chapter II

1. Writing in the middle of the second century B.C.E., Polybius (I:2) had no doubts as he compared Greeks, Macedonians, and Persians with the Romans: "The Romans, on the other hand, have brought not just mere portions but almost the whole of the world under their rule, and have left an empire which far surpasses any that exists today or is likely to succeed it."

2. For a contemporary account of the war and for its official history, see, respectively, Lodge (1899) and Halstead (1899); for a historical perspective consult Trask (1996).

3. By the treaty of Guadalupe Hidalgo, Mexico ceded 1.36 million km^2 (or 55%) of its territory. This cession encompassed the entire future states of California, Nevada, and Utah, most of Arizona, western parts of New Mexico and Colorado, and the southwestern corner of Wyoming, and it amounts to about 17% of the total area of the 48 contiguous states.

One of the most resolute critics of the Mexican war was Ulysses S. Grant, who eventually dictated magnanimous surrender terms at the end of the Civil War and who became the eighteenth president of the United States (1869–1877). He spent most of the war with Mexico as a regimental quartermaster but also led a company in combat. In his memoirs he was unequivocally critical of the Mexican conflict: "For myself, I was bitterly opposed to the measure, and to this day regard the war which resulted as one of the most unjust ever waged by a stronger against a weaker nation. It was an instance of a republic following the bad example of European monarchies, in not considering justice in their desire to acquire additional territory." (Grant 1885/6, 22). And one positive comment he made was more than outweighed by his belief that the roots of the Civil War were in the expansion: "It is to the credit of the American nation, however, that after conquering Mexico, and while practically holding the country in our possession, so that we could have retained the whole of it, or made any terms we chose, we paid a round sum for the additional territory taken; more than it was worth, or was likely to be, to Mexico. To us it was an empire and of incalculable value; but it might have been obtained by other means. The Southern rebellion was largely the outgrowth of the Mexican war. Nations, like individuals, are punished for their transgressions. We got our punishment in the most sanguinary and expensive war of modern times." (Grant 1885/6, 24).

4. Roman expansion beyond the Italian peninsula actually began during the First Punic War with the conquest of Sicilia (completed by 241 B.C.E.), followed by an unopposed takeover of Sardinia in 237 B.C.E. Its eastern Mediterranean phase was completed in 146 B.C.E. with the annexation of Greece and in 133 B.C.E. with the incorporation of Pergamum.

5. This is perhaps the best known and the most dissected period of Roman history. Rich sources include Caesar's meticulous account of the civil war (*Comentarii de bello civili*, a masterpiece to some, an over-detailed self-aggrandizement to others) and detailed descriptions of events in Tacitus and Suetonius.

6. This period of an increasingly precarious existence is covered in a great detail in Edward Gibbon's classic. Recent treatments of the period include those of Heather (2005), Ward-Perkins (2005), and Barbero (2007).

7. Constantin XI Palaiologos (Κωνσταντίνος Παλαιολόγος), who ruled for just five years a tiny remnant of a once grand empire, was killed at the end of the Muslim conquest of his capital on May 29, 1453.

8. Nerva, Trajan, Hadrian, Antoninus Pius, and Marcus Aurelius, if we do not count Lucius Verus, who held a temporary joint emperorship with Marcus.

9. The 1990s are a perfect example of stark contrasts when compared both with the 1980s and with the first decade of the twenty-first century: how rapidly America's international standing, its economic fortunes, and its overall confidence shifted from the gloom of the 1980s (record high oil prices, double-digit inflation, Reagan's costly military buildup, Japan's rising economic power, dollar/yen devaluation) to the exuberance of the 1990s and then again to fears and frustrations of the post-9/11 world.

10. Here is the complete text of the petition (available at <http://www.historiansagainstwar .org/>) *Historians Against the War Statement on the U.S. Occupation of Iraq (September 21, 2003).*

As historians, teachers, and scholars, we oppose the expansion of United States empire and the doctrine of pre-emptive war that have led to the occupation of Iraq. We deplore the secrecy, deception, and distortion of history involved in the administration's conduct of a war that violates international law, intensifies attacks on civil liberties, and reaches toward domination of the Middle East and its resources. Believing that both the Iraqi people and the American people have the right to determine their own political and economic futures (with appropriate outside assistance), we call for the restoration of cherished freedoms in the United States and for an end to the U.S. occupation of Iraq.

11. Alfred Thayer Mahan (1840–1914, a West Point–trained naval officer) became most famous for his massive work on *The Influence of Sea Power upon History* (1890) and for his advocacy of the possession of distant ports to serve the U.S. Navy. Brooks Adams (1848–1927, John Quincy's grandson) anticipated the emergence of New York as the world's capital of finance and published *America's Economic Superiority* (1900) and *The New Empire* (1902). Theodore Roosevelt (1858–1919) was the Secretary of Navy before the Spanish-American War, and during the war he organized and commanded the first volunteer cavalry regiment (Rough Riders). These were two key stepping stones to his becoming the twenty-sixth president (1901–1909). Henry Cabot Lodge (1850–1924) was, as a senator, instrumental in preventing the United States from joining the post–WW I League of Nations.

12. Gore Vidal's 1986 plea for the United States making "a common cause" with the USSR in order to match "the Sino-Japanese axis that will dominate the future" (2005, 53–54) is yet another example of how even an incisive thinker is not immune to ideological zeal that displaces critical thinking (Vidal was Mikhail Gorbachev's great admirer). Five years later the USSR was gone; a generation later there is no sign of Vidal's feared Sino-Japanese axis.

13. Quebec separatists will not be satisfied with any federal concession as long as they will not become complete *maîtres chez nous*. Canada's northern territories have only the powers ceded to them by the federal government, and these do not include the right of taxation.

14. During the early 1950s, Communist Czechoslovakia had (compared to other nations ruled from Moscow) a disproportionately large number of political prisoners in concentration camps; show trials copying the infamous proceedings in Moscow of the late 1930s ended up with the hanging of 11 prominent Communist party and government officials; and Prague had the world's tallest statue of Stalin on a plain above Vltava's steep left bank—all of it without any direct occupation by Soviet forces (that came only in August 1968, and it lasted until 1989).

15. The term thus straddled an abstract territory between constitutional law and religion: an individual was chosen to hold the *imperium* but "received it from, or at least with the active connivance of, the god" (Richardson 1991, 3).

16. Examples of these empires run through history; their prototype was the Phoenician expansion in the Mediterranean from a base at Tyre in southern Lebanon (Harden 1962; Moscati 1999). The Dutch and the Portuguese conquests are the best early modern examples of such leveraged empires. And, of course, Venetians enjoyed for centuries similar benefits without actually controlling any overseas territories.

17. This is how Deady (2005, 53) put it: "The United States topples an unsavory regime in relatively brief military action, suffering a few hundred fatalities. America then finds itself

having to administer a country unaccustomed to democratic self-rule. Caught unawares by an unexpectedly robust insurgency, the United States struggles to develop and implement an effective counterinsurgency strategy. . . . These events—from a century ago—share a number of striking parallels with the events of 2003 and 2004." Eventually a total of about 126,000 American soldiers fought in the Philippine war (although the peak troop level never surpassed 70,000) and 4,234 died. For comparison, in January 2007 (before the troop "surge") there were 132,000 U.S. troops in Iraq, and the total casualties (combat and accidents) were just short of 4,000 by the end of 2007.

18. America's multinationals continue to maintain global leadership in many industries and services. In 2007 (in an annual survey conducted by *Business Week*), seven out of the world's top ten best global brands were American: Coca Cola, Microsoft, IBM, GE, Intel, McDonald's, and Disney. Nokia (Finland) came fifth, Toyota (Japan) sixth, and Mercedes (Germany) tenth. U.S. companies also took seven spots in the next group of ten.

19. I chose the epigraph's translation by E. Fairfax Taylor, first published in 1907, because it reads well. At the same time, it exemplifies the contrast between Latin's admirable parsimony and an all-too-common tendency to embellish the translated text: the brevity and all-encompassing nature of *metas rerum* and *rerum dominos* surely has a superior ring to such dilatory phrasing as "bounds to their dominion" and "rulers of the land and sea."

20. The Latin text of *Res Gestae Divi Augusti* is available at the Latin Library (<http://www.thelatinlibrary.com/aug.html>); an English translation (*The Deeds of the Divine Augustus* by T. Bushnell), at the Internet Classics Archive <http://classics.mit.edu/>.

21. Ptolemy is known for his *Almagest* (summation of astronomical knowledge; the Arabic title is due to the ninth-century translation that preserved it) but above all for his *Geographia*. Its first, theoretical, part describes the techniques used to prepare the map of *oikoumene*, the second supplies the numerous coordinates. Berggren and Jones (2000) published an annotated and well-illustrated translation of the first part. Burton (1932) gave a brief general introduction to geographical knowledge in antiquity.

22. The *Periplus* is certainly one of the most fascinating documents that reached us from Roman antiquity. An anonymous author (most likely a Greek shipmaster who lived in Egypt) put together a unique combination of a mariner's handbook, a trade directory, and a historical and political guide to the waters, shores, ports (and even some hinterlands) of the Red Sea and Indian Ocean between Arabia, East Africa, and India. For an English translation, see Huntingford (1980).

23. These structures were built of turf and timber, and hence they left no above-ground traces (Fields 2005), unlike the sections of *vallum Antonini* and its more southerly twin *vallum Hadriani*, which cut the island from the Tyne to Solway Firth.

24. Pliny, who knew the distance between Carnuntum (in Austria) and the Baltic Sea fairly correctly, devoted a long section to amber and mentioned a Roman knight (*eques*) who traveled from the empire's Danubian border to the Baltic coast and brought back to Rome a rich hoard of *sucinum* that included a piece weighing 13 pounds (*Naturalis Historia* XXXVII; XI:30–45).

25. Cassius Dio, *Romaika* LXVIII:29: "Then he came to the ocean itself, and when he had learned its nature and had seen a ship sailing to India, he said: 'I should certainly have crossed over to the Indi, too, if I were still young.' For he began to think about the Indi and was

curious about their affairs, and he counted Alexander a lucky man" (E. Cary translation).

26. Pliny (*Naturalis Historia* XII;XIV:29) noted that other foodstuffs were imported from afar because of their sweetness or appearance "but pepper has nothing to recommend it in either fruit or berry." Hence his incredulous exclamation: "*Sola placere amaritudine, et hanc in Indos peti!*" (Its only pleasing quality is pungency, and we go all the way to India to get it!).

27. According to Pliny (*Naturalis Historia* VI;XX:54), the Seres were famous for their *lanicio silvarum nobiles, perfusam aqua depectentes frondium canitiem . . . tam multiplici opere, tam longinquo orbe petitur ut in publico matrona traluceat* (fine silk that their woods yield. They collect from the leaves of the trees their hoary down, and when it is steeped in water they card it . . . with so much labor and so far away is it sought after, that our matrons when they go abroad in the street may shine with transparency). As for their behavior, *Seres mites quidem, sed et ipsi feris similes coetum reliquorum mortalium fugiunt, commercia exspectant* (The Seres are a mild people, but they resemble beasts, in that they fly the company of other people when they desire intercourse with them).

28. Camels were introduced to the eastern Sahara (Sudan and Egypt) from southern Arabia during the second and first century B.C.E., and from there they slowly spread westward; the trans-Saharan camel-borne trade in western Africa dates only from the second to the fifth century C.E. (Bulliet 1975; Curtin 1984).

29. As a result, after more than four centuries of Roman rule of the North African littoral, the Romans did not know much more about sub-Saharan Africa than did the former Greek geographers (Snowden 1970). In contrast, the Phoenicians (under Hanno) had sailed as far as the Gulf of Guinea by 450 B.C.E. We have a fascinating brief summary of that journey from the lost *Periplous* of Xenophon of Lampsakos: the expedition included 60 ships of 50 oars and 30,000 men and women with provisions, and it eventually reached the land of *gorilla*, most likely today's Cameroon. For the brief account, see Irby-Massie and Keyser (2002).

30. Beloch's (1886) detailed measurements (using topographic maps where available) ended up with 3.3395 million km^2 in 14 C.E., including 2.231 million km^2 in Europe, 665,500 km^2 in Asia, and 443,000 km^2 in Africa. Taagepera (1978) used the total of 4.4 million km^2 for the greatest extent of the Roman Empire. My measurements, done on the maps in figure II.9, resulted in totals of 2.64 million km^2 in 44 B.C.E., 4.36 million km^2 in 117 C.E., and 4.58 million km^2 in 294 C.E.

31. Augustus, in his *Res Gestae* (XXIX), lists as one of his notable achievements the fact that he was able to compel the Parthians to restore the spoils and standards that three Roman armies lost at Carrhae and make them seek the friendship of the Roman people: *Parthos trium exercitum Romanorum spolia et signa reddere mihi supplicesque amicitiam populi Romani petere coegi.* He claimed that they were doing so as suppliants; but who got the spoils and standards and kept them for more than 30 years?

32. America's historically unique position as the sole nuclear power between 1945 and the early 1950s (the first test of the Soviet atomic bomb took place on August 29, 1949, but the USSR did not possess the number of bombs needed to launch an intercontinental airborne attack until a few years later) leads to some intriguing speculations. What would Hitler or Stalin have done in the same situation? What would have been the Roman course of action

if the emperor had commanded a weapon able to annihilate entire cities and destroy entire armies?

33. We can never reconstruct the GDP of even a single ancient nation with any satisfactory approximation, and any global figures are more in the realm of educated guesses. (In chapter IV, I review the best attempt at reconstructing the Roman per capita rate.) Nevertheless, Maddison (2001) boldly offered these regional breakdowns for the beginning centuries of c.e.: Western Europe about 11%; Asia, excluding Japan, 75%.

34. In Europe 16 countries were the beneficiaries of the Marshall Plan, which disbursed $13 billion (expressed in 2005 monies) between 1948 and 1952. Germany got most of this sum, about $9.3 billion. With other relief funds the total U.S. assistance to Germany amounted to $29.3 billion (60% of it as straight grants) between 1946 and 1952. During the same period Japan got $15.2 billion (77% of it as grants; both totals are in 2005 dollars). Only a small part of the aid received as loans was ever repaid. The aid included both badly needed food to ensure minimum dietary intakes and raw materials (above all, oil) and manufactured inputs (machinery, vehicles, agricultural equipment) required to speed up the economic recovery of the two nations (Serafino, Tarnoff, and Nanto 2006).

35. Large differences in the published grand totals are due to different assumptions regarding future Medicare, Medicaid, and Social Security claims and any intervening legislation to address these approaching crises.

36. In January 2006 even the Texan oilman who became the forty-third president of the United States finally acknowledged the country's addiction to foreign oil (Bush 2006). In 2007 the second largest oil exporters to the United States were Mexico and Saudi Arabia (each about 14%), followed by Venezuela (13%) and Nigeria (11%). What a group to be dependent on: a corrupt *narcotraficante* state, a country run by a family according to medieval rules, a nation led by a contemptuous Castroist, and Africa's leading cleptocracy. By the way, in 2007, Iraq supplied less oil to the United States than Angola (EIA 2008c).

37. U.S. oil imports are a complicated matter. The country imports crude (unrefined) oil as well liquefied petroleum gases and refined petroleum products (gasoline, kerosene, fuel oil), and it also exports fuels in the latter category. In 2006 its net crude and product imports amounted to about 670 Mt, equivalent to about 71% of the country's liquid fuel consumption. Canada is the leading supplier of imported oil, followed by Saudi Arabia, Mexico, Venezuela, and Nigeria. In addition, the United States has been a major importer of liquefied natural gas and a substantial buyer of Canadian electricity.

38. But these concerns are not new: during the late 1980s the same questions were asked as the yen was ascendant (Heldring 1988).

39. American intervention in Hungary or Czechoslovakia was not even considered: control of these two countries, and of Poland, was surrendered by Roosevelt to Stalin as a part of the Yalta agreements (Fenno 1972).

40. Just over 9 million Americans served in the Southeast Asia during the Vietnam War, with 2.6 million in South Vietnam and 1–1.6 million as combat troops. The official death toll due to hostile action was 47,378, and there were 10,800 nonhostile deaths and 2,318 missing in action. The conflict began officially in August 5, 1964, and direct U.S. military involvement ended on March 28, 1973. For details, see chapter 10 in Stewart (2005).

41. The commander of the rescue Delta Force acknowledged that "the assault plan was sketchy. Its chances for success were very slender indeed" (Beckwith and Knox 1983, 218). He also admitted that U.S. armed forces simply did not have resources or capabilities to pull off such a rescue. Appropriately, Lenahan's (1998) book on U.S. special operations between 1976 and 1996 was entitled *Crippled Eagle*. Reagan's later dealings with Iran—including a bizarre controversy involving a Bible and a cake (did Robert McFarlane, Reagan's security adviser, carry them to the ayatollahs, as a CIA man who accompanied him said he did, or did he not, as he maintained?), arms sales and diversion of monies for the Nicaraguan rebels—were hardly the actions worthy of a superpower.

42. The Committee on Armed Services of the U.S. House of Representatives (1983) produced an official report on the inadequate security of the U.S. Marine base. The history of the mission is detailed in Hammel (1985). Spiral wire (concertina) and a wall of sandbags were the only barriers protecting the barracks against a truck bomb attack. Imād Mughnīyah, the organizer of the bombing—as well as of the attack on the French troops that took place the same day (58 dead), the attack on the U.S. Embassy in Beirut in April 1983 (63 dead), the hijacking of a TWA flight in 1985, and numerous suicide missions in Israel—had spent a quarter century on the FBI's (and other countries') most wanted list before he was killed (by a car bomb) in Syria on February 12, 2008.

43. U.S. District Judge Royce C. Lamberth, who presided in a civil lawsuit of two plaintiffs against the Islamic Republic of Iran, called the attack "the largest non-nuclear explosion that had ever been detonated on the face of the Earth"; the expert testimony put the force of the explosive (pentaerythritol tetranitrate) equivalent to 6800–9500 kg TNT (CBS News 2003). In energy terms, the higher level is about 20 times that of a typical car or truck bomb, and a suicide bomber on foot explodes with just 0.25% of the energy of the 1983 bomb.

44. And, I should add, after a prevented attempt to fly an Air France jet into the Eiffel tower. A detailed timeline of these events is available at PBS (2005). A translation of al-Qaeda's training manual (discovered by the Manchester (England) Metropolitan Police during a house search) is available at <http://www.usdoj.gov/ag/manualpart1_1.pdf>.

45. Colin Powell ended his UN address on February 5, 2003, by saying that "the United States will not and cannot run that risk to the American people. Leaving Saddam Hussein in possession of weapons of mass destruction for a few more months or years is not an option, not in a post–September 11th world" (Powell 2003). In his 1995 memoirs, when he recalled his opposition to committing U.S. forces in Bosnia, he insisted that "American GIs are not toy soldiers to be moved around on some sort of global board" (Powell and Persico 1996, 576).

46. As far as I know, nobody has attempted to quantify the consequences of the war for the Iraqi economy, but the forfeited production of crude oil alone (calculated as the difference between the average outputs of 1998–2002 and 2003–2007) amounts to roughly $50 billion in five years. But I must add that as a former citizen of the Evil Empire, I have never had any doubts about the all too obvious parallels between Stalin and the Iraqi dictator and about the desirability of ending Hussain's murderous regime.

47. Joschka Fischer, a leftist and for men radical firebrand turned into a *Realo Grün*.

48. The intensity of Turkish anti-Americanism puts the country even ahead of Pakistan: in 2006 the Pew Global Attitudes Project found that only 12% of Turks had a favorable opinion

of the United States, compared to 27% in Pakistan and 43% in Russia; and a year later 64% of Turks identified the United States as a major threat to their country, the same share as in Pakistan (Pew Research Center 2007).

49. The French withdrew from the integrated military organization on March 7, 1966, and NATO removed its headquarters from Versailles on April 1, 1967. For details and the historical setting of these actions, see Bozo (2001). But two generations later a new French president turned out to be the only Western leader willing to offer some (albeit very limited) help: in the spring of 2008, America's call for more troops to stabilize Afghanistan was ignored by all of its NATO allies (countries with a combined population of more than 500 million) except for the French offer of an additional battalion, or 750 soldiers. And in 2009 Sarkozy's France rejoined NATO as a full member.

Chapter III

1. Modern civilization harnesses the following extrasomatic energies on commercial scales: *solar energy*, both directly (mainly through photovoltaic conversion to electricity) and indirectly, as flowing water (in hydroelectric plants) and wind (using wind turbines) and phytomass (by combustion of wood, charcoal, and crop residues and by conversion of crops to ethanol and biodiesel); *geothermal energy* of the Earth's crust (for electricity generation and heating); *chemical energy* of fossil fuels (released by combustion, with final uses as heat, electricity, and motion); and *nuclear energy* (by fissioning heavy nuclei to generate heat and then electricity).

2. Athena (Roman: Minerva), a goddess of wisdom and skill (but also of war and justice), was a child of Zeus (Roman: Jupiter) and Metis (another goddess of wisdom). Her most unusual gestation (Zeus devoured the pregnant Metis) led to an equally unorthodox birth (Athena sprang full-grown and armed from Zeus's forehead).

3. The mass of charcoal needed to produce 1 kg of iron declined from as much as 20 kg in antiquity to about 8 kg by the end of the eighteenth century. Ancient sailing ships could proceed only when the wind was directly astern or less than 30° off course; medieval ships could sail slowly with the wind on the beam (90°), and nineteenth-century clippers could come as close as 45° to the wind. Typical early medieval waterwheels rated mostly between 1 kW and 2 kW, whereas many nineteenth-century machines had power greater than 100 kW. For details on these technical advances, see Smil (1994; 2008a).

4. The following Renaissance masters were active at the turn of the sixteenth century: Sandro Botticelli (1445–1510), Leonardo da Vinci (1452–1519), Raphael (1483–1520), Michelangelo Buonarroti (1475–1564), and Tiziano Vecellio (Titian; 1477?–1576). What are the chances that artists of comparable caliber will once again be active during the same short period?

5. A good example of this temporary advantage is the British share of the world's economic product: in 1700, when Britain had about 1.4% of the world's population, its share of economic product was less than 3%; by 1870, when it had about 2.5% of the world's population, its share of economic product was nearly 15% (Maddison 2007).

6. Hughes (1983, 18) captured Edison's unique contribution perfectly: "Edison was a holistic conceptualizer and determined solver of the problems associated with the growth of systems."

7. During the nineteenth century the European innovators were often ahead of their American counterparts. Joseph Wilson Swan worked out the basic design of an electric lightbulb nearly two decades before Edison did, and he has official British recognition as the bulb's rightful pioneer (Bowers 1998). And German and French engineers and mechanics pioneered the design and development of gasoline-fueled internal combustion engines and early cars during the 1880s and 1890s. But it was General Electric that led the creation of electrified cities and households and the Ford Motor Company that transformed a car from an expensive oddity to the most commonly owned large machine.

Similar examples can be cited for the post-1945 period. Britain's de Havilland Comet (introduced in 1952) was the world's first commercial jetliner, and Concorde, a joint British-French project (conceived in 1956; money-losing flights only since 1976), was to be the future of intercontinental travel, but neither was a commercial success. A trio of American companies, Boeing, McDonnell Douglas, and Lockheed, led the jet revolution (Airbus came along only in the early 1970s), and wide-bodied jets, all derived from Boeing's pioneering 747, became the future of mass aviation.

8. That many American scientists publishing important findings and receiving patents and Nobel prizes are naturalized citizens does not weaken the conclusion about America's inventive and innovative primacy; just the opposite is true because the country provides conditions suitable for the expression of talent that might otherwise have remained unused or underused.

9. This is a suspect explanation. China's ancient intellectual tradition is not exactly brimming with descriptions of quotidian techniques and with odes to machinery, either, but the Han dynasty was a time of remarkably multifaceted innovation.

10. Ancient life dates in this and subsequent chapters one approximations.

11. According to Vitruvius (*De Architectura* IX:215), Archimedes discovered his famous displacement theorem when he stepped into a bath and noticed that the water level rose, understanding then that the volume of displaced water was equal to the volume of an object immersed in it. Having found a solution to the problem of calculating the volume of irregular objects, he exclaimed, *Eureka!* (εύρηκα! I have found it!). Pappus of Alexandria (*Synagoge* VIII), writing five centuries after Archimedes was killed (212 B.C.E.) during the siege of the Greek city of Syracuse by the Romans under Marcellus, attributed to him a hyperbolic summation of the power of mechanics; δος μοι που στω και κινω την γην (Give me a place to stand, and I shall move the Earth). Several accounts including *Plutarch's Lives: Marcellus*, describe Archimedes' death at the hands of a Roman soldier (who did not know him) while Archimedes was absorbed in geometric figures he had drawn on the ground, but the legendary last words attributed to him, Μη μου τους κύκλους τάραττε! (*Noli turbare circulos meos!* Do not disturb my circles!) are not found in them.

12. Eratosthenes was the head of Alexandria's famous library. Ironically, in his attempt to make a more accurate estimate of the Earth's size he inserted an erroneous observation into the previously accurate data (Rawlins 1982).

13. The best reconstruction of the Antikythera device and detailed explanations of its functions can be found in Freeth et al. (2008).

14. But there is a possibility that the water screw was invented much earlier, during the reign of the Assyrian king Sennacherib (704–681 B.C.E.) and that it was used to water palace gardens in Nineveh (Dalley and Oleson 2003).

15. Many modern commentators found this inexplicable and saw it as proof that Frontinus did not understand even such a basic concept as speed. For excellent reviews and possible solutions of the *quinaria* puzzle, see Hodge (1984) and Rodgers (1986).

16. The water supply for Pergamum (in Mysia, today's northwestern Turkey) was particularly impressive (Garbrecht et al. 1987). Its construction began during the second half of the third century B.C.E., and ten aqueducts were completed during the Hellenistic period, including the triple Madradag line of 42 km that contained a pressurized section and a siphon able to withstand pressures of up to 20 atmospheres when crossing a valley 180 m deep.

17. Pliny (*Historia Naturalis* XVIII:296) describes it clearly: *Galliarum latifundis valli praegrandes, dentibus in margine insertis, duabus rotis per segetem inpelluntur, iumento in contrarium iuncto; ita dereptae in vallum cadunt spicae* (In the vast domains of the provinces of Gaul a large hollow frame, armed with teeth and supported on two wheels, is driven through the standing corn, the beasts being yoked behind it; the result being, that the ears are torn off and fall within the frame) (Bostock and Riley 1855 translation). There are also a few extant depictions, but the machine disappeared with the demise of Roman rule. Two people were needed to operate it, one to guide the animal, the other (walking alongside or backward in front of it) to knock down the cut heads into a trough.

18. With about 0.5 m³ of stone and gravel and 5 m³ of soil handled per capita per day, the tasks of quarrying, cutting, crushing, and moving stone and gravel, fashioning embankments, preparing concrete and mortar, and laying the road required on the order of 1 billion labor days. If regular maintenance and repairs were to triple this labor, it would still amount to an annual mean of no more than 6 million labor days per year during the period of some 500 years, or an equivalent of some 20,000 full-time construction workers, an easily manageable feat in a state with a nonagricultural labor force of at least 1.5–2 million.

19. Lime (*calx*) has been produced for millennia by the calcination (heating) of limestone. The resulting CaO is hydrated to yield calcium hydroxide, slaked lime, which is used as a bonding agent. The reaction between the bonding agent and water (hydration) produces material that is very strong in compression (but weak in tension) and that can be fashioned into an endless variety of shapes. Davidovits's radical conclusion has apparently been confirmed by scanning and electron microscopy analysis of pyramid limestone samples and comparison with limestones from the site's vicinity (Barsoum, Ganguly, and Hug 2006).

20. The addition of *pulvere puteolano* had the effect (to use modern terms) of converting nonhydraulic Roman lime into hydraulic lime; they obtained the same effect by mixing crushed pottery with the mortar (Adam 1994).

21. This was a major metallurgical advance: previous smelting in hearths produced only relatively small masses of solid spongy iron that had to be transformed (by reheating and hammering) into wrought iron.

22. Rather than merely loosening the soil surface, as early ard plows did, the curved share of a moldboard turns the plowed-up soil to one side and thus buries the cut weeds and at the same time cleans the furrow bottom for the next turn and makes cross-plowing unnecessary. Incredibly, this great innovation, introduced in China before the first century B.C.E., was widely adopted in Europe only during the seventeenth century.

23. When Edwin Drake drilled his famous first Pennsylvania well in 1859, he used manila ropes rather than bamboo cables; multiple-strand steel wires came later.

24. The collar harness reached Europe by the end of the ninth century, and it came into general use three centuries later; then it remained largely unchanged until work horses were replaced by machines.

25. All grain grinding was originally done laboriously by rubbing stones or mortars and pestles, yielding at best 2–3 kg of flour per hour. Manual rotary querns date to the first century B.C.E., and when worked by two people, they could produce about 12 kg of flour per hour.

26. The best known, and also the most contentious, case is a poem *Mosella* by Ausonius (c.370 C.E.) with a description of water-driven saws cutting marble in the valley of the Ruwar (near Trier) whose power *praecipiti torquens cerealia saxa rotatu stridentesque trahens per levia marmora serras* (turns the millstones in rapid revolutions and drives the shrieking saws through smooth blocks of marble). Principal questions concern the poem's authenticity, its dating, and the technical details of converting the rotary power of waterwheels to a reciprocating power of saws. For details see Simms (1983).

27. *Lady Isabella*, an overshot wheel that worked between 1854 and 1926 on the Isle of Man, was the largest single-machine installation. The wheel's diameter was 21.9 m, and it delivered about 200 kW of useful power during normal operation (J. Reynolds 1970).

28. Sagui (1948) made unrealistic estimates of average water speed (2.5 m/s, whereas 0.8–1.0 m/s is most likely), water flow (1000 L/s), and average productivity (24 t of flour in 24 h, enough to produce bread for some 80,000 people). Sellin (1983) estimated the flow at 300 L/s and daily output of 4.5 t of flour. Leveau (2006, 7) put the flow at 260 L/s, and Russo (2004) suggested that the Barbegal mill might represent a pre-Roman technical tradition that the Romans found convenient to keep: an ancient Greek colony of mechanically adept Massilians controlled the area for centuries before the Romans. Sagui's assumption of converting 65% of water's kinetic energy to the millstone rotation was also too high. In 1759, Smeaton's calculations showed 63% to be the maximum efficiency of the much better built overshots and Denny's (2004) theoretical calculation put that limit at 71%.

29. I am assuming that a typical small Roman horse could work at a rate of 500 W, or about two-thirds of standard horsepower; but such a mill would need seven to eight good-sized donkeys.

30. I am assuming a total population of 60 million with 25 million adults working at an average rate of 60 W for 300 eight-hour days and 6 million draft and pack animals delivering average useful power at 300 W per head for 200 eight-hour days. The first total adds up to 20, the second one to 10, quadrillion joules of useful energy.

31. Ideally, the clearance between *meta* and *catillus* should have been the thickness of a grain of wheat. If the two parts came into contact in too many places the stones would overheat and burn the flour; if they were too far apart, the product would be too rough. Obviously, frequent adjustments and recutting of stones were needed.

32. His description (*Metamorphoses* IX, 12) is worth quoting at length because this is how the empire's staple was made: *Dii boni, quales illic homunculi vibicibus lividis totam cutem depicti dorsumque plagosum scissili centunculo magis inumbrati quam obtecti, nonnulli exiguo tegili tantum modo pubem iniecti, cuncti tamen sic tunicati, ut essent per pannulos manifesti, frontes litterati et capillum semirasi et pedes annulati, tum lurore deformes et fumosis tenebris vaporosae caliginis palpebras adesi atque adeo male luminati et in modum*

pugilum, qui pulvisculo perspersi dimicant, farinulenta cinere sordide candidati. (O good Lord what a sort of poore slaves were there; some had their skinne blacke and blew, some had their backes striped with lashes, some were covered with rugged sackes, some had their members onely hidden: some wore such ragged clouts, that you might perceive all their naked bodies, some were marked and burned in the heads with hot yrons, some had their haire halfe clipped, some had lockes of their legges, some very ugly and evill favoured, that they could scarce see, their eyes and facc were so blacke and dimme with smoake, like those that fight in the sands, and know not where they strike by reason of dust: And some had their faces all mealy. [Adlington translation, 1566])

33. That is nearly 50 times as much as the power of large machines (steam turbogenerators in fossil-fueled and nuclear plants, and turbines in hydro stations) used to generate electricity, but these large machines work almost continuously (70% to more than 90% of the time, that is, 6000–8000 h per year), whereas an average car covering a distance of about 30,000 km per year at 60 km/h works only about 500 h per year.

34. China's last dynasty, the Qing of the Manchus, withered away only in 1911, and despite the following decades of radical upheavals (civil war, war with Japan, the Communist takeover) many ancient perceptions and attitudes are readily identifiable even in currently modernizing China.

35. The total fossil fuel resources (all solid, liquid, and gaseous fuels present in the Earth's crust) may be equal to as much as roughly 4.75 trillion t of crude oil. At the 2008 rate of energy consumption this could support global civilization for another 500 years. That is a purely theoretical consideration because most fuels (being too deep or too expensive to recover) will remain untouched, and we will have turn to other sources (renewable or nuclear) for future supply.

36. Canada's slightly higher per capita energy use is due largely to two factors: high levels of energy production for export (it is America's largest supplier of both oil and natural gas) and cold climate; these aside, its per capita use would be much like America's.

37. A common denominator is needed to express the energy content of different sources, and quoting the rates in metric tons of oil (toe) is a better choice than using the scientific unit of energy, joule (J), with which few people are comfortable. One toe contains about 42 billion joules (GJ); for comparison, 1 tonne (1 t) of coal, commonly used for electricity generation, is equal to about 0.5 toe; 1 t of air-dried wood is equal to about 0.33 toe; and 1 m^3 of natural gas, with 35 million joules (MJ), has an energy content of less than 0.001 toe.

38. Apparent annual consumption rates in 2008 (all in toe per capita) were about 12.5 in Kuwait, 15 in Trinidad, 25 in Qatar, 29 in UAE, and 50 in Virgin Islands. The first four rates are explained by energy used to produce and export oil and gas; the last one by the refueling of cruise ships. In all these cases the actual domestic per capita energy use is less than in the United States.

39. The intensity of labor is conveniently expressed in terms of the metabolic equivalent (MET), the quotient of the work rate divided by the resting metabolic rate (1 MET is roughly equal to the energy cost of sitting). Standing needs 1.2–1.3 MET; light labor 1.8–2.0 MET; and moderate and heavy exertions common in traditional farming (plowing, planting, weeding, harvesting) 4–6 MET (Smil 2008a).

40. I calculated this total by assuming 40 million ha of annually sown croplands (the total derived from overall food requirements for 60 million people whose intakes were dominated by grains) and typical draft labor for 200 eight-hour days; the actual total may have been as low as 4 million but not higher than 6 million oxen.

41. This is a very difficult estimate to make because many oxen used for fieldwork were also used for transport.

42. Assuming average daily intake rate based on modern metabolic studies of horses (Smil 2008a).

43. I assume (all rates are per capita) 1 kg of wood per day for cooking and bread baking; 500 kg of wood per year for space heating (for roughly one-third of the empire's population); and average consumption of 2 kg of metals requiring about 60 kg wood per kilogram of metal. This results in an annual per capita demand of 650 kg of wood (or, in modern terms, the equivalent of about 230 kg of crude oil). Allen (2007) assumed daily rates of nearly 1 kg of wood per capita for a respectable household consumption basket and roughly 0.4 kg per capita for a bare-bones one.

44. There is a great deal of uncertainty regarding the precise meaning of *insula*, the total number of these structures in Rome (see chapter IV, note 37), their typical size, and their residential density (Hermansen 1978).

45. Inventive East Asians had come up with similar solutions. The Korean *ondol* (warm stone) used the hot combustion gases from the kitchen or additional fireplaces through brick or stone flues under concrete-covered granite floors, and North China's *kang* was a large (about 4–5 m²) heated platform used as a resting place during the day and a bed at night.

46. For historical comparisons of lighting efficiencies, see Fouquet and Pearson (2006).

47. This is what goes into *puls Juliana* according to the Roman collection of recipes known as *Apicius*: boiled cleaned *alica* (spelt), oil, a pair of pounded cooked brains, ground pork, lovage seed, peppercorns, fennel seed, meat stock and white wine. The final product is stirred and diluted until it has the thickness of a sauce (*ut quasi sucus videatur*). For more Roman recipes, see Faas (1994).

Chapter IV

1. Perhaps the best estimate, by the Pew Hispanic Center, was 11.5–12 million "unauthorized migrants" as of March 2006, about 5.4 million of them being adult males (Passel 2006). Other estimates are closer to 15 million. The U.S. Census Bureau put the total of illegal aliens at 3.3 million in 1990, and 8.7 million in 2000.

2. I hasten to add that even modern GDP figures must be seen as suspect. Perhaps the best recent example is a sharp reduction of China's GDP in PPP values: the World Bank's International Comparison Program now has it at about $4,100 per capita for 2005, compared to previously exaggerated estimates, which ranged from about $6,000 to well over $7,000 per capita for the same year (World Bank 2008).

3. A population expanding from 3 million to 7.5 million in about a century would be growing at an annual rate of roughly 1%, at least twice as fast as the highest posited growth rate in the Roman Egypt.

4. Naturally, plausible differences imply very different economic realities. For example, as Scheidel (2007) pointed out, either there was a densely populated Italy with a fairly high standard of living (that would be a great exception to the general pattern during antiquity), or with a stagnating economy, and increasingly impoverished population. No certainties are possible, just plausible arguments. That is why a really high Roman-Italian count is unlikely in comparison with later populations: after all, only 10–12 million people lived on the peninsula by 1850.

5. Such high residential densities prevail in Kwun Tong, the most densely populated part of Hong Kong's Kowloon (about 50,000 people/km^2). Tokyo's four central wards have about 55,000 people/km^2, and citywide densities are 40,000/km^2 in Manila and 20,000/km^2 in Paris. Manhattan's peak daily population is about 90,000 people/km^2. But all these modern examples include dwellings not just in multistoried buildings (in Paris typically five or six stories) but also in residential high-rises (Smil 2008a).

6. But it must be kept in mind that all comparisons of military mobilization based on simple shares of young men in active service (or in standing armies and reserves) tell us nothing about the level of preparedness and fighting prowess of a particular army or about the critical support its deployment enjoyed among the population.

7. Nor are the sources of Roman slaves clear (Harris 1999). We have no reliable information about any of the four ways of replenishing their numbers: specific fertility of the slave population; numbers of captured and imported slaves; self-enslavement; and enslaved foundlings (exposed children that were rescued and taken to slavery).

8. Egypt, unlike other provinces of the Roman Empire, had a most undesirable custom of endogamous marriages. Available data indicate that at least one-third of all brothers in families with marriageable sisters were married to them (K. Hopkins 1980; Bagnall and Frier 1994; Scheidel 1996). This practice was suppressed only with the Antoninian grant of Roman citizenship to the Egyptians in 212 C.E.

9. The only other affluent nations with total fertility around 2.0 in 2000–2005 were Iceland and New Zealand; in all other rich countries the rate was substantially below the replacement level, going as low as 1.3 in Japan, Spain, Italy, and Poland and 1.2 in the Czech Republic.

10. For details on the works of Domitius Ulpianus (160–228 C.E.), see Honoré (1982).

11. The Egyptian census data were not only limited but more than half the surviving lot came from the Fayum oasis, a stressful and unhealthy environment very different from conditions in the northern Mediterranean and even more so from those in Atlantic Europe. Given the large territorial extent of the Roman Empire, it makes little sense to offer a single life expectancy pattern. And while model life tables allow us to estimate basic vital statistics for populations that have no extant records, they are just abstract mathematical models, not descriptions of real populations. Moreover, no real populations are stable over extended periods of time, and given the heterogeneity of populations under Roman control, it would be unrealistic to expect one model to fit all.

12. Theodosius II reigned for 42 years (408–450 C.E.), but unlike Augustus he became the eastern emperor as a child, at age 7. On the other hand, five of the seven emperors that came after Commodus (in 180 C.E.) were assassinated, and, even worse, 14 out of 18 were murdered between 235 C.E. and 248 C.E. Being a Roman emperor during the third century was a perilous occupation by any standard.

13. Both the pace and the extent of future population aging are unprecedented in human history, and the process will affect everything from savings rates and consumption habits to values of real estate and stock markets.

14. The lowest infant mortalities (on the order of 3–4/1,000) are now experienced by such small or relatively homogeneous affluent populations as those of the Nordic countries and Japan. The American rate is elevated by higher infant mortalities among blacks (with many births to very young mothers and most births out of wedlock). In 2005 the nationwide mean for whites was 5.76; for blacks, 13.69, more than twice as much (CDC 2008). Infant mortalities are also higher than the mean among new poor Latino immigrants. But it must be stressed that infant mortality alone is not an ideal quasi-proxy for standard of living, and other factors must be considered. For example, infant mortality in a number of rapidly growing and industrializing cities of late-nineteenth-century Europe was still close to the Roman rate (well above 200), but the populations of those cities obviously had a standard of living much superior to the Roman (or today's sub-Saharan) way of life.

15. However, Faerman et al. (1998) reported on a cluster of mostly male infanticides in Roman Ashkelon that almost certainly had many counterparts elsewhere in the empire. They discovered skeletal remains of about 100 neonates thrown into a sewer beneath a Roman bathhouse (probably also a brothel). Ancient DNA could be recovered from 19 femurs, and its analysis showed that 14 were males. Such a high frequency of male infanticides suggests that the infants may have been children of the prostitutes working in the bathhouse who preserved many little girls for the continuation of their trade.

16. If it had been consumed without any losses, the average monthly Roman *anona* of 5 *modii* (that is 33.7 kg) of wheat per capita would have translated to no less than 15.4 MJ of food energy per day. Even if wheat had supplied a very high share (say 90%) of all food energy, the total availability would have reached about 17 MJ per day (about 4100 kcal per day), a total that is both substantially larger than the aggregate food energy supply in today's most affluent nations and much above the average food needs of Rome's population. On the other hand, if we assume (conservatively) transfer and storage losses totaling 10% and milling extraction of 85%, we get about 25 kg of wheat flour per month, or an equivalent of roughly 11.5 MJ per day (about 2750 kcal per day).

17. But according to Kron (2005), average male height during the Roman period equaled that of the mid-twentieth century mean.

18. The often cited water supply in Rome—on the order of 1 million m^3 (that is, 1 billion liters) per day—is impressive even in the modern context. Even with 1 million people it would prorate to 1000 L per capita. In contrast, daily per capita domestic water use (highly income-dependent) has ranged from about 700 L in the United States and 500 L in Canada to 400 L in Japan, 300 L in Italy, just over 100 L in Germany, and less than 50 L in low-income countries. But the estimates for ancient Rome are derived from aqueduct capacities, and because we cannot be sure about interannual and seasonal fluctuations of water flow or leakage rates, we do not know how much water was actually delivered.

19. Roman postelimination cleansing was done with a sponge on a stick. Our best information on these sponges reached us through an unexpected source, an epistle by Lucius Annaeus Seneca (*Epistulae morales*, LXX:20) describing the suicide of a German wild-beast gladiator who was facing the morning exhibition: "He withdrew in order to relieve himself, the only thing which he was allowed to do in secret and without the presence of a guard. While so

engaged, he seized the stick of wood, tipped with a sponge, which was devoted to the vilest uses, and stuffed it, just as it was, down his throat; thus he blocked up his windpipe, and choked the breath from his body" (Richard Gummers translation) (*secessit ad exonerandum corpus—nullum aliud illi dabatur sine custode secretum; ibi lignum id quod ad emundanda obscena adhaerente spongia positum est totum in gulam farsit et interclusis faucibus spiritum elisit*). The hygienic implications of such sponges need no elaboration.

20. Contemporary observations by Galen, the best known physician of Roman antiquity, describe black, ulcerated exanthema covering the entire body, a clear diagnostic sign of smallpox. But because the plague was still causing high mortality 14 years later, in 180 C.E., when Marcus Aurelius died, there may have been other pathogens involved (smallpox survivors would have acquired immunity).

21. As with other population-related quantifications, it is very difficult to come up with consistent, satisfactory estimates of the most likely annual immigration to Rome. For more on these challenges, see Lo Cascio (2001).

22. Using globalization in this context is yet another example of an inappropriate (frivolous, hyperbolic, anachronistic) use of a fashionable term.

23. In 2005 exports generated about 10% of U.S. GDP, but (as noted in chapter II) the country had a large trade deficit. For comparison, in 2005 exports accounted for 40% of Germany's and nearly 14% of Japan's GDP (WTO 2008).

24. American labor requirements were nearly 140 h/t of wheat at the beginning of the nineteenth century and about 50 h/t just before its end. In poor-weather years wheat yields during the late nineteenth century were as low in some Great Plains states as the Roman harvests in Italy (only about 0.5 t/ha), and the nationwide mean was below 1 t/ha. By 1950 it rose just above 1 t/ha, and by 2005 it was close to 3 t/ha, as was the average Italian yield (FAO 2008).

25. With a good pair of oxen it was expected to plow one *jugerum* (2675 m²) per day; one hectare (10,000 m²) took nearly four days, or on the order of 40 h of work. Plowing was followed by harrowing and seeding, manuring and occasional liming. Harvesting was done with sickles (the Gallic reaper was a relatively late invention and, in any case, was not in general use), threshing by driving animals over ears spread on the ground or by flailing. Reconstruction of inputs into Roman wheat farming indicates that 180–250 h of human labor and around 200 h of animal labor were needed to produce a typical grain harvest of about 500 kg/ha during the early centuries C.E. (Smil 1994).

26. These are simple gross supply rates, not actual food intakes, adjusted by applying the grain loss and milling rates outlined in note 16.

27. This was a major difference in comparison with America's pre–Civil War situation, when some slaves had relatively privileged positions inside a house but never as highly educated professionals.

28. By far the most convenient collections of historical reconstructions of national GDPs are by Maddison (2001; 2003; 2007).

29. The Roman *sestercius* (HS) was an ancient republican coin; HS 100 equaled one *aureus*, containing 8 g of gold, and hence the average Roman income of HS 380 would be equal to about 30 g of gold. In February 2008, when an ounce of gold reached $1,000, the income of HS 380 came to be almost exactly $1,000 (in 2008 dollars), the average per capita GDP

of Mali or Nepal; but taking the 1995–2008 mean gold value would more than halve the GDP rate and put it on par with those of the poorest sub-Saharan countries.

30. Taking 25 years as one generation and assuming a stationary population, such a doubling would require an annual GDP growth of 2.8%; with 20 years as one generation and population growth of 1% per year, annual GDP would have to grow by about 4.5%. Substantially higher rates during 20–25 year periods were achieved by Japan before 1990 and by China after 1980.

31. Maddison's (2007) provincial estimates imputed per capita rates as high as nearly $900 for peninsular Italy, $600 for Egypt, nearly as much for Roman Europe, and $550 for Roman Asia.

32. Allen's Mediterranean respectability basket includes the following quantities (all per year per capita): 182 kg of bread, 52 liters of beans, 26 kg of meat, 5.2 liters of olive oil, 5.2 kg of cheese, 52 eggs, 68.25 liters of wine, 2.6 kg of soap, 5 m of linen, 2.6 kg of candles, 2.6 liters of lamp oil, and an equivalent of about 350 kg of air-dried wood for fuel.

33. Allen's minimum subsistence basket (I consider it much closer to the modal consumption of Roman *plebs* than his respectability list) has 172 kg of wheat (or 155 kg of oats), 20 kg of beans or peas, 5 kg of meat, 5 liters of olive oil, 1.3 kg of soap, 3 m of linen, 1.3 kg of candles, 1.3 liters of lamp oil, and about 140 kg of wood. Its food energy prorates to about 1900 kcal per day.

34. U.S. sociologists put the share of middle class at only about 45% of the total population (Gilbert 2002; Beeghley 2004), but most Americans (more than 70%) perceive themselves to be in that category.

35. For comparison, Milanovic, Lindert, and Williamson (2007) also calculated analogical shares for Byzantium around the year 1000 at about 30%, for China of the 1880s at roughly 20%, and for Mughal India of 1750 at 15%. The recent U.S. share has been less than 7%.

36. But A. Reynolds (2007) argued that studies based on tax return data result in highly misleading comparisons and that, except for stock option windfalls during the late-1990s stock market boom, there has been little evidence of any significant or sustained rise in the inequality of America's incomes, wages, and wealth during the preceding 20 years.

37. Hermansen (1978) assumed that half of the city's area inside the Aurelian wall (total of 7.45 km^2) was taken up residential buildings, with 1,790 *domus* structures (average of 675 m^2) claiming 1.2 km^2, leaving 6.25 km^2 for *insulae*; with 250 m^2 per insula there would be some 25,000 structures.

38. Earlier reconstructions put the total area of Nero's megaproject, built between 65 and 69 C.E., at as much as 80 ha, but Warden's (1981) reevaluation of the best available evidence cut it to perhaps only half that size. I am using that much reduced total of 400,000 m^2. In any case, the madman who ordered its construction was satisfied with the result. When he moved in (according to Suetonius, *Vita Neronis* XXXI:2), he remarked that he could at last begin to live like a human being (*Eius modi domum cum absolutam dedicaret, hactenus comprobavit, ut se diceret quasi hominem tandem habitare coepisse*).

39. Diocletian's palace in Split, built between 295 C.E. and 305 C.E. as the emperor's retirement residence, was nearly as large: structures within its trapezoidal footprint (202 × 202 × 163 × 158 m) covered about 36,000 m^2 (Marasović 1994).

Part 3   Introduction

1. Edwards and Woolf (2003) offered a fascinating review of this infatuation with Rome, a city that was seen by the ancients as the epitome of the civilized world and its very nurturer (*cosmotrophos*), as the place where "whatever one does not see here neither did nor does exist" (Aristides) and which occupied the same space as the world: *Romanae spatium est urbis et orbis idem* (Ovid, *Fasti* 2.684).

2. I plead guilty on this account, although my fondness for Latin citations owes everything to my liking of that exacting language rather than to any infatuation with Rome's purported greatness.

Chapter V

1. Ancient architectural forms provided great inspiration to the Renaissance, Baroque, and neoclassical architects whose buildings adorn our cities. Rome's most iconic dome, the Pantheon, inspired structures such as the now demolished London PanTheon (1772), designed by James Wyatt; Berlin's Hedwigskirche (1747); Thomas Jefferson's building designs; and the Mosta Dome (church of Santa Maria) in Malta, built between 1833 and 1860 (MacDonald 1976). And, to be fair to Cullen Murphy (whose thoughtful book is sensibly full of caveats), in his "imperial" tour he also stressed the point about the misuse of oversimplified historical analogies.

2. Grant's harsh critique of the Mexican War was already noted (see chapter II, note 3). Douglas MacArthur, America's greatest wartime and peacetime military commander of the twentieth century (he contributed greatly to shaping modern Japan), came to the conclusion that "the entire effort of modern society should be concentrated on the endeavor to outlaw war as a method of the solution of problems between nations." And at the end of his presidency General Dwight Eisenhower famously warned Americans that "in the councils of government, we must guard against the acquisition of unwarranted influence, whether sought or unsought, by the military-industrial complex. The potential for the disastrous rise of misplaced power exists and will persist."

3. Japanese writings on corruption are voluminous. Good Western introductions are Mitchell (1996) and Blechinger (1998) for politics and corruption in general, B. Woodall (1996) for corrupt construction, Johnson (2004) for corrupt police practices, and Hill (2003) for Japan's organized crime.

4. TI's Corruption Perceptions Index is calculated from data obtained from 13 different sources that measure overall level of corruption (frequency and/or size of bribes) in the public and political sectors.

5. Emperor Qianlong's 1793 dismissive reply to the offer of King George III for trade between the two countries is a good illustration of fatal (for the Qing empire) miscalculation. Half a century after he ordered the king to "tremblingly obey," Britain inflicted the first Western defeat on China, ushering in the period of long decline. The text of Qianlong's letter is available at <http://academic.brooklyn.cuny.edu/core9/phalsall/texts/qianlong.html>.

6. Such complexities are the norm in all scientific, technical, and business advances. The Internet illustrates these challenges; besides yielding indubitable benefits it has also created

enormous problems (e.g., identity theft, electronic fraud, child pornography) that require complex and costly management.

7. In that respect, today's tabloid revelations are just tame family reading compared to what Suetonius had to say about Nero.

8. For detailed information on Roman gladiators and for critical assessments of the frequency and extent of gratuitously brutal gladiatorial combat in amphitheaters, see Hopkins and Beard (2005), Kyle (1998), and Barton (1993).

9. Rome saw more than 300 triumphal processions during the centuries of the republic and the empire. Unfortunately, these tasteless, boastful displays became the model for parades of many subsequent militaristic states, including fascist Germany and the Communist USSR, the two great Evil Empires of the twentieth century.

10. Minetti (2003) confirmed that average speed (usually 13–16 km/h) and daily distance covered by a Persian messenger horse (18–25 km) were carefully optimized in order to minimize the risk of damaging the animal's health; they avoided the emptying of spleen and anaerobic metabolism and allowed for adequate cooling. Stirrups (which diffused westward through Eurasia only after the third century C.E.) made riding easier but did not change the optimum speeds.

The fastest speeds of Roman shipping can be derived from those instances when urgent news had to travel as fast as possible. Duncan-Jones (1990) showed that the news of an emperor's death in Rome took 60–70 days to reach Alexandria, and another two to four weeks to travel up the Nile. That was the fast route, and westward sailings took twice as long.

11. Upon their arrival in Ostia, Rome's port on the Tyrrhenian shore, 30 km west of the city (now 3–4 km inland near the Fiumicino airport), these shipments had to be reloaded by *saccarii* onto barges that were dragged against the current to docksides in the city.

12. Even Murphy (2007, 65), generally a careful interpreter and one not given to hyperbolic claims, succumbed to this myth: "The Romans dominated most of the world they knew about, the *oikoumene* (though not all of it)." In reality, it was no more than one-seventh of the *oikoumene*.

13. The estimate of India's GDP for the first century C.E. (about 30% of the global total) is from Maddison (2007). Augustus noted in *Res Gestae* (XXXI), *Ad me ex India regum legationes saepe missae sunt, nunquam antea visae apud quemquam Romanorum ducem* (Embassies were often sent to me from the kings of India, a thing never seen before among the Roman rulers).

14. The latest place where the United States has been confronting these misperceptions is in Iraq. An anecdotal report illustrates this phenomenon. Totten (2007, 1) quotes an American lieutenant in Anbar province complaining that "they think we can do lot more for them than we can.... Like we're all-powerful... They say *hey, you're a sheikh, you can make stuff happen.* I say, well, that's just a nickname you gave me." Totten concurs: "I've heard that many Iraqis think the Americans are so powerful they can fix Iraq at will any time, which means there must be some sinister reason why they want Iraq to remain broken," and he recalls a similar sentiment expressed by a Beirut taxi driver: "President Bush can fix Lebanon in ten minutes.... So why *doesn't* he?"

15. Not only were the Romans incurious as far as the natural and applied proto-sciences were concerned, but they also cared little about their own origins and distant history, leaving

both of these to the retelling of absurd myths. As Johnston (1933, 42) put it, "To us this lack of interest in the past is incomprehensible. Yet no one saw any incongruity in the notion which made Augustus trace his descent from Venus and Aeneas, and made Virgil celebrate the theme." A notable modern analogue of the Roman lack of curiosity is the disappointing scientific and technical record of the Muslim world, an underachievement even more remarkable given the enormous amount of money some of its members (Algeria, Libya, Saudi Arabia, Iran and smaller Persian Gulf states, Indonesia, Malaysia) have made from the sales of their rich hydrocarbon resources.

16. The useful power delivered by a blindfolded (and often old and sickly) animal walking in a tight circle was as low as 30 W, an output smaller than the power of a modern coffee grinder.

17. The economic crisis of the 1930s marked tens of millions of Americans with painful memories, but the country is unique among the world's major nations in that it has never suffered a famine or even a prolonged period of serious large-scale malnutrition.

18. Isaac (1992) notes that these arguments often ignore what seems commonplace: it is sometimes difficult to determine if an army is engaged in defense or offense; the two parties involved many have very different motives; and the eventual aims of either side, or both sides, may change to such an extent that the aims may completely differ from initial anticipations.

19. But the meticulous war plans prepared by the OKW are also a perfect example of how grand designs succumb to unexpected events and brutal realities.

20. This conclusion does not exclude the formulation and pursuit of obviously transformative policies: the Marshall Plan, maintenance of the strategic parity with the USSR, efforts to build an effective shield against missile attacks. But in retrospect it is clear that reactions made more difference than planned actions: how different U.S. foreign policy would have been without the Japanese attack on Pearl Harbor, without Stalin's pre– and post–WW II paranoia, without the Soviet occupation of Afghanistan, without the unexpected demise of the USSR. And, of course, without the hijacked planes that were flown by Muslim terrorists into the World Trade Center and the Pentagon on 9/11.

21. All post–WW II U.S. administrations have supported the intolerant, undemocratic, secretive, family-run Saudi Arabia; all administrations since the Six Day War of 1973 helped to keep in power the quasi-dictatorships of Egyptian presidents; and America has been eager to excuse just about any human rights violations by China (ironically, in order to run record trade deficits with that country, bringing to mind Lenin's *bon mot* about the capitalists who "will sell us the rope with which we will hang them"). These are good examples of the clear limits on the promotion of democracy around the world.

22. Candidate Bush had this to say (in the second Bush-Gore debate) about nation building using the U.S. military: "Maybe I'm missing something here. I mean, we're going to have kind of a nation building corps from America? Absolutely not. Our military is meant to fight and win war. That's what it's meant to do. And . . . I'm going to be judicious as to how to use the military. It needs to be in our vital interest, the mission needs to be clear, and the exit strategy obvious." In his inaugural address on January 20, 2001, President Bush did not use even once the words *terror* or *terrorists*, *Islam* or *Muslim*, *Iraq* or *Afghanistan*, and *war* was used only once in a retrospective remark as he noted that "our national courage has

been clear in times of depression and war." So much for any grand national strategy and for the fate of best-laid plans.

23. Actually, given the many problems facing the U.S. military, Schmitt and Donnelly (2007) argue, defense spending should be raised to 5% of GDP and held at that level indefinitely, a recommendation beyond the capabilities of America's deeply dysfunctional economy.

24. My preference would be to stop referring to the *fall* of the (Western) Roman Empire and think of the change not as a discrete event but as a complex process of transformation.

25. The global economic downturn of 2008 is only the latest (and perhaps the most costly) example of this impossibility. The crisis may have started in the United States, but every major economy was almost instantly affected, and some of them may come out of a prolonged recession relatively worse off than the United States.

26. The stabilization factor explains why all the European states of the former Soviet Empire have rushed to join U.S.-led NATO, and why even Ukraine wants to be a member. U.S. intervention on behalf of Muslim Bosniaks (after Europe watched the Yugoslav slaughter passively for years) is a perfect example of an armed action that nobody else was willing to undertake.

References

Acar, F., S. Naderi, M. Guvencer, U. Türe, and M. N. Arda. 2005. Herophilus of Chalcedon: A pioneer in neuroscience. *Neurosurgery* 56: 861–867.

Adam, J.-P. 1994. *Roman Building: Materials and Techniques*. London: Routledge.

Adshead, S. A. M. 1992. *Salt and Civilization*. New York: St. Martin's Press.

Allen, R. C. 2007. How prosperous were the Romans? Evidence from Diocletian's price edict (301 AD). Economics Series Working Paper 363. Department of Economics, Oxford University.

Anderson, J. L., and T. Lewit. 1992. A contract with the barbarians? Economics of the fall of Rome. *Explorations in Economic History* 29: 99–115.

Arterburn, S., and D. Merrill. 2004. *Every Man's Bible: New Living Translation*. Carol Stream, Ill.: Tyndale House.

ARWU (Academic Ranking of World Universities). 2007. *Top 500 World Universities*. Shanghai: Institute of Higher Education, Jiao Tong University. <http://www.arwu.org/rank/2007/ARWU2007TOP500list.htm>.

Bacevich, A. J. 2002. *American Empire: The Realities and Consequences of U.S. Diplomacy*. Cambridge, Mass.: Harvard University Press.

———, ed. 2003. *The Imperial Tense: Prospects and Problems of American Empire*. Chicago: Ivan R. Dee.

Bacevich, A. J., and S. Mallaby. 2002. New Rome, new Jerusalem. *Wilson Quarterly* 26 (3): 50–58.

Bagnall, R. S., and B. W. Frier. 1994. *The Demography of Roman Egypt*. Cambridge: Cambridge University Press.

Bagnall, R. S., B. W. Frier, and I. C. Rutherford, eds. 1997. *The Census Register P.Oxy 984: The Reverse of Pindar's Paeans*. Brussels: Fondation égyptologique Reine Élisabeth.

Bakker, J. T., ed. 1999. *The Mills-Bakeries of Ostia: Description and Interpretation*. Amsterdam: J. C. Gieben.

Bang, P. F. 2007. Trade and empire: In search of organizing concepts for the Roman economy. *Past & Present* 195: 3–54.

Barbero, A. 2007. *The Day of the Barbarians: The Battle That Led to the Fall of the Roman Empire*. New York: Walker.

Barfield, T. J. 2001. The shadow empires: Imperial state formation along the Chinese-Nomad frontier. In *Empires, Perspectives from Archaeology and History*, ed. S. E. Alcock, T. N. D'Altroy, K. D. Morrison, and C. M. Sinopoliet, 10–41. Cambridge: Cambridge University Press.

Baring, E. (Lord Cromer). 1908. The government of subject races. *Edinburgh Review*, January, 1–27.

Barsoum, M. W., A. Ganguly, and G. Hug. 2006. Microstructural evidence of reconstituted limestone blocks in the Great Pyramids of Egypt. *Journal of the American Ceramic Society* 89: 3788–3796. DOI:10.1111/j.1551–2916.2006.01308.x.

Barton, C. 1993. *Sorrows of the Ancient Romans: The Gladiator and the Monster*. Princeton, N.J.: Princeton University Press.

Bastomsky, S. J. 1990. Rich and poor: The great divide in ancient Rome and Victorian England. *Greece & Rome* 37: 37–43.

BBC News. 2007. Gorbachev criticises US "empire." June 3. <http://news.bbc.co.uk/2/hi/europe/6717037.stm>.

BEA (Bureau of Economic Analysis, U.S. Dept. of Commerce). 2008. U.S. net international investment position at year end 2007. <http://bea.gov/newsreleases/international/intinv/intinvnewsrelease.htm>.

Beard, M. 2007. *The Roman Triumph*. Cambridge, Mass.: Belknap Press.

Beare, W. 1959. The Roman achievement. *Greece & Rome* 6: 3–13.

Beckwith, C., and D. Knox. 1983. *Delta Force: The Army's Elite Counterterrorist Unit*. New York: Harcourt Brace Jovanovich.

Beeghley, L. 2004. *The Structure of Social Stratification in the United States*. Boston: Allyn and Bacon.

Begley, V., and R. D. de Puma, eds. 1991. *Rome and India: The Ancient Sea Trade*. Madison: University of Wisconsin Press.

Belasco, A. 2008. *The Cost of Iraq, Afghanistan, and Other Global War on Terror Operations Since 9/11*. Washington, D.C.: Congressional Research Service.

Beloch, K. J. 1886. *Die Bevölkerung der griechischen-römischen Welt*. Leipzig: Duncker and Humblot.

Bender, P. 2003a. *Weltmacht Amerika das neue Rom*. Stuttgart: Klett-Cotta.

———, 2003b. America: The new Roman Empire. *Orbis* 47: 145–159.

Benoit, F. 1940. L'usine de meunerie hydraulique de Barbegal (Arles). *Revue Archeologique* 15: 19–80.

Berggren J. L., and A. Jones. 2000. *Ptolemy's Geography: An Annotated Translation of the Theoretical Chapters*. Princeton, N.J.: Princeton University Press.

Billington, D. P., and D. P. Billington Jr. 2006. *Power, Speed, and Form: Engineers and the Making of the Twentieth Century*. Princeton, N.J.: Princeton University Press.

bin-Lādin, U. 2004. Message to the American people. Videotape. October 29. Transcript at <http://www.cnn.com/2004/WORLD/meast/10/29/bin.laden.transcript/>.

Blackman, D. R., and A. T. Hodge. 2001. *Frontinus' Legacy: Essays on Frontinus' de aquis urbis Romae*. Ann Arbor: University of Michigan Press.

Blank, W. 2004. *Rome* is Rome. *The Church of God Daily Bible Study.* <http://www.keyway.ca/htm2004/20040129.htm>.

Blechinger, V. 1998. *Politische Korruption in Japan: Ursachen, Hintergründe und Reformversuche.* Hamburg: Institut für Asienkunde.

Bloch, M. 1928. Pour une histoire comparée des sociétés européennes. *Revue de synthèse historique* 46: 15–50.

BLS (Bureau of Labor Statistics, U.S. Dept. of Labor). 2008. *Current Employment Statistics.* <http://www.bls.gov/ces/>.

Bowden, M. 1999. *Black Hawk Down: A Story of Modern Warfare.* New York: Penguin.

———, 2006. *Guests of the Ayatollah: The First Battle in America's War with Militant Islam.* New York: Atlantic Monthly Press.

Bowers, B. 1998. *Lengthening the Day: A History of Lighting.* Oxford: Oxford University Press.

Bowersock, G. W. 1983. *Roman Arabia.* Cambridge, Mass.: Harvard University Press.

Bozo, F. 2001. *Two Strategies for Europe: De Gaulle, the United States, and the Atlantic Alliance.* Lanham, Md.: Rowman and Littlefield.

BP (British Petroleum). 2008. *Statistical Review of World Energy.* <http://www.bp.com/>.

Bradley, K. 2000. Animalizing the slave: The truth of fiction. *Journal of Roman Studies* 90: 110–125.

Branscomb, L. M., and P. E. Auerswald. 2002. *Between Invention and Innovation: An Analysis of Funding for Early-Stage Technology Development.* Report to the Economic Assessment Office, Advanced Technology Program, National Institute of Standards and Technology (NIST). GCR-02-841. <http://www.atp.nist.gov/eao/eao_pubs.htm>.

Braudel, F. 1972. *The Mediterranean and the Mediterranean World in the Age of Philip II.* New York: Harper and Row.

Brogan, O. 1936. Trade between the Roman Empire and the Free Germans. *Journal of Roman Studies* 26: 195–222.

Brunt, P. A. 1987. *Italian Manpower, 225 BC–AD 14.* Oxford: Oxford University Press.

Bryce. J. 1886. *The Holy Roman Empire.* New York: Lovell, Coryell.

———, 1914. The Roman Empire and the British Empire in India. In *Two Historical Studies*, 1–79. Oxford: Oxford University Press.

Buchanan, P. 1999. *A Republic, Not an Empire: Reclaiming America's Destiny.* Washington, D.C.: Regnery.

Bugh, G. R. 2006. *The Cambridge Companion to the Hellenistic World.* Cambridge: Cambridge University Press.

Bulliet, R. W. 1975. *The Camel and the Wheel.* Cambridge, Mass.: Harvard University Press.

Burnham, G., R. Lafta, S. Doocy, and L. Roberts. 2006. Mortality after the 2003 invasion of Iraq: A cross-sectional cluster sample survey. *Lancet* 368: 1421–1428.

Burton, H. E. 1932. *The Discovery of the Ancient World.* Cambridge, Mass.: Harvard University Press.

Bush, G. W. 2002. Graduation speech at West Point. June 1. <http://www.teachingamericanhistory.org/library/index.asp?document=916>.

———, 2006. State of the Union Address. January 31. <http://www.gpoaccess.gov/sou/index.html>.

Butler, D. 1985. *Fall of Saigon*. New York: Simon and Schuster.

Cain, P. J., and A. G. Hopkins. 2001. *British Imperialism 1688–2000*. 2d ed. London: Longman.

CBS News. 2003. Beirut barracks attack remembered. October 23. <http://www.cbsnews.com/stories/2003/10/23/world/main579638.shtml>.

CDC (Centers for Disease Control and Prevention). 2007a. *Deaths: Preliminary Data for 2005*. National Center for Health Statistics. <http://www.cdc.gov/nchs/products/pubs/pubd/hestats/prelimdeaths05/prelimdeaths05.htm>.

———, 2007b. United States life tables, 2004. *National Vital Statistics Reports* 56 (9). National Center for Health Statistics. <http://www.cdc.gov/nchs/products/pubs/pubd/lftbls/life/1966.htm>.

Chamberlin, J. 2004. *Comparisons of U.S. and Foreign Military Spending: Data from Selected Public Sources*. Washington, D.C.: Congressional Research Service.

Chase-Dunn, C., R. Giem, A. Jorgenson, T. Reifer, J. Rogers, and S. Lio. 2002. *The Trajectory of the United States in the World-System: A Quantitative Reflection*. Riverside, Calif.: Institute for Research on World-Systems.

Christian, D. 2000. Silk roads or steppe roads? The silk roads in world history. *Journal of World History* 11: 1–26.

Cipolla, C. M. 1966. *Guns, Sails, and Empires*. New York: Pantheon.

Claude, J. 1968. *L'Empire américain*. Paris: B. Grasset.

Coale, A. J., and P. Demeny. 1983. *Regional Model Life Tables and Stable Populations*. San Diego: Academic Press.

Cockburn, A., and J. St. Clair. 2005. *Imperial Crusades: Iraq, Afghanistan and Yugoslavia—A Diary of Three Wars*. New York: Verso.

Cohen, E. A. 2004. History and the hyperpower. *Foreign Affairs* 83 (4): 49–63.

Comptroller (New York City). 2002. Thompson releases report on fiscal impact of 9/11 on New York City. Press release. <http://comptroller.nyc.gov/press/2002_releases/02-09-054.shtm>.

Constable, G., and B. Somerville. 2003. *A Century of Innovation: Twenty Engineering Achievements That Transformed Our Lives*. Washington, D.C.: Joseph Henry Press.

Cox, M. 2008. Europe's enduring anti-Americanism. *Current History* 107 (709): 231–235.

Craddock, P. T. 1995. *Early Metal Mining and Production*. Washington, D.C.: Smithsonian Institution Press.

Crawford, M. H. 1974. *Roman Republican Coinage*. Cambridge: Cambridge University Press.

Cummings, L. V. 2004. *Alexander the Great*. New York: Grove Press.

Curtin, P. D. 1984. *Cross-Cultural Trade in World History*. Cambridge: Cambridge University Press.

Dalley, S., and J. P. Oleson. 2003. Sennacherib, Archimedes, and the water screw. *Technology and Culture* 44: 1–26.

Davidovits, J. 2002. *Ils ont bâti les pyramides*. Paris: Godefroy Editions.

Deady, T. K. 2005. Lessons from a successful counterinsurgency: The Philippines, 1899–1902. *Parameters* 35 (1): 53–68.

Denny, M. 2004. The efficiency of overshot and undershot waterwheels. *European Journal of Physics* 25: 193–202.

Dew-Becker, I., and R. J. Gordon. 2005. Where did the productivity growth go? Inflation dynamics and the distribution of income. *Brookings Papers on Economic Activity* 36 (2): 67–127.

Dickeman, M. 1975. Demographic consequences of infanticide in man. *Annual Review of Ecology and Systematics* 6: 107–137.

Dignas, B., and E. Winter. 2007. *Rome and Persia in Late Antiquity: Neighbours and Rivals*. Cambridge: Cambridge University Press.

Doyle, M. 1986 *Empires*. Ithaca, N.Y.: Cornell University Press.

Duncan-Jones, R. 1990. *Structure and Scale in the Roman Economy*. Cambridge: Cambridge University Press.

Edwards, C., and G. Woolf. 2003. Cosmopolis: Rome as world city. In *Rome the Cosmopolis*, ed. C. Edwards and G. Woolf, 1–20. Cambridge: Cambridge University Press.

EIA (Energy Information Administration). 2008a. *Annual Energy Review 2007*. Report DOE/EIA-0384(2007). <http://www.eia.doe.gov/emeu/aer/overview.html>.

———, 2008b. Energy flow 2007. <http://www.eia.doe.gov/emeu/aer/pdf/pages/sec1_3.pdf>.

———, 2008c. *Petroleum Basic Statistics*. <http://www.eia.doe.gov/basics/quickoil.html>.

Engels, D. 1980. The problem of female infanticide in the Graeco-Roman world. *Classical Philology* 75: 112–120.

Erdkamp, P. 2005. *The Grain Market in the Roman Empire*. Cambridge: Cambridge University Press.

Erskine, A. 1995. Culture and power in Ptolemaic Egypt: The Museum and Library of Alexandria. *Greece & Rome* 42: 38–348.

Evans, H. B. 1994. *Water Distribution in Ancient Rome: The Evidence of Frontinus*. Ann Arbor: University of Michigan Press.

Evans-Pritchard, A. 2004. Art show sees Europe as "new Roman Empire." *Telegraph*, September 13. <http://telegraph.co.uk>.

Faas, P. 1994. *Around the Roman Table: Food and Feasting in Ancient Rome*. Chicago: University of Chicago Press.

Faerman, M., G. K. Bar-Gal, D. Filon, C. L. Greenblatt, L. Stager, A. Oppenheim, and P. Smith. 1998. Determining the sex of infanticide victims from the late Roman era through ancient DNA analysis. *Journal of Archaeological Science* 25: 861–865.

Fagan, G. 2001. "Pliny the Elder on Science and Technology" by J. F. Healy. Book review. *Journal of Roman Studies* 91: 248–249.

Falk, R. A. 2004. *The Declining World Order: America's Imperial Geopolitics*. New York: Routledge.

FAO (Food and Agriculture Organization). 2008. FAOSTAT: Agriculture. <http://faostat .fao.org/default.aspx>.

Farwell, B. 1963. *Burton*. London: Penguin.

Fears, J. R. 2004. The plague under Marcus Aurelius and the decline and fall of the Roman Empire. *Infectious Disease Clinics of North America* 18: 65–77.

———, 2005. The lessons of the Roman Empire for America today. Heritage Lecture 917. December 19. Washington, D.C.: Heritage Foundation.

Fenno, R. F. 1972. *The Yalta Conference*. Lexington, Mass.: D. C. Heath.

Fenton, J. 1985. *The Fall of Saigon*. London: Granta Books.

Ferguson, N. 2004. *Colossus: The Price of America's Empire*. New York: Penguin.

Fields, N. 2005. *Rome's Northern Frontier AD 70–235*. Oxford: Osprey Publications.

Finkel, C. 2005. *Osman's Dream: The History of the Ottoman Empire, 1300–1923*. London: John Murray.

Finley, M. I. 1965. Technical innovation and economic progress in the ancient world. *Economic History Review* 18: 29–45.

———, 1973. *The Ancient Economy*. Berkeley: University of California Press.

FitzGerald, C., S. Saunders, L. Bondioli, and R. Macchiarelli. 2006. Health of infants in an imperial Roman skeletal sample: Perspective from dental microstructure. *American Journal of Physical Anthropology* 130: 179–189.

Forbes, R. J. 1965. *Studies in Ancient Technology*. Vol. 2. Leiden: Brill.

———, 1966. Heat and heating. In *Studies in Ancient Technology*, vol. 6, 1–103 Leiden: Brill.

Fouquet, R., and P.J.G. Pearson. 2006. Seven centuries of energy services: The price and use of light in the United Kingdom (1300–2000). *Energy Journal* 27: 139–177.

Fraser, P. M. 1972. *Ptolemaic Alexandria*. Oxford: Oxford University Press.

FRB (Federal Reserve Board). 2008. *G.19 Consumer Credit*. <http://www.federalreserve. gov/Releases/g19/current/>.

Freedland, J. 2002a. *Rome: The Model Empire*. TV program. Broadcast on September 21, 18:50 GMT.

———, 2002b. Rome, AD . . . Rome, DC? *Guardian*, September 18.

Freeth, T., A. Jones, J. M. Steele, and Y. Bitsakis. 2008. Calendars with Olympiad display and eclipse prediction on the Antikythera mechanism. *Nature* 454: 614–617.

Frier, B. W. 1993. Subsistence annuities and per capita income in the early Roman Empire. *Classical Philology* 88: 222–230.

———, 2000. Demography. In *The Cambridge Ancient History*. 2d ed. Vol. 11: *The High Empire, A.D. 70–192*, ed. A. K. Bowman, P. Garnsey, and D. Rathbone, 787–816. Cambridge: Cambridge University Press.

———, 2001. More is worse: Some observations on the population. In *Debating Roman Demography*, ed. W. Scheidel, 139–159. Leiden: Brill.

Galloway, J. A., D. Keene, and M. Murphy. 1996. Fuelling the city: Production and distribution of firewood and fuel in London's region, 1290–1400. *Economic History Review* 49: 447–472.

Garbrecht, G., ed. 1987. *Die Wasserversorgung antiker Städte*. Mainz: P. von Zabern.

Garnsey, P. 1988. *Famine and Food Supply in the Graeco-Roman World*. Cambridge: Cambridge University Press.

Garnsey, P., and R. Saller. 1987. *The Roman Empire: Economy, Society and Culture*. Berkeley: University of California. Press.

Geraghty, R. M. 2007. The impact of globalization in the Roman Empire, 200 BC–AD 100. *Journal of Economic History* 67: 1036–1061.

Giardina, A. 1993. Roman man. In *The Romans*, 1–15. Chicago: University of Chicago Press.

Gibbon, E. 1776–1788. *The History of the Decline and Fall of the Roman Empire*. London: Strachan and Cadell.

Gilbert, D. 2002. *The American Class Structure in an Age of Growing Inequality*. Belmont, Calif.: Wadsworth.

Gillette, B. 2007. The revived Roman Empire. *BrittGillette.com*. May 28. <http://brittgillette.com/WordPress/?p=35>.

Gilmour, D. 2007. *The Ruling Caste: Imperial Lives in the Victorian Raj*. London: Pimlico.

Ginouvès, R. 1962. *Balaneutikè: Recherches sur le bain dans l'antiquité grecque*. Paris: de Boccard.

Glavas, C. B. 1994. *The Place of Euclid in Ancient and Modern Mathematics*. Athens: Korfi.

Go, J. 2007. The provinciality of American Empire: "Liberal exceptionalism" and U.S. colonial rule, 1989–1912. *Comparative Studies in Society and History* 49: 74–108.

Goldsmith, R. W. 1984. An estimate of the size and structure of the national product of the early Roman Empire. *Review of Income and Wealth* 30: 263–288.

Goncharov, S. N., J. W. Lewis, and X. Litai. 1993. *Uncertain Partners: Stalin, Mao, and the Korean War*. Stanford, Calif.: Stanford University Press.

Goodyear, F. 1982. *Cambridge History of Literature*. Vol. 2: *Latin Literature*, 670–672. Cambridge: Cambridge University Press.

Gowan, P. 2004. Contemporary intra-core relations and world systems theory. *Journal of World-Systems Research* 10: 471–500.

Grant, U. S. 1885/6. *Personal Memoirs of U.S. Grant*. 2 vols. New York: C. L. Webster.

Greatrex, G., and S. N. C. Lieu. 2007. *The Roman Eastern Frontier and the Persian Wars AD 363–628*. London: Routledge.

Greene, K. 1990. Perspectives on Roman technology. *Oxford Journal of Archaeology* 9: 209–219.

————, 2000. Technological innovation and economic progress in the ancient world: M. I. Finley reconsidered. *Economic History Review* 53: 29–59.

Greenwood, J., and A. Seshadri. 2002. The U.S. demographic transition. *AEA Papers and Proceedings* 92: 153–159.

Grew, R. 1980. The case for comparing histories. *American Historical Review* 85: 763–778.

Gunderson, G. 1976. Economic change and the demise of the Roman Empire. *Explorations in Economic History* 13: 43–68.

Halstead, M. 1899. *Full Official History of the War with Spain.*

Hammel, E. M. 1985. *The Root: The Marines in Beirut, August 1982–February 1984.* San Diego: Harcourt Brace Jovanovich.

Harden, D. B. 1962. *The Phoenicians.* New York: Praeger.

Hardy, G., and A. B. Kinney. 2005. *The Establishment of the Han Empire and Imperial China.* Westport, Conn.: Greenwood Press.

Hardy, T. 1901. Embarcation (Southampton Docks: October, 1899). In *Poems of the Past and the Present.* Reprinted in *The Complete Poetical Works of Thomas Hardy*, ed. S. Hynes. Vol. 1, 116. Oxford: Oxford University Press.

Harris, W. V. 1979. *War and Imperialism.* Oxford: Oxford University Press.

————, 1982. The theoretical possibility of extensive infanticide in the Graeco-Roman world. *Classical Quarterly* 32: 114–116.

————, 1994. Child-exposure in the Roman Empire. *Journal of Roman Studies* 84: 1–22.

————, 1999. Demography, geography and the sources of Roman slaves. *Journal of Roman Studies* 89: 62–75.

Harrison, S. J. 1997. The survival and supremacy of Rome: The unity of the Shield of Aeneas. *Journal of Roman Studies* 87: 70–76.

Heath, T. L. 1931. *A History of Greek Mathematics.* Oxford: Clarendon Press.

Heather, P. 2005. *The Fall of the Roman Empire: A New History of Rome and the Barbarians.* New York: Oxford University Press.

Heer, F. 1968. *The Holy Roman Empire.* London: Weidenfeld and Nicolson.

Heldring, F. 1988. Can the U.S. dollar survive as a world reserve currency? *Annals of the American Academy of Political and Social Science* 500 (1): 23–32.

Herman, D. 2000. The new Roman Empire: European envisionings and American premillennialists. *Journal of American Studies* 34: 23–40.

Hermansen, G. 1978. The populations of Rome: The regionaries. *Historia* 27: 129–168.

Hill, P. B. 2003. *The Japanese Mafia: Yakuza, Law, and the State.* New York: Oxford University Press.

Hiro, D. 2007. Seizing American supremacy. *Salon.com.* August 22. <http://www.salon.com/news/feature/2007/08/22/american_decline/print.html>.

Hobsbawm, E. 2003. The empire expands wider and still wider. *Counterpunch.* June 11. <http://www.counterpunch.org/hobsbawm06112003.html>.

Hockenos, P. 2007. *Joschka Fischer and the Making of the Berlin Republic: An Alternative History of Postwar Germany*. New York: Oxford University Press.

Hodge A. T. 1981. Vitruvius, lead pipes and lead poisoning. *American Journal of Archaeology* 85: 486–491.

———, 1984. How did Frontinus measure the quinaria? *American Journal of Archaeology* 88: 205–218.

———, 1990. A Roman factory. *Scientific American* 263 (5): 106–111.

———, 2002. *Roman Aqueducts and Water Supply*. London: Gerald Duckworth.

Holt, R. 1988. *The Mills of Medieval England*. Oxford: Oxford University Press.

Honoré, T. 1982. *Ulpian*. Oxford: Clarendon Press.

Hopkins, C. 1979. *The Discovery of Dura-Europos*. New Haven: Yale University Press.

Hopkins, K. 1966. On the probable age structure of the Roman population. *Population Studies* 20 (2): 245–264.

———, 1980. Brother-sister marriage in ancient Egypt. *Comparative Studies in Society and History* 22: 303–354.

———, 1993. Novel evidence for Roman slavery. *Past & Present* 138: 3–27.

———, 1995/6. Rome, taxes, rents, and trade. *Kodai* 6/7: 41–75.

Hopkins, K., and M. Beard. 2005. *The Colosseum*. Cambridge, Mass.: Harvard University Press.

Howe, S. 2003. American Empire: The history and future of an idea. *openDemocracy*. <http://www.opendemocracy.net/conflict-americanpower/article_1279.jsp>.

Howgego, C. 1992. The supply and use of money in the Roman world 200 B.C. to A.D. 300. *Journal of Roman Studies* 82: 1–31.

Hua, J. 1983. The mass production of iron castings in ancient China. *Scientific American* 258 (1): 120–128.

Huet, V. 1999. Napoleon I: A new Augustus? In *Roman Presences: Receptions of Rome in European Culture, 1789–1945*, ed. C. Edwards, 53–69. Cambridge: Cambridge University Press.

Hughes, T. P. 1983. *Networks of Power*. Baltimore, Md.: Johns Hopkins University Press.

Huntingford, G. W. 1980. *The Periplus of the Erythrean Sea*. London: Hakluyt Society.

Hyland, A. 1990. *Equus: The Horse in the Roman World*. New Haven: Yale University Press.

Ikenberry, J. 2002. America's imperial ambitions. *Foreign Affairs* 81 (5): 44–60.

Illich, I. D. 1974. *Energy and Equity*. New York: Harper and Row.

Iraq Body Count. 2007. <http://www.iraqbodycount.org/>.

Irby-Massie, G., and P. T. Keyser. 2002. *Greek Science of the Hellenistic Era: A Sourcebook*. London: Routledge.

Isaac, B. 1992. *The Limits of Empire: The Roman Army in the East*. Oxford: Oxford University Press.

Jansen, M. 2002. *The Making of Modern Japan*. Cambridge, Mass.: Belknap Press.

Johnson, C. 2000. *Blowback: The Costs and Consequences of American Empire*. New York: Metropolitan Books.

———, 2004. *The Sorrows of Empire: Militarism, Secrecy, and the End of the Republic*. New York: Metropolitan Books.

Johnston, E. I. 1933. How the Greeks and Romans regarded history. *Greece & Rome* 3: 38–43.

Jones, H. M. 1971. *The Age of Energy: Varieties of American Experience 1865–1915*. New York: Viking Press.

Jones, M. W. 2000. *Principles of Roman Architecture*. New Haven: Yale University Press.

Julien, C. 1968. *L'Empire américain*. Paris: B. Grasset.

Kagan, D. 1992. *The Fall of the Roman Empire: Decline or Transformation?* Lexington, Mass.: D. C. Heath.

Kagan, K. 2006. Redefining Roman grand strategy. *Journal of Military History* 70: 333–362.

Kamiya, G. 2007. "Are We Rome?" by Cullen Murphy. Book review. *Salon.com* <http://www.salon.com/books/review/2007/06/07/rome/>.

Kane, T. 2006. *Global U.S. Troop Deployment, 1950–2005*. Center for Data Analysis Report 06-02. Washington, D.C.: Heritage Foundation. <http://www.heritage.org/research/nationalsecurity/cda06-02.cfm>.

Kenen, P. B. 2002. The euro versus the dollar: Will there be a struggle for dominance? *Journal of Policy Modeling* 24: 347–354.

Kennedy, P. 1988. *The Rise and Fall of the Great Powers: Economic Change and Military Conflict from 1500 to 2000*. London: Unwin Hyman.

———, 2002. The greatest superpower ever. *New Perspectives Quarterly* 19 (2): 8–18. <http://www.digitalnpq.org/archive/2002_spring/kennedy.html>.

Kertzer, D. I., and R. P. Saller, eds. 1991. *The Family in Italy: From Antiquity to the Present*. New Haven: Yale University Press.

Kessler, D., and P. Temin. 2007. The organization of the grain trade in the early Roman Empire. *Economic History Review* 60: 313–332.

Khan, Y. 2007. *The Great Partition: The Making of India and Pakistan*. New Haven: Yale University Press.

Kirwan, L. P. 1957. Rome beyond the southern Egyptian frontier. *Geographical Journal* 123 (1): 13–19.

Koepke, N., and J. Baten. 2005. The biological standard of living in Europe during the last two millennia. *European Review of Economic History* 9: 61–95.

Krokodil. 1989. *Soviet Humor: The Best of Krokodil*. Kansas City, Kans.: Andrews McMeel.

Kron, G. 2005. Anthropometry, physical anthropology, and the reconstruction of ancient health, nutrition, and living standards. *Historia* 54: 68–83.

Kuhn, T. S. 1962. *The Structure of Scientific Revolutions*. Chicago: University of Chicago Press.

Kurth, W., ed. 1927. *The Complete Woodcuts of Albrecht Dürer*. London: W. & G. Foyle.

Kyle, D. G. 1998. *Spectacles and Death in Ancient Rome*. London: Routledge.

Laack-Michel, U. 1974. *Albrecht Haushofer und der Nationalsozialismus; ein Beitrag zur Zeitgeschichte*. Stuttgart: E. Klett.

Lanciani, R. 1888. *Ancient Rome in the Light of Recent Discoveries*. Boston: Houghton Mifflin.

Lardner, J., and D. A. Smith, eds. 2005. *The Growing Economic Divide in America and Its Poisonous Consequences*. New York: New Press.

Lee, J., and F. Wang. 1999. *One Quarter of Humanity: Malthusian Mythology and Chinese Realities, 1700–2000*. Cambridge, Mass.: Harvard University Press.

Lenahan, R. 1998. *Crippled Eagle: A Historical Perspective of U.S. Special Operations 1976–1996*. Charleston, S.C.: Narwhal Press.

Leveau, P. 2006. Les moulins de Barbegal (1986–2006). *Traianus*. <http://traianus.rediris.es/textos/barbegal.pdf>.

Levick, B. 2004. The Roman economy: Trade in Asia Minor and the niche market. *Greece & Rome* 51: 180–198.

Levy, B.-H. 2003. Anti-Americanism in the Old Europe. *New Perspectives Quarterly* 20: 4–10.

Lewis, M. J. T. 1997. *Millstone and Hammer: The Origins of Water-Power*. Hull, UK: University of Hull Press.

Lind, M. 2002. Is America the new Roman Empire? *Globalist*, June 12, 2002.

Lindsey, H. 1970. *The Late Great Planet Earth*. Grand Rapids, Mich.: Zondervan.

Lintott, A. 1981. What was the "Imperium Romanum"? *Greece & Rome* 28: 53–67.

Lipset, S. M. 1996. *American Exceptionalism: A Double-edged Sword*. New York: W. W. Norton.

Littman, R. J., and M. L. Littman. 1973. Galen and the Antonine plague. *American Journal of Philology* 94: 243–255.

Litwak, R. S. 2002. The imperial republic after 9/11. *Wilson Quarterly* 26 (3): 76–82.

Lo Cascio, E. 1994. The size of the Roman population: Beloch and the meaning of the Augustan census figures. *Journal of Roman Studies* 84: 23–40.

———, 2001. Recruitment and the size of the Roman population from the third to the first century. In *Debating Roman Demography*, ed. W. Scheidel, 111–137. Leiden: Brill.

Lodge, H. C. 1899. *The War with Spain*. New York: Harper.

Looney, R. 2002. Economic costs to the United States stemming from the 9/11 attacks. *Strategic Insights* 1 (6). <http://www.ccc.nps.navy.mil/si/aug02/homeland.asp>.

Lucas, A. R. 2005. Industrial milling in the ancient and medieval worlds. *Technology and Culture* 46: 1–30.

Lucas, C. P. 1912. *Greater Rome and Greater Britain*. Oxford: Clarendon Press.

Lucchini, F. 1996. *Pantheon*. Rome: Nova Italia Scientifica.

Lugard, L. F. 1910. British Empire. In *Encyclopaedia Britannica*, 11th ed., vol. 4, 606–615.

Luks, L. 2002. *Tretii Rim? Tretii Reikh? Tretii Put Istoricheskie ocherki o Rossii, Germanii i Zapade*. Moscow: Moskovskii filosofskii fond.

Luttwak, E. 1976. *The Grand Strategy of the Roman Empire: From the First Century A.D. to the Third*. Baltimore, Md.: Johns Hopkins University Press.

Lyall, A. 1906. *The Rise and Expansion of the British Dominion in India*. London: John Murray.

MacDonald, W. L. 1976. *The Pantheon: Design, Meaning, and Progeny*. Cambridge, Mass.: Harvard University Press.

———, 1982. *The Architecture of the Roman Empire: An Introductory Study*. New Haven: Yale University Press.

MacMullen, R. 1988. *Corruption and the Decline of Rome*. New Haven: Yale University Press.

Maddison, A. 2001. *The World Economy: A Millennial Perspective*. Paris: OECD.

———, 2003. *The World Economy: Historical Statistics*. Paris: OECD.

———, 2007. *Contours of the World Economy, 1–2030 AD*. Oxford: Oxford University Press.

Mann, C. L. 2002. Perspectives on the U.S. current account deficit and sustainability. *Journal of Economic Perspectives* 16: 131–152.

Mann, M. 2003. *Incoherent Empire*. London: Verso.

Manzi, G., E. Santandrea, and P. Passarello. 1997. Dental size and shape in the Roman Imperial age: Two examples for the area of Rome. *American Journal of Physical Anthropology* 102: 469–479.

Marasović, T. 1994. Diocletian's Palace—World Cultural Heritage: Split, Croatia. 2d ed. Zagreb, Croatia: Dominović and Buvina.

Martin, D. B. 1996. The construction of the ancient family: Methodological considerations. *Journal of Roman Studies* 86: 40–60.

McEvedy, C., and R. Jones. 1978. *Atlas of World Population History*. London: Allen Lane.

McNeill, W. H. 1989. *The Age of Gunpowder Empires, 1450–1800*. Washington, D.C.: American Historical Association.

Meredith, R. C. 2004. A new Caesar in Europe? *Tomorrow's World* 6 (1). <www.tomorrowsworld.org/>.

Milanovic, B., P. H. Lindert, and J. G. Williamson. 2007. Measuring ancient inequality. NBER Working Paper 13550. National Bureau of Economic Research.

Millar, F. 1993. *The Roman Near East 31 BC–AD 337*. Cambridge, Mass.: Harvard University Press.

Minetti, A. E. 2003. Efficiency of equine express postal systems. *Nature* 426: 785–786.

Minor, H. H. 1999. Mapping Mussolini: Ritual and cartography in public art during the Second Empire. *Imago Mundi* 51: 147–162.

Mitchell, R. H. 1996. *Political Bribery in Japan*. Honolulu: University of Hawaii Press.

Mokyr, J. 2002. *The Gifts of Athena: Historical Origins of the Knowledge Economy*. Princeton, N.J.: Princeton University Press.

Molenaar, A. 1956. *Water Lifting Devices for Irrigation*. Rome: FAO.

Moore, R. W. 1936. Decline and fall. *Greece & Rome* 5: 65–72.

Morgan, M. J. 2006. American empire and the American military. *Armed Forces & Society* 32: 202–218.

Moritz, L. A. 1958. *Grain-Mills and Flour in Classical Antiquity*. Oxford: Clarendon Press.

Morley, N. 2006. The poor in the city of Rome. In *Poverty in the Roman World*, ed. M. Atkins and R. Osborne, 21–39. Cambridge: Cambridge University Press.

Moscati, S. 1999. *The Phoenicians*. New York: Rizzoli.

Mras, G. P. 1961. Italian Fascist architecture: Theory and image. *Art Journal* 21 (1): 7–12.

Murphy, C. 2007. *Are We Rome? The Fall of an Empire and the Fate of America*. Boston: Houghton Mifflin.

Mustafa, S. G. 1971. *Legacy of Britain: A Brief Educational and Cultural Survey of British Rule in India*. Karachi: Pak Publishers.

Needham, J. 1965. *Science and Civilization in China*. Vol. 4., Pt II: *Physics and Physical Technology*. Cambridge: Cambridge University Press.

Needham, J., with L. Wang and G. Lu. 1971. *Science and Civilisation in China*. Vol. 4, Part III: *Civil Engineering and Nautics*. Cambridge: Cambridge University Press.

Nelis, J. 2007. Construing Fascist identity: Benito Mussolini and the myth of *Romanità*. *Classical World* 101: 391–415.

New York Times. 2007. The imperial presidency 2.0. Editorial. January 7.

Newport, F. 2007. One-third of Americans believe the bible is literally true. *Gallup*. <http://www.gallup.com/poll/27682/OneThird-Americans-Believe-Bible-Literally-True.aspx>.

Nobel Foundation. 2008. All Nobel laureates. <http://nobelprize.org/nobel_prizes/lists/all/>.

Nye, J. S. 1991. *Bound to Lead: The Changing Nature of American Power*. New York: Basic Books.

Yale University Press, 2007. xxi, 251 p.:

———, 2002a. The new Rome meets the new barbarians: How America should wield its power. *Economist*, March 23, 23–25.

———, 2002b. *The Paradox of American Power: Why the World's Only Superpower Can't Go It Alone*. New York: Oxford University Press.

———, 2004. *Soft Power: The Means to Success in World Politics*. New York: Public Affairs.

Oleson, J. P. 1984. *Greek and Roman Mechanical Water-Lifting Devices: The History of a Technology*. Toronto: University of Toronto Press.

———, ed. 2008. *The Oxford Handbook of Engineering and Technology in the Classical World*. New York: Oxford University Press.

Panarin, A. S. 1996. *"Vtoraia Evropa" ili "Tretii Rim"?: Izbrannaia sotsialno-filosofskaia publitsistika.* Moscow: Rossiiskaia akademiia nauk.

Papaioannou, E., R. Portes, and G. Siourounis. 2006. Optimal currency shares in international reserves: The impact of the euro and the prospects for the dollar. *Journal of the Japanese and International Economies* 20: 508–547.

Parkin, T. G. 1992. *Demography and Roman Society.* Baltimore, Md.: Johns Hopkins University Press.

Passel, J. S. 2006. *The Size and Characteristics of the Unauthorized Migrant Population in the U.S.: Estimates Based on the March 2005 Current Population Survey.* Washington, D. C.: Pew Hispanic Center.

PBS (Public Broadcasting Service). 1996. Oral history: Norman Schwarzkopf. *Frontline: The Gulf War.* <http://www.pbs.org/wgbh/pages/frontline/gulf/oral/commanders.html>.

———, 2005. Al-qaeda's global context. *Frontline: The Man Who Knew.* <http://www.pbs.org/wgbh/pages/frontline/shows/knew/etc/cron.html>.

Peddie, J. 1994. *The Roman War Machine.* Stroud, UK: Sutton Publishing.

Pekáry, T. 1968. *Untersuchungen zu den römischen Reichsstrassen.* Bonn: R. Habelt.

Perdue, P. C. 2005. *China Marches West: The Qing Conquest of Central Eurasia.* Cambridge, Mass.: Belknap Press.

Peters, J. 1998. *Römische Tierhaltung und Tierzucht: Eine Synthese aus archäozoologischer Untersuchung und schriftlich-bildlicher Überlieferung.* Rahden, Germany: Leidorf.

Pew Research Center. 2007. *Global Opinion Trends 2002–2007.* Washington, D.C.

Pleket, H. W. 1990. Wirtschaft. In *Europäische Wirtschafts- und Sozialgeschichte in der römischen Kaiserzeit,* ed. F. Vittinghoff, 25–160. Stuttgart: Klett-Cotta.

Powell, C. 2003. Address to U.N. Security Council. February 5. <http://www.cnn.com/2003/US/02/05/sprj.irq.powell.transcript/>.

Powell, C., and J. Persico. 1996. *My American Journey.* New York: Random House.

Preston, S. H., N. Keyfitz, and R. Schoen. 1972. *Causes of Death: Life Tables for National Populations.* New York: Seminar Press.

Quataert, D. 2005. *The Ottoman Empire, 1700–1922.* Cambridge: Cambridge University Press.

Rast, J. 2003. Is the E.U. the revived Roman Empire? *Contender Ministries.* <http://contenderministries.org:80/prophecy/romanempirePF.php>.

Raven, S. 1993. *Rome in Africa.* London: Routledge.

Rawlins, D. 1982. Eratosthenes' geodesy unraveled: Was there a high-accuracy Hellenistic astronomy? *Isis* 73: 259–265.

Rawski, E. S. 1998. *The Last Emperors: A Social History of Qing Imperial Institutions.* Berkeley: University of California Press.

Rawson, B. 1991. *Marriage, Divorce, and Children in Ancient Rome.* Oxford: Oxford University Press.

Raymer, A. J. 1940. Slavery—the Graeco-Roman defence. *Greece & Rome* 10: 17–21.

Reilly, T., and A. M. Williams. 2003. *Science and Soccer.* London: Routledge.

Revel, J. F. 2003. Contradictions of the anti-American obsession. *New Perspectives Quarterly* 20: 11–27.

Reynolds, A. 2007. *Has U.S. Income Inequality Really Increased?* Washington, D.C.: Cato Institute.

Reynolds, J. 1970. *Windmills and Watermills.* London: Hugh Evelyn.

Ribbe, C. 2005. *Le crime de Napoléon.* Paris: Privé.

Rice, E. 1990. *Captain Sir Richard Francis Burton.* New York: Da Capo Press.

Richardson, J. S. 1991. *Imperium Romanum*: Empire and the language of power. *Journal of Roman Studies* 81: 1–9.

Riddle, J. M. 1999. *Eve's Herbs: A History of Contraception and Abortion in the West.* Cambridge, Mass.: Harvard University Press.

Robinson, E. W. 2005. American Empire? Ancient reflections on modern American power. *Classical World* 99: 35–50.

Rodgers, R. H. 1986. *Copia Aquarum*: Frontinus' measurements and the perspective of capacity. *Transactions of the American Philological Association* 116: 353–360.

Rollins, A. 1983. *The Fall of Rome: A Reference Guide.* Jefferson, N.C.: McFarland.

Rowland, D. B. 1996. Moscow—The Third Rome or the New Israel? *Russian Review* 55: 591–614.

Russell, J. C. 1958. Late Ancient and medieval population. *Transactions of the American Philosophical Society*, New Series 48 (3), 1–152.

Russo, L. 2004. *The Forgotten Revolution: How Science Was Born in 300 BC and Why It Had to Be Reborn.* Berlin: Springer.

Ryan, Paul B. 1985. *The Iranian Rescue Mission: Why It Failed.* Annapolis, Md.: Naval Institute Press.

Ryn, C. G. 2003. The ideology of American Empire. *Orbis* 47: 383–397.

Sagui, C. L. 1948. Le meunerie de Barbegal (France) et les roués hydrauliques les ancients et au moyen âge. *Isis* 38: 225–231.

Sale, K. 2005. Imperial entropy: Collapse of the American Empire. Book review of *Imperial Crusades* by A. Cockburn and J. St. Clair. *Counterpunch.* February 22. <http://www.counterpunch.org/sale02222005.html>.

Sallares, R. 2002. *Malaria and Rome: A History of Malaria in Ancient Italy.* New York: Oxford University Press.

Sallares, R., A. Bouwman, and C. Anderung. 2004. The spread of malaria to Southern Europe in antiquity: New approaches to old problems. *Medical History* 48: 311–328.

Saller, R. P. 1984. *Familia, Domus,* and the Roman conception of the family. *Phoenix* 38: 336–355.

Scheidel, W. 1996. *Measuring Sex, Age, and Death in the Roman Empire: Explorations in Ancient Demography. Journal of Roman Archaeology* Suppl. Ser. 21. Ann Arbor, Mich.

———, 1999. Emperors, aristocrats, and the grim reaper: Towards a demographic profile of the Roman elite. *Classical Quarterly* 49: 254–281.

———, 2001. Roman age structure: Evidence and models. *Journal of Roman Studies* 91: 2–26.

———, 2003. Germs for Rome. In *Rome the Cosmopolis*, ed. C. Edwards and G. Woolf, 158–176. Cambridge: Cambridge University Press.

———, 2006a. Republics between hegemony and empire: How ancient city-states built empires and the USA doesn't (anymore). Princeton/Stanford Working Papers in Classics 020601.

———, 2006b. Stratification, deprivation, and quality of life. In *Poverty in the Roman World*, ed. M. Atkins and R. Osborne, 40–59. Cambridge: Cambridge University Press.

———, 2007. Roman population size: The logic of the debate. Princeton/Stanford Working Papers in Classics 070706.

———, 2008. Real wages in early economies: Evidence for living standards from 2000 BCE to 1300 CE. Princeton/Stanford Working Papers in Classics 030801.

Scheidel, W., and S. Friesen. 2008. The size of the economy and the distribution of income in the Roman Empire. Princeton/Stanford Working Papers in Classics 110801.

Schlesinger, A. M. 1973. *The Imperial Presidency*. Boston: Houghton Mifflin.

Schmitt, G. J., and T. Donnelly. 2007. *Of Men and Materiel: The Crisis in Military Resources*. Washington, D.C.: AEI Press.

Schroeder, P. 2003. Is the U.S. an empire? *History News Network*. February 3. <http://hnn.us/articles/1237.html>.

Scobie, A. 1986. Slums, sanitation, and mortality in the Roman world. *Klio* 68: 399–433.

Scott, J. C. 1990. *Domination and the Arts of Resistance: Hidden Transcripts*. New Haven: Yale University Press.

Sellin, H. J. 1983. The large Roman water mill at Barbegal (France). *History of Technology* 8: 91–109.

Semenov, M., ed. 1983. *Krokodilu—60 let: iubileinaia letopis'*. Moskva: Izdatel'stvo Pravda.

Serafino, N., C. Tarnoff, and D. K. Nanto. 2006. *U.S. Occupation Assistance: Iraq, Germany, and Japan Compared*. Washington, D.C.: Congressional Research Service.

Simms, D. L. 1983. Water-driven saws, Ausonius, and the authenticity of the Mosella. *Technology and Culture* 24: 635–643.

SIPRI (Stockholm International Peace Research Institute). 2008. SIPRI Military Expenditure Database. <http://www.sipri.org/contents/milap/milex/mex_database1.html>.

Sitwell, N. H. 1981. *Roman Roads of Europe*. New York: St. Martin's Press.

Smil, V. 1994. *Energy in World History*. Boulder, Colo.: Westview Press.

———, 2003. *Energy at the Crossroads: Global Perspectives and Uncertainties*. Cambridge, Mass.: MIT Press.

———, 2005. *Creating the Twentieth Century: Technical Innovations of 1867–1914 and Their Lasting Impact*. New York: Oxford University Press.

———, 2006. *Transforming the Twentieth Century: Technical Innovations and Their Consequences*. New York: Oxford University Press.

————, 2008a. *Energy in Nature and Society: General Energetics of Complex Systems*. Cambridge, Mass.: MIT Press.

————, 2008b. *Global Catastrophes and Trends: The Next 50 Years*. Cambridge, Mass.: MIT Press.

————, 2008c. *Oil: A Beginner's Guide*. Oxford: Oneworld Publications.

Snowden, F. M. 1970. *Blacks in Antiquity: Ethiopians in the Greco-Roman Experience*. Cambridge, Mass.: Belknap Press.

Sobotka, T. 2004. Postponement of Childbearing and Low Fertility in Europe. Amsterdam: Dutch University Press.

Statistics Bureau (Japan). 2008. *Japan Statistical Yearbook*. Tokyo.

Stewart, R. W. 2002. *The United States Army in Somalia, 1992–1994*. Washington, D.C.: U.S. Army Center of Military History.

————, 2005. *The United States Army in a Global Era, 1917–2003*. Washington, D.C.: U.S. Army Center of Military History.

Taagepera, R. 1978. Size and duration of empires: Systematics of size. *Social Science Research* 7: 108–127.

Talbert, R. J. A., ed. 2000. *Barrington Atlas of the Greek and Roman World*. Princeton, N.J.: Princeton University Press.

Temin, P. 2001. A market economy in the early Roman empire. *Journal of Roman Studies* 91: 169–181.

Temple, R. 1986. *The Genius of China: 3,000 Years of Science, Discovery, and Invention*. New York: Simon and Schuster.

Thompson, B. 2007. Imperial Washington: The author of "Are We Rome?" takes in the sights and similarities. *Washington Post*, June 30, C01.

Thorley, J. 1969. The development of trade between the Roman Empire and the East under Augustus. *Greece & Rome* 16: 209–223.

————, 1971. The silk trade between China and the Roman Empire at its height, circa A.D. 90–130. *Greece & Rome* 18: 71–80.

Thornton, R. C. 2001. *Odd Man Out: Truman, Stalin, Mao, and the Origins of the Korean War*. Washington, D.C.: Brassey's.

TI (Transparency International). 2008a. *Bribe Payers Index*. <http://www.transparency.org/policy_research/surveys_indices/bpi/bpi_2008>.

————, 2008b. *Corruption Perceptions Index*. <http://www.transparency.org/policy_research/surveys_indices/cpi/2008>.

Totman, C. D. 1980. *The Collapse of the Tokugawa Bakufu*. Honolulu: University Press of Hawaii.

Totten, M. 2007. The Peace Corps with muscles. *Michael Totten's Middle East Journal*, October 1. <http://www.michaeltotten.com/archives/2007/10/the-peace-corps-with-muscles.php/>.

Trask, D. F. 1996. *The War with Spain in 1898*. Lincoln: University of Nebraska Press.

Twain, M. 1889. *A Connecticut Yankee in King Arthur's Court.* New York: C. L. Webster.

UN (United Nations). 2006. World Population Prospects: The 2006 Revision Population Database. <http://esa.un.org/unpp/>.

UNDP (United Nations Development Programme). 2008. *Human Development Report.* <http://hdr.undp.org/en/reports/>.

USCB (U.S. Census Bureau). 1976. *Historical Statistics of the United States: Colonial Times to 1970.* Bicentennial Edition. Parts 1, 2. <http://www.census.gov/prod/www/abs/statab .html>.

———, 2006. *U.S. International Trade in Goods and Services—Annual Revision for 2005.* <http://www.census.gov/foreign-trade/Press-Release/2005pr/final_revisions/>.

———, 2007. *Historical Income Inequality Tables.* <http://www.census.gov/hhes/www/ income/histinc/ineqtoc.html>.

———, 2008. *U.S. International Trade in Goods and Services—Annual Revision for 2007.* <http://www.census.gov/foreign-trade/Press-Release/2007pr/final_revisions/>.

———, 2009. *Statistical Abstract of the United States.* <http://www.census.gov/compendia/ statab/>.

USDL (U.S. Department of Labor). 2006. *Comparative Civilian Labor Force Statistics, 10 Countries, 1960–2005.* <http://www.bls.gov/fls/flslforc.pdf>.

USDOD (U.S. Department of Defense). 2006. *Base Structure Report—FY 2006 Baseline.* <http://www.defenselink.mil/pubs/BSR_2006_Baseline.pdf>.

USDOT (U.S. Department of Transportation). 2008. Research and Innovative Technology Administration (RITA). Bureau of Transportation Statistics. <http://www.bts.gov/>.

USDT (U.S. Department of Treasury). 2008. *Gross Federal Debt History.* <http://www.treas. gov/education/fact-sheets/taxes/fed-debt.shtml>.

USGAO (U.S. Government Accountability Office). 2007. *Transforming Government to Meet the Demands of the 21st Century.* GAO-07-1188CG. <http://www.gao.gov/cghome/ d071188cg.pdf>.

USPTO (U.S. Patent and Trademark Office). 2008. *Patent Counts by Country/State and Year, January 1, 1963–December 31, 2007.* <http://www.uspto.gov/go/taf/cst_utl.pdf>.

van Tilburg, C. 2007. *Traffic and Congestion in the Roman Empire.* London: Routledge.

Viansino, G. 2005. *Impero romano, impero americano: Ideologie e prassi.* Milan: Punto Rosso.

Vidal, G. 1992. *The Decline and Fall of the American Empire.* Berkeley, Calif.: Odonian Press.

———, 2005. *Imperial America: Reflections on the United States of Amnesia.* New York: Nation Books.

Wade, R. H. 2003. The invisible hand of American Empire. *Ethics and International Affairs* 17 (2): 77–88.

Walker, M. 1994. *The Cold War: A History.* New York: Henry Holt.

———, 2002. America's virtual empire. *World Policy Journal* 19 (2): 13–20.

Wallace-Hadrill, A. 1990. Pliny the Elder and man's unnatural history. *Greece & Rome* 37: 80–96.

———, 1994. *Houses and Society in Pompeii and Herculaneum*. Princeton, N.J.: Princeton University Press.

Ward-Perkins, B. 2005. *The Fall of Rome and the End of Civilisation*. Oxford: Oxford University Press.

Warden, P. G. 1981. The Domus Aurea reconsidered. *Journal of the Society of Architectural Historians* 40: 271–278.

Weigel, D. 2007. Quo vadimus? *Reason Online*. July 9. <http://www.reason.com/news/show/121274.html>.

Wheeler, E. 1993. Methodological limits and the mirage of Roman strategy. *Journal of Military History* 57: 7–41, 215–240.

Wheeler, M. 1954. *Rome Beyond the Imperial Frontiers*. London: G. Bell and Sons.

Wikander, Ö. 1981. The use of water-power in Classical Antiquity. *Opuscula Romana* 13: 91–104.

———, 1983. *Exploitation of Water-Power or Technological Stagnation?* Lund, Sweden: CWK Gleerup.

Wild, A. 2001. *Remains of the Raj: The British Legacy in India*. New York: HarperCollins.

Wilson, A. 2002. Machines, power, and the ancient economy. *Journal of Roman Studies* 92: 1–32.

Woodall, B. 1996. *Japan under Construction: Corruption, Politics, and Public Works*. Berkeley: University of California Press.

Woodall, F. P. 1982. Water wheels for winding. *Industrial Archaeology* 16: 333–338.

Woods, R. 2007. Ancient and early modern mortality: Experience and understanding. *Economic History Review* 60: 373–399.

Woolf, G. 1992. Imperialism, empire, and the integration of the Roman economy. *World Archaeology* 23: 283–293.

World Bank. 2008. *Gross Domestic Product 2007 PPP*. <http://siteresources.worldbank.org/DATASTATISTICS/Resources/GDP_PPP.pdf>.

WTO (World Trade Organization). 2008. *International Trade and Tariff Data*. <http://www.wto.org/english/res_e/statis_e/statis_e.htm>.

Young, G. K. 2001. *Rome's Eastern Trade: International Commerce and Imperial Policy, 31 BC–AD 305*. London: Routledge.

Zhou, P., and L. Leydesdorff. 2006. The emergence of China as a leading nation in science. *Research Policy* 35: 83–104.

Name Index

Adams, Brooks, 43
Ahmedinejad, Mohammed, 76
Albright, Madeleine, 73
Alexander the Great, 58, 87, 152–153
Allawi, Ayad, 49
Antipater of Thessalonica, 99
Antoninus Pius, 59, 130
Antonius, Marcus (Antony), 37–38
Apollonius of Perga, 88
Apuleius, Lucius, 102
Archimedes, 87
Aristarchos of Samos, 88
Aristotle, 137
Augustus Octavianus, 4, 6, 9, 37–38, 55, 134
Aurelius, Marcus, 28, 39–40, 59, 130

Baring Evelyn (Lord Cromer), 6
Belisarius, 39, 170
Bell, Alexander G., 83
Bender, Peter, 21
bin-Lādin, Usama, 72–73
Bonaparte, Napoleon, 3, 6, 25, 152–153
Boot, Max, 16
Botticelli, Sandro, 81–82
Bryce, James W., 7
Bush, George W., 18, 49, 164

Caesar, Gaius Julius, 37–38, 46, 60, 147
Caracalla, 130, 165
Castro, Fidel, 51–52
Cato, Marcus Porcius (Cato the Elder), 137
Charlemagne, 3–4
Cicero, Marcus Tullius, 30

Clinton, William J., 73
Commodus, 39
Constantine, 8, 38, 127
Constantius II, 166
Crassus, Marcus Licinius, 58, 165
Ctesibius, 88
Cyrus the Great, 157

de Gaulle, Charles, 76
Dio, Cassius, 58, 87, 133
Diocletian, 38, 130, 141, 150
Dole, Samuel, 36
Domitian, 39, 145

Edison, Thomas A., 83–84
Eratosthenes, 88
Euclid, 87, 90

Filofei, 5
Finley, Moses I., 85–86, 99
Flavius, Julius Valens, 38
Flavius, Romulus, 38
Ford, Henry, 84
Francis II, 4
Freedland, Jonathan, 20–21
Frontinus, 90–91, 132

Galerius, 166
Gates, Bill, 146
Genghis Khan, 152–153
Gibbon, Edward, 3, 38–39, 147, 168
Gorbachev, Mikhail S., 23
Gordian III, 166–167
Gratian, 127

Subject Index